Wittgenstein and Derrida

Wittgenstein and

Don't *for heaven's sake*, be afraid of talking nonsense! But you must pay attention to your nonsense.

Ludwig Wittgenstein, Culture and Value

by Henry Staten

Derrida

. . . as though literature, theater, deceit, infidelity, hypocrisy, infelicity,
parasitism, and the simulation of real life were not part of real life!

Jacques Derrida, *Limited Inc.*

University of Nebraska Press, *Lincoln and London*

First Bison Book printing: 1986
Most recent printing indicated by first digit below:
1   2   3   4   5   6   7   8   9   10

Library of Congress Cataloging in Publication Data
Staten, Henry, 1946–
    Wittgenstein and Derrida.
    Includes index.
    1. Wittgenstein, Ludwig, 1889–1951.   2. Derrida,
Jacques.   I. Title.
B3376.W564S78   1984   192   84-3525
ISBN 0-8032-4138-0
ISBN 0-8032-9169-8 (paper)

The paper in this book meets the guidelines for perma-
nence and durability of the Committee on Production
Guidelines for Book Longevity of the Council on Library Resources.

Second cloth printing 1986

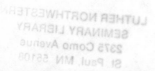

For Diana Potts,
who taught me the most
essential things

Contents

Abbreviations of Works by Husserl, Derrida, and Wittgenstein

Husserl

CM *Cartesian Meditations*. Translated by Dorion Cairns. The Hague: Martinus Nijhoff, 1960.

Crisis *The Crisis of European Sciences and Transcendental Phenomenology*. Translated by David Carr. Evanston: Northwestern University Press, 1970.

EJ *Experience and Judgment*. Revised and edited by Ludwig Langrebe. Translated by James S. Churchill and Karl Ameriks. Evanston: Northwestern University Press, 1973.

Ideas I *Ideas: General Introduction to Pure Phenomenology*. Translated by W. R. Boyce Gibson. New York: Collier Books, 1975.

ITC *The Phenomenology of Internal Time-Consciousness*. Translated by James S. Churchill. Bloomington: Indiana University Press, 1973.

LI *Logical Investigations*. Translated by J. N. Findlay. New York: Humanities Press, 1970.

Logic *Formal and Transcendental Logic*. Translated by Dorion Cairns. The Hague: Martinus Nijhoff, 1969.

Origin *The Origin of Geometry*. Translated by David Carr, published as appendix to Derrida's *Edmund Husserl's Origin of Geometry: An Introduction*.

Derrida

Diss.   *Dissemination*. Translated by Barbara Johnson. Chicago: University of Chicago Press, 1981.

Gramma.   *Of Grammatology*. Translated by Gayatri Chakravorty Spivak. Baltimore: Johns Hopkins University Press, 1976.

Intro.   *Edmund Husserl's "Origin of Geometry": An Introduction*. Translated by John P. Leavey, Jr. Stony Brook, N.Y.: Nicholas Hays, 1978.

Ltd Inc   *Limited Inc abc*. Translated by Sam Weber. Published in *Glyph 2*, pp. 162–254. Baltimore: Johns Hopkins University Press, 1977.

Margins   *Margins of Philosophy*. Translated by Alan Bass. Chicago: University of Chicago Press, 1982.

Pos.   *Positions*. Translated by Alan Bass. Chicago: University of Chicago Press, 1981.

S&P   *Speech and Phenomena*. Translated by David B. Allison. Evanston: Northwestern University Press, 1973.

W&D   *Writing and Difference*. Translated by Alan Bass. Chicago: University of Chicago Press, 1978.

Wittgenstein

BB   *The Blue and Brown Books*. New York: Harper and Brothers, 1958.

Culture   *Culture and Value*. Edited by G. H. von Wright in collaboration with Heikki Nyman. Translated by Peter Winch. Chicago: University of Chicago Press, 1980.

L&C   *Lectures and Conversations on Aesthetics, Psychology, and Religious Belief*. Edited by Cyril Barrett. Berkeley and Los Angeles: University of California Press, 1972.

OC   *On Certainty*. Edited by G. E. M. Anscombe and G. H. von Wright. Translated by Denis Paul and G. E. M. Anscombe. New York: Harper Torchbooks, 1969.

PI   *Philosophical Investigations*. Translated by G. E. M. Anscombe. 3rd ed. New York: Macmillan Company, 1958.

RFM   *Remarks on the Foundations of Mathematics*. Edited by G. H. von Wright, R. Rhees, and G. E. M. Anscombe. Translated by G. E. M. Anscombe. Cambridge: MIT Press, 1967.

Z   *Zettel*. Edited by G. E. M. Anscombe and G. H. von Wright. Translated by G. E. M. Anscombe. Berkeley and Los Angeles: University of California Press, 1970.

Wittgenstein usually divided his writing into numbered "remarks," but not always. Citations of his work will thus sometimes follow the usual page-reference form (e.g., *BB*, p. 11); but where only a number is given, the reference is to a remark rather than a page (e.g., *PI* 46). The first part of *PI* is numbered by remarks, the second part, by pages.

Preface

The most difficult problem in the writing of this book was the heterogeneity of its presumed audience. How could it be made readable for both literary critics and philosophers, and within these large divisions, for such equally heterogeneous subgroups as traditional humanistic critics and radical theorists, or phenomenologists and analytical philosophers? In the end, I tried to include enough explanation and bibliography so that no reasonably hard-working reader would feel bewildered by my presuppositions, regardless of his specialized background. But though there is something of the "introduction" about this book, that is not its main purpose, and I have striven for rigor as much as for clarity in my presentation.

A reading of the philosophical bearings of deconstruction seemed necessary because in this country Derrida's work has been taken up almost exclusively by literary critics, who have had little to say about it except as it happened to coincide with what they were already interested in.[1] For these writers, Derrida belongs in the context of structuralism and post-structuralism. One would not guess, from the ease with which it is often declared that Derrida has "deconstructed" the boundary between literary and philosophical discourse, that Derrida remains in most of his work a careful and systematic, if unorthodox, philosopher. In this study I try to redirect the discussion of Derrida by two maneuvers.

The first is by not giving a summary of his results but rather, by trying to show how we work through philosophical texts to get to these results. Many available accounts of Derrida's "deconstructions" of philosophical texts give the impression that deconstruction is a sudden and rather simple operation, in which a philosophical argument is dispatched when it is found to be merely figurative or rhetorical, or is found to privilege speech over writing. But Derrida does not merely point out fundamental metaphors; he analyzes, in great detail, arguments and conceptual structures.

And one of the things we learn by reading his texts is that the "logos" in "logocentric" cannot be understood simply in relation to *speech*. *Logos* must first be understood in relation to *eidos*, "form," a concept that occupies a far more important place in metaphysical thematics than does speech. One can argue that speech occupies a more important place in metaphysics than metaphysicians have explicitly given it; but this argument is based on the analysis of the concept of form. If speech is privileged by philosophy, it is because it names what is, as what it truly is, in its intelligibility; and the principle of intelligibility is form.

Second, I have tried to bring Derrida's project into relation with Wittgenstein's in order to suggest an Anglo-American context within which deconstruction makes philosophical sense.[2] The predecessors who provide the philosophical context of Derrida's project in France—Heidegger, Levinas, Bataille—are not well known in this country, and that is an important reason why Derrida has found almost no philosophical audience here. If we see Derrida's project as paralleling Wittgenstein's, this offers an alternative to seeing him as some sort of structuralist and suggests how and why we should read his texts on Husserl and Aristotle as well as those on Saussure and Rousseau.

Reading Derrida as an ally of Wittgenstein raises the question of "ordinary language." Derrida's language is certainly not ordinary, and one might legitimately wonder how his work could possibly be compatible with Wittgenstein's. The question is not, however, whether the language of a given text is "ordinary" in any fixed or predetermined fashion, but rather whether we can find the pathways that lead from language that makes clear sense to us to the new, strange language we are trying to figure out. I understand "ordinary language" not as something that is just there for us to see but as an operational concept, a hint associated with a technique for criticizing and sharpening the language by which we carry on our meditations and polemics. I agree with the "therapeutic" school that we need Wittgenstein's treatment to get us unstuck from a too literal or uncritical or fixated attachment to the formulas of traditional philosophy.[3] On the other hand whatever liberation we get from such therapy should be the liberty to read philosophy in more supple and interesting ways than formerly, and not to chuck the old texts as mistakes.[4] In this I agree with John Wisdom, who held the therapeutic view but argued that the peculiar verbal usages of philosophers, properly read, give us a new apprehension of the familiar, a claim that sounds exactly like what literary critics say about the peculiar usages of poets.

This brings us again to the underlying theme of this whole book, the question of what kind of functioning of language is involved in deconstructive discourse, which is neither poetry nor (quite) philosophy. Derrida picks up the view of language developed first by the symbolists and then by the modernists, that language is a quasi-material medium that is worked not by fitting words to the requisite meanings but by attentiveness to the way the words as words (sounds, shapes, associative echoes) will allow themselves to be fitted together. This is called in contemporary jargon "the play of signifiers" and has probably always been the way poets choose their words (recall Dante speaking of his "hairy" words and "smooth" words), but it has generally not been a very respectable view among philosophers. "Linguistic philosophy" may recognize the dependence of meaning on language, but this recognition hardly ever extends so far as to include the signifying potential of the "accidental" sensual properties of signs. I will argue that Wittgenstein himself did treat language this way, and so does the rare Wittgensteinian (viz., O. K. Bouwsma; but then, Bouwsma was fond of *Finnegans Wake*), yet the orthodox mainstream (whether Wittgensteinian or not) continues the old Platonic quarrel with poetry. Not that contemporary philosophers would be so crass as to put down *poems*; it's a matter of their attitude toward language. Thus Newton Garver, in his otherwise fine preface to the first volume of Derrida's work published in English, warned readers that they would experience "frequent discomfort" from Derrida's style, and remarked that, fortunately, "students of Wittgenstein are already familiar with the problem of having to read *through* someone's language in order to see the point lying behind it" (*S&P*, p. xxvi). J. N. Findlay has gone so far as to claim that in the case of Wittgenstein "one was tempted to confuse beauty with clarity and strangely luminous expression with perspicuous truth." Wittgenstein's "immense influence," says Findlay, was due to a "magic of stylistic tellingness" that concealed the "logical holes" in his work.[5]

Deconstructive discourse, which relies in part on powers of language which philosophy routinely declares illegitimate for the purposes of rationality, must free itself of the charge of sorcery and must not use any sorcery in so doing. This cannot quite be accomplished. Derrida makes the argument as logical as possible, but he attempts certain stretchings of language that must appear out of bounds so long as we remain within the closed circle of philosophical concepts that finds no place for the play of signifiers. Philosophy is like Desdemona's father, convinced that Othello must have used sorcery to persuade Desdemona, and proving it by the fact that Othello succeeded, which Othello could not have done unless he used sorcery. All this looks like one vast begged question from outside the philosophical discourse on truth; and of course from within it deconstruction looks like wordplay and confusion. That is why the summary accounts of deconstruction that declare philosophy vanquished by *fiat* do nothing to improve the situation, and why I try in this book to give a more detailed account of the arbitrations between the two positions, arbitrations which cannot be dealt with in one fell swoop.

What is proposed here is an approach adapted to a particular purpose. That purpose may be rejected, and with it the approach, but the approach ought not to be judged in terms of some other purpose. The purpose here is not to speak about the truth of anything—neither that it is right to attempt to refer directly to reality nor that it is not. Because the aim is to disentangle the deconstructive style of discourse from that of philosophy, it will often look exactly as though I am attempting to refute propositions of philosophy and replacing them with others having a superior claim to truth. But that is not the purpose. In this book we do not ever get so far as to contest anybody's theories. At the end of the book I only reach the point at which one first picks up one's pen. From that point on one can advance or refute theories. The questions raised in this book concern how one situates oneself ethically as linguistic subject, regardless of what views about truth or reality one may espouse, and, if one situates oneself in the way recommended, what techniques for working language become available. Thus all the remarks about reduction of object-talk to talk of "grammar" should be understood, not as saying we must reject "realism," but rather as enjoining a strategic suspension of the realist perspective in order to look at something we are inclined to overlook. Not: "don't think in terms of objects," but: "don't do it *yet*; there's quite a lot to meditate upon before we turn our attention away from language." Afterwards, many things are possible. My own view is that deconstruction and everything else are ultimately contained by Darwin's tale—but that is another story and will wait for another day.

II

Some remarks on the strategy of presentation of this book.

Wittgenstein's work is usually divided into three phases—early, transitional, and late. There is controversy over whether the late work (the phase of the *Philosophical Investigations*) constitutes a radical break with the early work (the *Tractatus* phase), or whether there is fundamental continuity. Everyone agrees that there are many continuities and many discontinuities: the question is what it all amounts to. Here I assume discontinuity and base my discussion on texts from the *Blue Book* on, when, I believe, Wittgenstein's work became consistently deconstructive.

The work of Derrida's discussed here, on the other hand, is mostly early. I wanted to trace the beginnings of his method, beginnings which have been largely ignored by American readers, who rarely give close study to Derrida's work on Aristotle and Husserl. Derrida's relation to Husserl provides a remarkably perspicuous area in which to trace the similarities between his work and Wittgenstein's. Garver has pointed out that "Wittgenstein's *Tractatus* bears close affinities to Husserl's *Logical Investigations*," and that thus Derrida's "penetrating consideration and ultimate rejection of the basic principles of Husserl's philosophy of language is the historical analogue of Wittgenstein's later consideration and rejection of his own earlier work, the *Tractatus Logico-Philosophicus*" (*S&P*, p. xxii; see also xix–xxi). The argument may be made even more strongly. The more one reads the *Logical Investigations* next to the *Philosophical Investigations*, the more striking the relation between the two becomes. It seems almost as though Wittgenstein is replying to Husserl's views. A number of writers have commented on the likelihood that Wittgenstein was influenced by the Husserl of the *Logical Investigations*;[6] if this is so, the very name of Wittgenstein's own *Investigations* acquires a special significance. For the purposes of the present study, however, what matters is not the historical fact of influence but the existence of such important correspondences that they could lead one to suspect an influence.

The Introduction presents an overview of the relation of deconstruction to the philosophical concept of form, especially as it is developed in Aristotle, and outlines the readings of Derrida and Wittgenstein that are developed in Chapters 1 and 2. In Chapter 1 it proved necessary to go into considerable detail on Husserl and not only for the reasons given above. None of the accounts I had seen of Derrida's concept of the trace or of his analysis of the sign had taken account of the transcendental/phenomenological basis of Derrida's argument, an omission which makes the philosophical pertinence of the argument incomprehensible. The whole chapter may be thought of as a commentary on pages 44–65 of the *Grammatology*, and particularly of the concluding paragraph of that section (p. 65). Chapter 2 lays out a deconstructive reading of Wittgenstein's later work, focusing on the *Philosophical Investigations*. Much of what I say here will be familiar to students of Wittgenstein, but there is a new twist in the direction of the "play of the signifier." In Part Two I contrast the deconstructive view of communication with other modern and classical views and suggest the difference in fundamental aims between deconstruction and these other views.

The argument of each chapter and of the book as a whole is consecutive and cumulative, but the chapters are designed to be capable of being read independently, so there is some repetition of fundamental arguments. For many readers the arguments will be unfamiliar enough that this repetition should in any case prove helpful.

III

This book owes more than most to other people. Above all, I am indebted to O. K. Bouwsma, my teacher and friend, for whom philosophy was not a profession but a life. Gayatri Spivak read the original essay out of which this book grew and was the one who first suggested a larger-scale study. Since then she has read successive versions and made acute criticisms. It was through her superb introduction to the *Grammatology* that I was first introduced to Derrida, and she remains the most sophisticated reader of Derrida we have. My thanks to Jacques Derrida for his interest in my work, for his encouragement, which got me over some desperate moments, and for his generosity with his time. Paul Haanstad shared his detailed knowledge of Husserl with me in numerous lengthy conversations and helped me immensely in trying to get all the nuances right in the chapter on Husserl. Of course, what errors remain are my own responsibility. Charles Altieri, Sam Weber, and Virgil Aldrich read drafts of the book and made helpful suggestions. Not only I, but every reader of this book owes a debt of gratitude to Diana Potts, whose luminous sense of style has much improved its readability. Finally, my thanks to Margery Stricker Durham and Lonnie Durham, who initiated me into the fundamental conceptions of language and the ethical position of the subject of language that have here come to some sort of fruition.

I am grateful to the University of Utah College of Humanities for a quarter's leave and a research grant in the fall of 1981.

Wittgenstein and Derrida

Introduction: From Form to *Differance*

In the case of both Wittgenstein and Derrida, deconstruction is generated by an intense, sustained confrontation with philosophy; and the language arising out of this confrontation remains marked by its relation to the language of philosophy. But why call Wittgenstein's style of philosophy deconstruction? Are we now going to go back and discover that many of our great thinkers were, without knowing it, or at least without having this name for it, really practicing deconstruction, just as a short time ago we were informed that many of them were really structuralists?

I have no objection to the current expansion of the application of the term *deconstruction*, which no one owns or ought to own, but in this study a much more restrictive conception of its sense will be in force.

Deconstruction here will be strictly defined in terms of Derrida's practice, and the extension of the term to what Wittgenstein does will be guided by this definition. This single extension does not open the door to further inclusions; on the contrary, as deconstruction is here understood, Wittgenstein is unique among Derrida's predecessors in having achieved, in the period beginning with the *Blue Book*, a consistently deconstructive standpoint.

The deconstructive standpoint is not to be understood as a passing beyond philosophy into a higher or more advanced level of awareness or theoretical vision. Derrida describes it, rather, as something like a lateral displacement, a method of writing, each moment of which is oriented toward the precise articulation of some moment of philosophical discourse, and which proceeds to veer away from philosophy while taking its bearings, in a disciplined and methodical fashion, from this articulation. Someone practicing deconstruction while looking at philosophy would thus resemble the people in those odd cases Wittgenstein often postulated—for example, the person who "naturally react[s] to the gesture of pointing with

1

the hand by looking in the direction of the line from finger-tip to wrist, not from wrist to finger-tip" (*PI* 185; cf. *Z* 317); or the geometer who follows a line with one leg of his compass while altering the opening of the compass, "apparently with great precision," looking at the line that is supposedly his rule, but with no observable regularity in the line he draws. We cannot learn his way of following the line from observing what he does, and so must conclude that the line is not a "rule" (*PI* 237).

Such remarks are commonly taken by Wittgenstein's commentators to point to the necessity for communal agreement in how we understand signs and rules. I want to emphasize that Wittgenstein's own practice has (or at least had, when it was new) just the sort of peculiar status with respect to established norms as have the practices of the aberrant people in his examples, and that consequently, Wittgenstein in such examples implicitly questions the status of his own practice. Observers of Wittgenstein's practice have often found themselves feeling just the sort of exasperation at trying to figure out the "rules" of what he does that one would feel watching the errant geometer of the example.[1] But how do we know whether the fault lies with the geometer or with us? Perhaps he *is* responding to the guide-line according to a learnable technique, but we can't figure it out because it's different from any technique we're familiar with, and we haven't tried hard enough or been smart enough to understand it. I want to stress both the methodical character of Wittgenstein's practice, the fact that the "rule" he is following can be understood, and its strangeness, the fact that his rule deviates from what we are accustomed to and requires radical readjustment on our part if we are to learn it.

The philosophical world has had several decades now to digest Wittgenstein's works and the radicality of his approach has lost much of its bite. His arguments have been interpreted, and his results are common coin; this obscures the extent to which the nature of his *practice* remains a mystery. Both the strangeness of Wittgenstein's practice and its methodical character can be understood as a form of what Derrida calls deconstruction. Deconstruction makes sense only in relation to philosophy, to what, following Derrida, I will call "the text of philosophy," treating the chain of philosophical works since Plato as "one great discourse" (*Margins*, p. 177) to be read and interpreted. Since deconstruction makes sense only in terms of this relation, it follows that extensive reading of the reference text is required for an understanding of the "rules" of deconstruction. (I speak of "rules" here, though the concept of a rule will be one of those that become problematic for us as we go.)

To say this much is already to cast the problem in strongly Derridean terms. Apart from scattered references, Wittgenstein paid little attention to the history of philosophy. He wanted to be self-engendered; the only reference text he wanted for the *Philosophical Investigations*, his great deconstructive work, was the *Tractatus Logico-Philosophicus*, his own earlier masterpiece against which the *Investigations* reacted. Wittgenstein treated the problems of philosophy as though they could be addressed in a highly generalized form—namely, in terms of his own elliptical recension of the tradition; but for Derrida the problems of philosophy are always embodied in particular philosophical texts. Whereas Wittgenstein's style of deconstruction erases from its surface its relation to, and dependence upon, the parent language, Derrida traces this dependence in great detail and outlines his deviations against its background. For Derrida, the reference text is the whole body of Western philosophy, from Plato and Aristotle to Husserl and Heidegger, and the deconstruction of philosophy's discourse on truth is a way of tracing a path from one body of discourse to another. The closeness of the deconstructive interrogation of a text is a way of carefully tying the emerging text of deconstruction to the text of philosophy. There is a filiation between the texts, and the new threads must be twisted onto the old ones with the tightness appropriate to philosophical textuality.

Wittgenstein may have succeeded in freeing himself from most of the philosophical urges he inherited, but he remained trapped by the urge toward final liberation, which may be the original philosophical urge. Derrida emphasizes the impossibility of a simple exit from the inherited web of language, which we can escape no more than we can escape history or culture or our parentage. Thus Derrida's language is more directly dependent upon the language of classical metaphysics (especially that of transcendental phenomenology); yet this dependence is a function of his refusal to take the lure that catches Wittgenstein. By bringing Wittgenstein into relation with Derrida, we can overcome the historical amnesia Wittgenstein can cause, without betraying the fundamental radicality of his method. Derrida is in every way as alert as Wittgenstein, his language as tense and original. On the other hand, Derrida's language, precisely because it is so much like the language of metaphysics, carries dangers of its own—namely, that it will come to seem too much like another version of what it seeks to distinguish itself from. So we can use Wittgenstein's language to remind ourselves of how much there is to be suspicious of in the metaphysical tendencies of Derrida's style. Not that Derrida ever succumbs to these tendencies, but there are many traps in his style for the unwary reader. Each technique has the limitations of its virtues, and we can use each to supplement the other.

II

There is a widespread belief, obviously based on nonreading, that Derrida removes all constraint from, and sanctions arbitrary distortion in, the interpretation of texts. In fact, Derrida consistently *defends* philosophical texts against less than informed and rigorous reading. For example, in his critique of Benveniste's reading of Aristotle, Derrida takes pains to emphasize "the aporias that appear to engage anyone who takes on the task of defining the constraints which limit philosophical discourse," aporias to which Benveniste has not been alert enough (*Margins*, p. 180). In particular, Derrida insists that "it is a mistake to believe in the immediate and ahistorical legibility of a philosophical argument." A "prerequisite and highly complex elaboration" that takes account of the full articulation of a philosophical text, both internally and in its relation to the history of philosophy, must precede the application of an interpretive "grid," whether linguistic, psychoanalytic, or other, to the philosophical text (*Margins*, p. 188).

Derrida's own texts are no more immediately legible than the texts he comments on, and because the status of the critical operation called deconstruction is so uncertain, these texts call even more exigently for a working out of their relation to the history of philosophy. Thus we need in the first place to consider the relation of Derrida's work to that of Husserl, since it was in an extensive reading of Husserl that Derrida worked out the foundations of his practice; and in order to understand this relation we have to understand as well something of Husserl's relation to his own predecessors. Husserl considered his phenomenology to be something like the fulfillment or culmination of the history of philosophy, which, by a radical and presuppositionless reflection on the ground of its own possibility in preconceptual experience, had opened the way to the elaboration of "the *one* philosophy which as Idea underlies all the philosophies that can be imagined" (*Ideas*, p. 20). Though not underwriting this claim precisely as stated, Derrida takes it very seriously and accords phenomenology what he calls a "juridical priority" in philosophical discourse (*Intro.*, p. 151); that is, he argues that it is necessary to go through the reduction of empirical being to phenomenological "sense" in order to separate out completely the ideal from the factual (see below, Chap. 1). This separation is what philosophy has always aimed at in its pursuit of "being," and Derrida in linking Husserl to the metaphysical tradition follows Husserl's own conception of phenomenology as "authentic metaphysics," in "the sense with which metaphysics, as 'first philosophy,' was instituted originally" (*CM*, p. 139; cited in *S&P*, pp. 5–6).

But if phenomenology is the fulfillment of the work begun by the Greeks, the *telos* toward which Greek philosophy already aimed, then reading Husserl takes us back to the Greeks and to the "opposition between form and matter—which inaugurates metaphysics" (*S&P*, p. 6). In the key essay linking Derrida's reading of Husserl to his reading of Greek philosophy, "Form and Meaning: A Note on the Phenomenology of Language," we read the following:

Whether it is a question of [Husserl's] determining *eidos* in opposition to "Platonism," or form (*Form*) . . . or *morphe* . . . in opposition to Aristotle, the force, vigilance, and efficacity of [Husserl's] critique remain intrametaphysical. . . . Only a form is *self-evident*, only a form has or is an *essence*, only a form *presents itself* as such. . . . Form is presence itself. Formality is whatever aspect of the thing in general presents itself, lets itself be seen, gives itself to be thought. . . . [M]etaphysical thought . . . is a thought of Being as form. (*Margins*, pp. 157–58)

The notion of "presence," derived from Heidegger, has achieved currency in discussion of Derrida's thought, but Derrida's linking of it to the concept of form (*eidos* or *morphê*) is less familiar though at least as important. Its elucidation takes us back to classical philosophy and especially to Aristotle's *Metaphysics*. Derrida's remarks on Aristotle, especially in "The Supplement of Copula" and "Ousia and Grammē," are among the most important passages for understanding how Derrida's work is oriented to the history of philosophy and what Derrida calls "the general code of metaphysics," which bears "the decisive mark of Aristotelianism" (*Margins*, p. 192).

This decisive mark is also to be found in the features of philosophical thought that Wittgenstein worked against, especially in philosophical theories of language.[2] In fact, Wittgenstein's own system in the early phase of his work, which in his later work became a paradigm of what he wanted to do away with, may itself in certain essential respects be called Aristotelian, and especially with respect to the crucial notion of Form. The philosophical investigation of language is often summed up as involving the relation of words to things; but it is more accurately seen as involving the relation of the ideality of the sense of words (the form of the *Logos*) to the form of the entity (the form of *ousia*). The key term is *form*, the eidos; and the basic structure of concepts by means of which we think the relation of words to thought and thought to things through the mediation of ideality as form was laid down by Aristotle. The famous "picture theory" of the *Tractatus* is really a theory of Form, since a picture, in order to be a picture of a reality, must have the same "logical form" as that reality. A proposition can then be a "picture" of reality because it too can share this logical form.[3] Thought as well, in order to represent reality, must have logical form; in fact "thoughts are logical pictures *par excellence* since logical structure is *the whole* of their logical form."[4] In the *Investigations*, Wittgenstein summed up his own former view in this way: "These concepts: proposition, language, thought, world, stand in line one behind the other, each equivalent to each" (*PI* 96). This equivalence is a transformation of the old Aristotelian equivalence of *logos* (verbal expression, especially the "formula of essence"), *noésis* (thought), and *ousia* (traditionally but obscurely translated "substance"; in this study, I will render it as "entity"), and for the Wittgenstein of the *Tractatus* as for Aristotle what circulates among them and makes them equivalent is form.

For Aristotle the form, or eidos, is the ultimate root or cause of the being of entities and at the same time of their knowability. Matter without form is the principle of indefiniteness; therefore it is not ousia, "being" or "entity" (*Metaphysics*, 1029a). Only when joined with form does matter become an individual, knowable existent, a this-here of a definite kind (*tode ti*). Aristotle uses the word *eidos* to refer to both the form of the individual entity we perceive and the species to which the individual belongs; this means that the eidos is prior to the distinction between singular and universal.[5] As primary entity or essence (*ti en einai*), form is at once the being of the concrete individual (ousia) and its abstractable intelligible content which can be fixed in a logos or verbal formula.[6]

The concept of form thus cuts across the categories of epistemology and ontology, for the being of the particular is itself exhaustively defined according to the requirements of knowledge. "The Form alone defines the thing," writes Joseph Owens, and "expresses all the Being in the singular thing . . . as knowable and definite" (pp. 361–62), whereas matter, in itself unknowable, only enters into the light of being, of actuality (*energeia* or *entelecheia*), as it is given to form. Thus for Aristotle the form remains "in some way—the thing itself" (Owens, p. 196). This is "the strange sameness of *noein* and *einai* [thought and being] spoken of in Parmenides' poem" to which Derrida refers as the background of Aristotle's thought (*Margins*, p. 182), a connection Owens too remarks (p. 194). Thought, word, and thing are defined in relation to thinkable form, and thinkable form is itself in a relation of reciprocal definition with the concept of entity. That is, the being of the entity is determined as form, but conversely, form itself is conceived as co-incident with the presence to sense intuition of an object. When we perceive an object as *what* the object is, we perceive it as entity, but this means that we perceive it as form, since only the form without the matter can enter the mind. But to perceive form is to perceive an individual entity, since all knowledge of forms is given through sense perception of particulars.[7] Hence we have a peculiar blending of the being of the entity with the ideality of form that led Werner Jaeger to remark that Aristotle really "abolishes the 'things' of naive realism by making them conceptual." According to Jaeger, "the object of sense-experience can come to the knowledge of the thinking subject only so far as it becomes a conceptual form; on the other hand it *is* only so far as it is form. The complete determination of reality by the forms of the understanding and by the categorical multiplicity of their conceptual stratification is rooted not in transcendental laws of the knowing conscious but in the structure of reality itself."[8] Curt Arpe, commenting on the final sentence of the foregoing passage, wrote that for a "non-Kantian" it was "meaningless," since the closing reference to "the structure of reality itself" negated the opening reference to the "determination of reality by the forms of the understanding."[9] It is true that Jaeger was careless in his manner of stating things here; to speak of "form" as "conceptual" or as belonging to the "understanding" is certainly to assimilate Aristotle's way of talking too closely and too quickly to the terms of modern philosophy. On the other hand, as we have seen, even someone like Owens, who shares with Arpe the intention of interpreting Aristotle out of Aristotle himself, arrives at the conclusion that Aristotle remains in some way within the Parmenidean assimilation of being to thinking. Thus if Jaeger's way of putting it is misleading, still it points to something in Aristotle which might be legitimately brought out by a more nuanced explication. If the eidos is not "conceptual," still it is the matching double of the act of mind; nothing in it is opaque or alien to consciousness. If it is not a "form of understanding," still it is a form whose essence is defined in terms which are precisely the same as those by which understanding is defined.[10]

In some sense the eidos, which is the cause of the being of entities, is made of the substance of the ideal, or at least exists in a medium homogeneous with soul or mind. Aristotle himself suggests as much in *De Anima* 3.8, where he writes that "in a way the soul [*psyche*] is all existing things" because the faculties of the soul must be "identical" with the forms of things. The intellect (*nous*) is the *form of forms* (*eidos eidōn*). The homogeneity of intellect and being is also suggested by the way in which Aristotle sometimes uses *logos* interchangeably with *eidos* (*Metaphysics* 1039b20 ff; *De Anima* 412b10–413a3), so that entity seems to be not just correlative with logos but in some way the same as logos.

The intraphilosophical question of being with respect to Plato and Aristotle addresses the relation between the intelligible form and the sensible thing; what is significant from a deconstructive viewpoint is that the sensible thing, even in a "realist" like Aristotle, is itself unthinkable except in relation to intelligible form. Hence, the crucial boundary for Aristotle and for philosophy generally does not pass between thought and thing or between word and thing *but, within each of these, between form and formlessness or indefiniteness.*

All of philosophy works on the other side of the line that separates being according to the logos from the indeterminate, and for Derrida the full weight of this separation comes to rest on the role within philosophy of the third-person present indicative of the verb "to be." The word "is" speaks the being of the thing, and so marks the relation of language to what is outside language (*Margins*, p. 183); it is the linguistic passageway between form as what is knowable and speakable and form as the presence of the entity. Though it is still a word, the "is" seems to be the thinnest membrane, offering almost no distortion or deformation of the being it brings to expression, so that thought by its means could come into the closest relation with being. But thought and being have already been teleo-logically predestined to meet, since they are part of the same mutually de-termined circle of concepts: "One might think then that the *sense of Being* has been limited by the imposition of the *form* which, . . . since the origin of philosophy, seems to have assigned to Being, along with the authority of the *is*, the closure of presence, the form-of-presence, presence-in-form, form-presence. . . . on the other hand, that formality . . . is limited by the sense of Being which . . . has never been separated from its determination as presence" (*Margins*, p. 172).[11]

III

The issue between deconstruction and philosophy does not concern the rights of language or of thought as against the rights of things. Rather, deconstruction questions the determination of the essence of language, thought, and things at once by form-as-presence. Let us now look more closely at the concept of form as determined by Aristotle in the *Metaphys-ics*. Form is the cause of entity (ousia), of a thing's being just that thing which it is and of its being knowable and definable as such. But this means that the concept of form is inseparable from *unity* and *self-identity*, and we are thus led to the principle of contradiction as the "most certain of all principles" (1005b ff.). There is considerable confusion in the expression of this principle in *Metaphysics Four*,[12] but no matter how we explicate it Aristotle's main purpose is clear; he is, as Owens says, "fighting against the flux," looking for a principle that will make a thing be a "definite abiding something," the same as itself and different from anything else (Owens, p. 376). The principle of contradiction is a formal explication of the "is"; it tells us the most general and unyielding constraint that is laid by being upon the language that speaks and the thought that thinks being. Entity is preeminently one and indivisible; this means that the logos that declares its being must also be one and indivisible, and so must be the act of mind that grasps this logos (1016b). The principle of contradiction is thus the expres-sion in logical terms of the ontological principle of form; Owens writes that Aristotle "seems to look upon the principle of contradiction as merely the expression of the formal cause in the act of intellect. . . . one belongs primarily to the thing, the other as such belongs primarily to thought" (p. 286).

It seems as though, whether we like it or not, whether we choose to admit it or not, whether we deny it or affirm it, we presuppose the principle of contradiction by the very fact that we say or think anything that can be understood. Aristotle admits as legitimate the use of the same word in different senses, or "equivocally" (*kath' homonymian*), but each different use of a word will be *one* and distinguishable from the other uses. Even a term like "white," which is accidental as predicated of a subject, will essentially designate the being of the categorical kind to which it belongs (white as such) and thus have a unitary essence (*ti en einai*) in the secondary sense which Aristotle assigns to the being of the categories predicable of primary ousia (1030a–b).[13] This means that equivocality is a movement on the surface of language, while underneath we find the stasis of unitary essences with their corresponding names. "It is not possible for anyone to think of anything if he does not think one thing, and if it is possible, he could then posit one name for this thing" (1006b). Here the principle of contradiction invades the inmost recesses of thought, becomes the origin and wellspring which thought cannot get behind or under or beyond, because it seems that it is the generative principle out of which any thought comes into being. Form is the *horismos*, or boundary of definition, that makes an object be what it is and not anything or everything else, the bulwark that holds it together against the indefinite, and, correlatively, the guarantee of the unity and self-identity of thought.

For the moment, the point I want to emphasize is the way the concept of form shows up in various transformations, first as the form of an object, then as the foundational principle of the formalism of logic, then as what we could call a "psycholinguistic" principle. We are not here worried about whether Aristotle has gotten all his distinctions clear; rather, we are interested in the persistence through these varied manifestations of the same kernel of doctrine. The subsequent history of metaphysics, though shifting Aristotle's emphasis, has to a large degree merely developed doctrines that are already implicit in the basic schema he drew up.

If what is is identical with what is knowable, it becomes easy to lose sight of the distinction between being-in-itself and being-for-knowledge, as in fact happened during the sixteenth and seventeenth centuries, when the modern concept of "ontology" began to be developed. J. F. Mora's sketch of the history of this concept is instructive, since it shows that "ontology" begins as an equivalent for Aristotle's "first philosophy" (the most general science of being, as distinguished from "metaphysics," the science of the branches of being or specific types of beings) and winds up being defined by Clauberg in a way that leaves us on the verge of Kantianism.

The concept of ontology will appear as designating *the* "theoretical science" insofar as it has not yet been divided into branches. Unfortunately . . . despite the claims that the "theoretical science" in question is, as Clauberg once maintained, "at an infinite distance from "rational [purely rational, namely logical] knowledge," it will be increasingly common to cram logical principles into "ontological principles." This is probably due to the fact that Ontology was also considered as purely rational, but since Ontology was to deal with reality (although reality as such, and not any specific types or parts of it), the distinction between Ontology and Logic appeared considerably less clear than the difference between Ontology and Metaphysics proper.[14]

When Clauberg in 1656 defines the subject matter of ontology, "ens," as "whatever can be thought or spoken about," we are not far from the Kantian problematic.

Clauberg and the others who developed the concept of ontology were not simply confused in their reading of Aristotle; the opening to their confusions is given in Aristotle's *Metaphysics*. "First philosophy," the science of being qua being that Aristotle tries to define in the *Metaphysics*, is not the science of specific beings but of the most general principles of any and all beings, and it is at that level of generality that the ambiguity between principles of knowledge and principles of being becomes possible.[15] Since the principles of being are identical with the principles of knowledge, it is easier to stipulate their independence from subjectivity than it is consistently to maintain this independence.

In all its manifestations, form is the transphenomenal boundary of the phenomenon by virtue of which the phenomenon becomes accessible to knowledge. It is the common element in thing, thought, and word that makes them able to line up with each other in truth. Thus form is, as Derrida says, the form of presence, of the accessibility to the knower of the known. Form is the a priori, the necessary predetermination or bounding of the form of a possible cognition, whether as predetermining the experiencing through the form of the experienced (realism), or the experienced through the form of the experiencing (transcendental idealism), or both together (as is perhaps the case in Husserl's phenomenology). From the deconstructive point of view what matters is not where the form is ultimately located, but the form of form or form-in-general, and the relation between the concept of form and that of an object-in-general.

Even for Kant, the unity and self-identity of thought remains tied to the concept of an object.[16] Kant, of course, was as much as Aristotle "fighting against the flux," looking for a *necessary* boundary against formlessness. Thus he writes in the *Critique of Pure Reason* (A 111) that "unity of synthesis according to empirical concepts would be altogether accidental, if these latter were not based on a transcendental ground of unity. Otherwise it would be possible for appearances to crowd in upon the soul, and yet to be such as would never allow of experience. Since connection in accordance with universal and necessary laws would be lacking, all relation of knowledge to objects would fall away."[17] The disconnected flux of empirical intuitions must be subject to an a priori condition that makes possible its synthesis into unity, into a connected whole, and this condition is the transcendental unity of apperception—the "pure original unchangeable" unity of consciousness that "precedes all data of intuitions" (A 104–8). This necessary unity of consciousness unites the manifold of intuition into connected object-representations through the concept of an object in general or "transcendental object," a concept which has no content but its reference to the unity which must be found in the manifold of knowledge as a consequence of its relation to the unity of consciousness (A 109). That is, the transcendental object = X is only the most general concept of "something" within which a manifold of representations can be united as belonging to a single, unified, selfsame thing, a unified phenomenon belonging to the unity of consciousness for which it is an object.

For Kant this problem of establishing the unity of consciousness arises in relation to time. The manifold of intuition is not only a multiplicity but a temporal succession, and Kant is worried about the problem of linking together the moments of this sequence in consciousness. The problem is that phenomena must always be *reproducible* in successive moments, for if I think of a line or the number "787," the representation will take time to be completed in my consciousness. But "if I were always to drop out of thought the preceding representations (the first parts of the line, the antecedent parts of the time period, or the units in the order represented), and did not reproduce them while advancing to those that follow, a complete representation would never be obtained" (A 102). Furthermore, the reproduced representation must be identifiable as belonging to the same whole as the present representation to which it is added: "If we were not conscious that what we think is the same as what we thought a moment before, all reproduction in the series of representations would be useless. For it would in its present state be a new representation which would not in any way belong to the act whereby it was to be gradually generated. The manifold of the representation would never, therefore, form a whole, since it would lack that unity which only consciousness can impart to it" (A 103).

The failure of unity in the manifold of representation would be correlative with the disintegration of the knowing self: "For otherwise I should have as many-coloured and diverse a self as I have representations of which I am conscious to myself" (B 134). The concept of an object-as-unity serves as the rule representing the identity of the function by which consciousness binds together the flow of representations across time. By fixing the identity of this unifying function, the pure concept of an object makes possible the reproduction, as belonging to a unity, of the manifold elements of any given phenomenon.

With Kant we move into the problematic of time that Heidegger has identified as the key to the deconstruction of the philosophy of presence; yet Kant still remains bound to the form of entity. Heidegger's representation of Kant in *Kant and the Problem of Metaphysics* distorts Kant's view of time, presenting it in terms that are really closer to Husserl than to Kant.[18] Kant contrasts the unity of consciousness with the discontinuity of its contents as given in time, and achieves this unity through the unity of the timeless concept of an object. Kant thus remains bound to the thought of form as the self-identity of the form of entity.

IV

In general, then, according to Kant, "the concept of body serves as a rule to our knowledge of external phenomena." Here we find the concept of form, as the form of an object-in-general, translated into a rule for the unification of successive representations, and thus into a version of form that has a relation to time, that gives the form of unity to time. A rule is the form of moments in a temporal sequence, rather than of an entity, yet the form it bestows on this sequence—form as boundary of unity constituting intelligible presence—remains conceivable only on the model of the form of entity. This form, the form of an object-in-general, remains, as with Aristotle, the guardrail of unity and self-identity, both in what is known and in the act of mind by which it is known. Beyond the distinctions between metaphysics and critical philosophy or between ontology and epistemology there remains a thread of continuity between Aristotle and Kant, a thread that may perhaps, if Karl Bärthlein is right, be called strictly *transcendental*.[19]

However, I want to appropriate the term *transcendental* for use in this study not in the strict sense but in a special sense, as a synonym for what Wittgenstein calls the "*super*-order between—so to speak—*super*-concepts" (*PI* 97); that is, for that dimension of heightened power and generality that philosophy tries to gain for its language. Wherever philosophy speaks of necessity, whether essential or logical, or of universality or the *a priori* or the *in principle*—in general, wherever the impulse to safeguard identities leads to "philosopical superlatives" (*PI* 192) that define the transphenomenal boundaries of mere phenomena—that is what in this study will be called the "superhard" or "transcendental." Bärthlein has attempted to link Kant to Aristotle and the Scholastics through the kernel doctrine of the transcendental validity of the Principle of Contradiction, but for the purposes of the present study transcendentality in the strict sense, as going beyond the categories, is only the most extreme version of a transcendentality that from a deconstructive point of view is always at work in philosophy, or is that towards which philosophy always works.

The heightened function of langauge by which Kant attempts to establish transcendental rules for the cognitive functions of consciousness is, from this point of view, only the hyperbolic expression of a transcendentality that shows up in other conceptions of rules. It was one of Wittgenstein's main purposes to unmask this widespread, transcendental conception of rules and to offer an alternative, nontranscendental view. Wittgenstein thought that we commonly misconceive the way rules function in such a way that rules come to seem a unique kind of predetermination of a process. Thus, when I give someone the order to continue a numerical series by adding two to form each successive term (2, 4, 6, 8, 10, . . .), I have the impression that in some way each term of the series, to infinity, is traced out in advance by the order, and needs only to be filled in.

> Your idea was that that act of meaning the order had in its own way already traversed all those steps: that when you meant it your mind as it were flew ahead and took all the steps before you physically arrived at this or that one.
>
> Thus you were inclined to use such expressions as: "The steps are *really* already taken, even before I put them in writing or orally or in thought." And it seemed as if they were in some *unique* way predetermined, anticipated. (*PI* 188)

> "All the steps are really already taken" means: I no longer have any choice. The rule, once stamped with a particular meaning, traces the lines along which it is to be followed through the whole of space. (*PI* 219)

The precursory movement or imagined running-on-ahead-of-itself of consciousness is crystallized in imagination, through the agency of the rule, as determinability and determinacy—that is, as the boundary of *form*—of a sequence of steps not yet taken. Form-as-rule is the frozen trace of the imagined movement of mind running on ahead of itself, a concept historically determined on the model of form as the intelligible presence of an object-in-general.

The deconstructive critique of philosophy focuses on the most general structure of thought that makes it possible to think predetermination as form; that is, it focuses on the form of form. For both Wittgenstein and

Derrida philosophy thinks formal predetermination by imagining that thought secretly or silently runs on ahead of itself—for example, through the manifold of intuition—through all the steps that would be required actually to fill in the outline of an object (or a temporal sequence) and then imagining the determinacy of the object (or temporal sequence) as the outline already traced in imagination. Determinacy is imagined as determinability-in-principle, and determinability-in-principle means "I can imagine someone, perhaps a god, going through these steps."

The transcendental determination of being, cognition, or rule-following guarantees a priori the rational order of that which is so determined—establishes beyond the empirical possibility of accidents, deviations, and unknowabilities a necessary order of the eidos and the logos. Thus the rule "add 2" may be misunderstood or disobeyed, or mistakes might be made in its application, but yet it seems that *in itself*, as *just this rule*, it necessarily determines in a precise and unbendable way a unique series of terms. We do not normally think of our conception of a simple rule like this as "transcendental," yet as a form of ideal predetermination settling atemporally and in a "superhard" fashion the order of the series, that is what it is. Wittgenstein believed that such an attitude toward rules was visible "everywhere in our lives," not only in the technique of calculating but in "innumerable related practices" (*Z*, p. 279). His critique of the concept of a rule is aimed at showing that the form of a rule is essentially multiple and that it is always possible to deviate from the established application of a rule while continuing to adhere to its form. In Wittgenstein's later work there is no inviolable boundary of form to meaning. It is true that for Wittgenstein words have meaning only in the context of "language-games" and "forms of life." But neither language games nor forms of life are to be conceived as structured by some self-identical form that marks their boundaries and makes their varying manifestations instances of the same.[20] Wittgenstein's account runs counter to those views that see human activities as structured by "implicit rules"; for him the actual instances of usage are our "rules."[21] The instances of usage are spatiotemporal phenomena, and are to be "applied" to the understanding of new cases, not as a rule conceived as logos or intelligible form is applied, but rather as an actual physical ruler is applied to a swatch of material for purposes of comparison. In fact, even the ordinary wooden ruler, though less "hard" than the logos-substance of which essence and a priori are made, is more rigid than the "rule" provided by instances of usage. Language samples are more like the elastic ruler of which Wittgenstein speaks in the *Remarks on the Foundation of Mathematics* than they are like the standard meter-stick at Paris.

The "rule for the use of a word" cannot, then, in Wittgenstein's text be construed as a form that makes the meaning present by predetermining it.

And, at the same time, since meaning for Wittgenstein can no longer be simply present, this means that meaning is no longer determined by the "is," by the being of the object. Meaning is neither itself a present form nor does it make present the form of an entity. Wittgenstein's rejection of rules as transcendental forms imposing transcendental necessity is a break with the classical metaphysics of entity, a metaphysics which Kant retained through the form of an object = X. This retention is especially revealing in contrast with Wittgenstein's project because Kant himself accomplished the translation of the form of the object into a rule for a sequence of representations and thus provided a version of the concept of form intermediate between classical metaphysics and the deconstructive picture of meaning as temporally extended syntax, or *differance*.

V

Aristotle speaks of accidents in two senses. In one sense, an accident is a necessary or intrinsic property of an entity, but a property that is not named in the definition of essence. Though not strictly part of the essence, this kind of property belongs within the circle that is traced by the essence definition. The second kind of accident, however, lies outside this circle; it is the sort of individual variation that occurs by chance and that cannot be reliably predicted on the basis of knowledge of the essence. This kind of accident cannot be "known" in the scientific or philosophical sense; it cannot be submitted to law or generalization. Knowing more than Aristotle did about causation, we would have to draw the line between the "regular" and the "chance" accident differently than he does. For him, a man's being white is a "chance" variation, since it is neither always nor usually the case; we would recognize such a variation as law-bound and consistent with the "essence" of man. But regardless of where we draw the line, the basic distinction between the essential (as what is continuous with essence, including law-bound variation) and the accidental (as what escapes the law of essence) must sooner or later come into play.

Accidents in the second sense are the infinite possibilities of variation in the course of things that, because they are infinite, cannot be subjected to rule, cannot be mastered by intellect and language (1007a). Knowledge, says Aristotle, can only be of what is the case always or at least for the most part; but beyond the regularities whose formula the mind can discover there is the illimitable realm of "accidental being," and accidental being is close to "nonbeing." Accidents in this sense, says Aristotle, are not *really* real—they are only names. Now, "accidents" may be innocuous, as when a man happens to be pale, or even happy, as when a man digging a hole for a plant finds a treasure; but the *principle* of accidents (if we can call it a principle) is not innocuous; accidents have no *aition horismenon*, no cause with a definite boundary drawn or drawable about its limits. Accidents come by chance (*to tuchon*), and chance lacks a boundary of definition or definiteness; it is *aoriston* (1025a). Matter, indefinite in itself and capable of bearing infinite predication, is the cause of accidents (1027a), and indefiniteness threatens the principle of being and of knowability, the determinate, unified selfsameness of the same, *kath'auton*—as such.

Derrida's question with respect to this schema is so simple that it can scarcely be misunderstood and so radical in its implications that it can scarcely be understood. It is this: if essence is *always* exposed to the possibility of accidents, is this not then a necessary, rather than a chance, possibility, and if it is always and necessarily possible, is it not then an *essential* possibility?

We said that the accident in the bad sense is for Aristotle whatever cannot be captured by a generalization, and involves in general the indefiniteness or infinitude of possible particularization of the matter, or of the possible relations that it has with everything around it. By the same principle of indefiniteness, it includes also those occurrences that are accidents in the English sense of the word—disruptions of the normal course of things in accordance with purpose, as when a ship is blown off course by a storm (1025a). Generalizing the principle of the accidental, then, we can say that it is the "outside" of essence, the solvent in which the knowable and speakable could lose its form; accidents as catastrophic disruptions in a sense express the essence of the accidental, its character as violation of the eidos boundary. Derrida works something like a figure-field switch on this conception and takes the outside to be *necessary* to the constitution of a phenomenon in its as-such, a condition of the possibility of the "inside." Thus, in "Signature Event Context" Derrida argues that the possibility of infelicity, since it is always possible, ought to be treated as an essential predicate or law of the nature of speech acts. We could call this an instance of the "general" law of accidents, the principle that something can always go wrong with the normal course of things because of the illimitability of its relations with its "outside." But each particular kind of thing will also have a "special" accident that will be the limit appropriate to its own as-such and that will constitute it as that particular kind of as-such. In this sense of a "constitutive outside," the outside is not "accidental" as indefinite, since it is necessary for a given kind of as-such; it is accidental as non-essence that befalls essence.

Now, Derrida works out of the Kant-Husserl "transcendental" tradition; thus, the application of the as-such in his usage is not to things-in-themselves but to things-for-consciousness and to concepts, specifically those concepts that have played an important role in philosophy, such as language, meaning, intention, idea, mimesis, memory, time, origin, representation, sign, and so on—the same kinds of concepts that Wittgenstein is concerned with. There is no question here of looking for the "constitutive outside" of a chair or even of the idea of a chair, which plays no role in the constitution of philosophical conceptuality; but we *are* interested in the concept of "entity" or "object-in-general," which does play such a role. Let us schematize Derrida's concept of constitution in this way: X is constituted by non-X.[22] X here means essence or self-identity as conceived by philosophy, and non-X is that which functions as the "outside," or limit, to the positive assertion of this self-identity, that which keeps ideality from complete closure, yet in *limiting* it remains the *positive* condition of the possibility of the positive assertion of essence. The "special" application of this schema takes many forms. For example, Derrida points out that the necessary condition for the definition of "memory" is that it must be subject to forgetfulness: "a limitless memory" would be "not memory but infinite self-presence" (*Diss.*, p. 109). But there is one form of constitution by non-X that underlies several of Derrida's most important deconstructions, and that is the opposition of *original presence* and *repetition*. In his reading of Husserl, as we will see in detail in the next chapter, Derrida will apply the argument "original presence is constituted by repetition" (i.e., by the non-original, the return or "again" of the original) repeatedly, to the pairs primal impression/reproduction, Now/not-now, and sign-identity/sign-repetition.

This move of Derrida's seems as far as it can be from Wittgenstein's approach. Rather than attacking ideality directly, Derrida appropriates it for his own purposes and uses it against itself. American readers unaccustomed to the metaphysical style of European philosophy may find such twists of thought tedious—perhaps no more than linguistic tricks. I want to suggest, following Wittgenstein, that we can treat the concept of "essence" *grammatically*, that is, as a general term whose principles of operation sum up or schematize the principles of operation of a whole set of other, less metaphysical-sounding terms. Derrida argues that the characteristic move of metaphysics is to set up a binary opposition and then hierarchically subordinate one term of the opposition to the other. Here I take "essence" and "accident" as the most general rubrics under which to range all other instances of this opposition and subordination: all concepts in general of opposition between positive value and privation, inside and outside, purity and contamination, ideal or logical and empirical, a priori and contingent, and more restricted expressions of these oppositions, such as meaning and sign, soul and body, man and animal, and so on. Everything that is said here concerning essence is therefore intended as relevant wherever any of these oppositions, or any others of their type, occurs, and not as a critique of an outmoded style of metaphysical speculation.

Wittgenstein's own attack on the conception of rules as transcendental, or "superhard," is a special case of this general structure. In remarks 193–94 of the *Investigations*, for example, he contrasts a real machine, in which there may always be a "distortion of the parts," with the *picture* of a machine or machine-as-symbol, in which no such distortion is possible. The possibility of a particular movement as given in the *diagram* of the machine or ideal machine seems absolute and immutable, whereas an actual machine is subject to accidents; Wittgenstein wants us to stop thinking of the operation of rules on the model of the machine-as-diagram and think, rather, in terms of something actual that is subject to contingency, to which *accidents may happen*. To think an essential law of contingency, as Derrida does, is to generalize as a "grammatical rule" the principles of the kind of critique that Wittgenstein here instantiates. Whereas "metaphysical grammar" subordinates accident to essence, the empirical to the logical, and so on, "deconstructive grammar" does not. Rather, it attempts to let accidental being operate upon deconstructive writing, deforming it and preventing it from achieving transcendental form. (Hence the "zigzag" movement of Wittgenstein's *Philosophical Investigations*.) The grammatical structures or syntactic exemplars that Derrida devises thus develop the transformations into various terminologies or idioms of the notion of a "constitutive outside," of the non- or anti-essence that violates the boundary of positivity by which a concept has been formerly thought to be preserved in its as-such, but in violating it becomes the positive condition of the possibility of the assertion of that positive boundary. The question still remains as to whether such a paradoxical-sounding formulation as this makes sense, or whether the sense that it makes is worth making in such a peculiar fashion. Can it not be stated in more commonsense and less jarring terms? I believe it cannot. To do so would be to lose the connection with the philosophical tradition and with what has been positively established by that tradition. Derrida does not want to deny the self-identity of concepts or of entities-as-given-to-knowledge; he only denies what we could call the impermeability of the as-such, the transcendentality or logical superhardness of the barrier that marks off the conceptual purity of X from everything that is not-X. It is not that identity is drowned in otherness, but that it is *necessarily* open to it, contaminated by it. Yet the necessity or essential character of this contamination cannot be named unless we first grasp the concept of essence or form as purity, as pure positive self-identity. Otherwise either there is nothing to contaminate, or the force of the contamination is not felt. Furthermore, the claims of positive self-identity are undeniable. The Now cannot be reduced to the not-now. Its essential linkage with the not-now compromises the purity of its positive identity without destroying it.

The point of departure of deconstruction from philosophy is thus quite subtle. The value and necessity of pure concepts and categories are not denied, but they are no longer the last word. We no longer simply note and then set aside the factual or empirical contamination of our unities, but see that they are impure always and in principle, and pursue the implications of this essential law of impurity.

VI

We have already touched on the problem of the Now in Husserl's analysis of time consciousness. It is part of Husserl's own analysis that the present Now "retains" within it a former Now; the issue Derrida raises is whether this retention amounts to a contamination of the full presence of the present Now with what is essentially nonpresence, something that Husserl denies.

We could take this moment in Derrida's critique of Husserl as the opening to the deconstructive divagation from classical philosophy. Husserl himself prepared the way for Derrida; even though Husserl maintains the privilege of the Now in classical fashion, the concept of retention of a past Now within the present Now provides Derrida with the basic structure that he will adapt for his own purposes. It is what he calls the structure of the "trace." In the *Grammatology*, Derrida elaborates the concept of the trace as the general structure of the sign, but before it is the structure of signs in the usual sense of signs, the trace is the general structure of experience as lived time:[23] "Such would be the originary trace. Without a retention in the minimal unit of temporal experience, without a trace retaining the other as other in the same, no difference would do its work and no meaning would appear. It is not the question of a constituted difference here, but rather, before all determination of the content, of the *pure* movement which produces difference. *The (pure) trace is différance*" (*Gramma.*, 62).

Following Heidegger, Derrida sees the privilege of the Now-point as defining classical metaphysics, the "metaphysics of presence," which has determined the form of entity as presence in the Now, the Now as "the intemporal kernel of time," and time itself as the not-now and therefore not-being.[24] The trace as a "retention" in the "minimal unit of temporal experience" fundamentally displaces the privilege of the Now as the intemporally present form of time, and experience can be thought of as structured by "différance," by the relation, in the first instance, to a not-now that inhabits the Now, and then by the relation to a constitutive outside in general—that is, by the relation to a whole series of determinations of the outside, such as space, materiality, animal nature, the unconscious, and the female, all of which have been classically defined as the Other to the corresponding series of privileged terms that flows from form, *nous*, and the Logos.

Derrida's emphasis on language and signification is not a "privileging" of language but one way of explicating the very general structure I have just outlined, of which the core is the "reference" within the Now to a past Now. Experience-in-general as experience in time has a trace- or sign-structure, as reference of a present to a nonpresent term.[25]

The strict integrity of the present is either the self-identical form of time within which an entity or truth could be present to the knowing intellect, or the form of the entity itself, in itself, as that which is present. As soon as this strict integrity is violated by *differance*, by the essential constitution of the present by the reference inscribed within it to what is nonpresent, the door is open to nonessence and thus to what would classically be conceived as formlessness or the flux (though, as we shall see, the flux is not our only alternative). The question of language must be understood within this more general problematic; otherwise we misconceive deconstruction as simply asserting some such doctrine as that "we cannot get outside of language." The question, What is language? must be answered before we can know the sense of such a doctrine. The deconstructive answer or non-answer is so radically different from the classical philosophical conception of language that the actual situation turns out to be more accurately conceived as the inverse of what it appears: it could in fact be argued that deconstruction is a challenge to the covert privileging of language by classical philosophy. Despite all their expressed mistrust of the medium of words, philosophers have generally maintained a confident optimism in the possibility of purifying language, of finding its core of truth-telling power. The aim has been subordination of language to the reality which that language is to describe; yet that reality is itself postulable only in language. Deconstruction could be seen as founded in a skeptical questioning of the power of philosophical language to give us a reality that is more than reality-as-presented-by-philosophical-language. And yet this skepticism might go with a feeling of perfect at-homeness in the world and of quite unbothered satisfaction, for ordinary purposes, with our ordinary ways of talking about the world—that is, with talk about "objects" and "reality" that does not seek to generalize and formalize itself, to give itself a transcendental reassurance of its connection with reality.

The deconstructive critique of language could even be phrased as a *denial that there is language*. Not, of course, a denial that we speak and write, that we have dictionaries and Berlitz schools and so on, but a denial that there is any *boundary of essence* between what we call language and what we think of as nonlanguage. The question of the privileging of language can arise only when we have first given language an identity as something distinctive, as having its very own form. Let us consider what the philosophical concept of language is that deconstruction criticizes. We do not mean by "language" sounds we make with our mouths or marks we make with our pens; there is only language where there is that ideality we call "meaning." The essence of a word *as word*, beyond its appearance as a spatiotemporal thing or event, is derived from this added dimension of meaningfulness. Derrida in his commentary on Husserl's *Origin of Geometry* (pp. 67–72) finds that Husserl distinguishes three levels of ideality of meaning. The ideality of the word—its self-identity as "type" over against its individual manifestations—is the lowest level of ideality; the "single" word *lion* can be repeated by any number of speakers, can be spoken or written, and so on. This identity is "bound" to the sensuous configurations within a given language (in this case, English) that will count as instances of "the same word." Ingarden, Husserl's disciple, calls this level of ideality the "word-sound" (roughly equivalent to Saussure's "signifier") and distinguishes it from the "phonic material." [26] A second, higher level of ideality is the unity of the word's sense or signification. I need not know the sense of *lion* to recognize it as the same word across its different occurrences (first level of ideality); when I do know its sense, I can "intend" or think this sense (second level) on the basis of the word. The identity of the sense is, unlike the identity of the word, not bound to any particular set of signs in a given language; I can intend the sense of *lion* in other languages through words that are completely different in their sensuous appearance from the word *lion*.

Yet the *sense* of *lion* is still bound to its referent, and depends upon the actual experience of actual lions. Here, the *ideality* of the sense is still grounded in empirical *actuality*, and in order for the word to have sense it must ultimately be referred back to the existence of an actual, perceivable lion. Only the highest level of ideality is free from dependence on contingent realities. The ideal objectivities of logic and mathematics exist timelessly, and their sense is in principle always accessible to rationality, beyond any particular language or particular experience of any actual individual existent. As Husserl puts it in *Experience and Judgment*, "free idealities" are "bound to no territory, or rather, they have their territory in the totality of the universe and in every possible universe" (p. 267). It is true that even free idealities must be embodied in language, but, as Derrida says, they "are rooted only in language in general, not in the factuality of languages and their particular linguistic incarnations" (*Intro.*, p. 66).

But even the first level of ideality, the ideality of the "word-sound," is, in this schema, derived from ideality at the level of sense. Even if, knowing a language, I can here and there encounter sounds and recognize them as repeatable word-sounds though I do not know what they mean, this is only possible because I model my recognition of them on my recognition of words whose sense I do understand, and because they are given in a context that signals their word character. And in words whose meaning I do know, as Ingarden puts it, the "form" of a "word-sound" is "bestowed on the concrete phonic material through the identical meaning."[27] The varying occurrences of the sensuous material of the sign (tokens) are given unity as occurrences of the same sign (type) by this ideal meaning. Free ideality, then, the independence in principle of meaning from its particular embodiments, would seem to be the essence or *telos* of language. What we normally call words would derive their identity as words from that which is in its essence independent of words; the primacy of words would then be the primacy of that ideality that makes the word a word. And if the field of signification is oriented hierarchically toward the *telos* of pure meaning, then the ideality that is in its essence *most free of language*, ideality of the third level, would appear to be that which most fully manifested the essence of what we call language.

Thus it is misleading to say that Wittgenstein, for example, "wants to establish the *primacy* of language in thought"[28] so long as we have not carefully distinguished the word whose essence is ideality, *Verbum* or *Logos*, from the word as what Wittgenstein calls "spatio-temporal phenomenon" and Derrida calls the "remainder."

Now, there is no denying the validity, within limits, of the picture of meaning as free ideality, nor has Derrida ever denied it. From his earliest work onward, he has always recognized the necessity of "identity of sense" as "ground" of the possibility of the "reactivation" of a text by the consciousness of someone other than its creator (*Intro.*, pp. 103–5). But for Derrida the domination of the signifying substance by the ideality of its identity is restricted and *is itself constituted* by the necessity that this identity must be essentially capable of being spread around in a variety of tokens. Whereas the classical analysis of the sign has split it neatly along a presumed conceptual fault-line between matter and form, with matter as the spread of particulars subordinated to the ideality of their identity, Derrida treats the relation between ideality and embodiment, as it were, horizontally. The varying phenomenal occurrences of a sign are an empirical fact, but the necessity that the sign-type must always appear in such contingent and different repetitions is essential. The sign-type is constituted in its conceptual essence by its "iterability," its repeatability in principle in a series of tokens that, as distinct spatiotemporal things, to some extent differ from each other. This iterability is no accident; if the type were not iterable it would not be a sign, could not perform the signifying function. On the other hand, if there were not "a certain self-identity" of the sign that would permit its recognition "across empirical variations of tone, of voice, etc.," the varying sign phenomena could not function as signs either (*Margins*, p. 318). The structure of iteration "implies both identity *and* difference," and Derrida places difference on a par with identity as having essential status. Iterability, or the capacity to be multiple, constitutes the identity or essence of the sign as sign and, as Derrida says, "splits the identity of the sign *a priori*" (*Ltd Inc*, p. 190); while unity, the capacity to remain in some measure itself, makes iterability possible. Thus Derrida whittles down the purity or self-containedness of ideal identity to what he calls "a minimal remainder" of selfsameness made possible by a "minimum of idealization," (*Ltd Inc*, p. 190), a minimum which is essentially subject to having its ideality nibbled away at, in each of its iterations, by the deformations of material incarnation.[29] Whereas in the classical account the ideality of the type was sealed off from contamination by the variability of the particulars, in Derrida's account the two are essentially linked, and identity and difference coexist on the same level of dignity, instead of difference being cast out and down from the purity of the Logos.

There is in fact nothing paradoxical about Derrida's formulation, or if there is, it is the paradox of the One and the Many that has been with us since the beginning of philosophy. The elevation of the One to a status essentially or logically sealed off from the contingency of the Many creates its own characteristic paradox of what the relation can be between two sorts of things having essentially distinct natures. Plato of course pushed the paradox to its ultimate conclusion with the doctrine of the separate Ideas, which Aristotle rejected, but Aristotle's own doctrine of the eidos, which is capable of manifesting itself both as particular and as universal, turns out to be just as paradoxical in its own way.[30]

The notion of a constitutive outside is the deconstructive alternative to the fundamental philosophical concept of form or essence—that is, of unity and self-identity as the most general and inviolable boundaries (whether strictly transcategorical or not) of being and knowledge. As the admission of the not-itself into the citadel of the as-such, this notion appears to open the way to the flux Aristotle and Kant feared. This flux is the flux of particulars. The transcendental function of language is the heightening of the abstracting and generalizing power of words; transcendentality in the strict sense is only the highest flight of this power of generalization. To know is always to categorize, and even for Aristotle the name of that which guarantees the unity and self-identity of *this* individual here is the same as the name of its membership in a category: *eidos* means both "form" (of the individual) and "species." All of philosophy takes place within the medium of nous or Logos, within which form is possible. Outside the Logos, says Aristotle, is primary matter (*prōtē hylē*), the principle of indefiniteness, pure potentiality, absolutely unknowable in itself. Beyond the boundary of the eidos with its unitary formula (logos), unformed matter would bear infinite predication, a limitless spread of particularization, which would be nothing but babble.

But must we really restrict ourselves to these two alternatives of form and chaos? Is this not a rather lurid picture? We know that Wittgenstein's hostility toward philosophy was a hostility toward its love of generalization and "contempt for the particular case." His own method could be described as a systematic and regulated leakage across the boundaries of established categories, a method for allowing what seemed accidental to acquire cognitive centrality—at least momentarily. Deconstruction is not a defense of formlessness, but a regulated overflowing of established boundaries, and Derrida has formulated the most general principle of this overflowing as the principle of a constitutive outside. But when the principle of the constitutive outside is applied to the analysis of language itself, it turns back upon the medium within which all analysis must be formulated. In order to find the logos or formula of essence of any determined being, we must have available the medium of Logos as the ideality of sense within which particular ideal unities can be fixed. Thus to turn the question of the constitutive outside back upon language itself, and to restrict the field of its ideality while opening out its capacity to differ from itself ever anew, seems to be to strike directly at the bulwarks of sense.

The question that arises is, then, What does one do once one has given up the idealizing project of knowledge, the effort to unify ever more particulars under ever more powerful subsumptive formulas? Part of the answer is that we *cannot* give up—at least, not entirely—the project of idealization. Even to use language at all is already to idealize, to classify; and to practice anything so closely related to philosophy as deconstruction is to idealize and generalize on a large scale. It is not a question of giving up idealization, but of modulating it, of allowing it to open out onto some possibilities that have not been conceivable under the old formulas.

In particular, limiting the claim of ideality to determine the essence of language opens up once more the question of the status of metaphor and figuration in general. So long as reason and order are conceived in relation to the ideality of Logos, uses of language that draw upon the resources of its phenomenality can be judged inferior, inessential, or merely ornamental compared to the objective sense uttered by the discourse on truth of philosophy or science.[31]

The limitless iterability of the sign, its capacity to appear again and again in new contexts where its meaning differs, however slightly, from its meaning in any previous context (even if only because this is now and that was then), means that in order to understand each appearance in its difference we must study its context or syntax.[32] Only in relation to its surroundings in each particular occurrence does the "minimal remainder" that we identify as the same word acquire the charge of differentiation that is required to fill out its "iterated" (repeated yet also transformed, made "other," "iter") sense. We can see the convergence between Derrida and Wittgenstein in this notion of continually different contextualized meaning as the focus of investigation. The "spatio-temporal phenomenon of language" that is the object of their investigation cannot, obviously, be pure sensuous material, and must retain enough ideality to make it perceptible *as language*; but, on the other hand, the permeability to context of its identity makes this identity shade off into its surroundings; and since the surroundings which determine its meaning are both linguistic and nonlinguistic, the identity of the sign as language also shades off into what is not-language.[33]

The "materiality of the sign" of which Derrida speaks can thus not be reduced either to simple materiality nor to the materiality of the signifier as defined by Saussure: "The remainder is not that of the signifier any more than it is that of the signified, of the 'token' or the 'type,' of a form or of a content" (*Ltd Inc*, p. 189). It is closer to the materiality of dream language as Derrida discusses it in one of his essays on Freud ("Freud and the Scene of Writing"), the "materiality" that makes words capable of being replaced ("condensed") by things so that things can then stand in pictorially or hieroglyphically for the words (*W&D*, p. 219). Speech, word-language, is "subordinated" on the "dream-stage": "Far from disappearing, speech then changes purpose and status. It is situated, surrounded. . . . It figures in dreams much as captions do in comic strips, those picto-hieroglyphic combinations in which the phonetic text is secondary and not central in the telling of the tale" (p. 218). Wittgenstein's *Investigations* can be seen as similarly resituating speech within the scenes in which it occurs and finds its place, and most strikingly philosophical speech, which is transcendental speech itself, speech that attempts to transcend the particularity of any particular context. "Ask yourself: On what occasion, for what purpose, do we say this? What kind of actions accompany these words? (Think of a greeting.) In what scenes will they be used; and what for?" (*PI* 489).

If we think of the highest dignity of language as its capacity to correspond in the ideality of its sense to the form of Entity, of what really is (whether empirically, ideally, or logically), then its variable phenomenal surface can be set apart as having no essential role, as a deficient or inferior stratum of the Logos. The spatiotemporal phenomenon of language is insufficiently distinguishable from the scenes in which it occurs, from the gestures and things and events whose form language ought to be able to liberate, rather than disappearing into their phenomenality. But if words become things among other things, and both wordhood and thinghood cease to mean what they mean so long as the boundary of form holds, then the work of figuration in language can no longer be relegated to a position of inessentiality. In order to present the sense of words we must present the scenes of their use; and these scenes are themselves presented in words; the words *are* scenes when their materiality and power of figuration are unleashed. Derrida and Wittgenstein both rely heavily, though in very different ways, on figuration, on image and metaphor, in general on *style*.

And now of course the insistent philosophical question arises once again. When we give ourselves up to the shifting phenomenality of language, where are the boundaries against nonsense? The answer is: in the method or technique of writing, in the character of the syntax or concatenation of terms and scenes. We no longer rely on a correspondence between the form in the Logos and the form of the Entity, because we deny that such a relation can be constituted without a relation to the outside, and especially not without the relation to a past Now. There is no sense without syntax, *différance*: "Now suppose I sit in my room and hope that N. N. will come and bring me some money, and *suppose one minute of this state could be isolated, cut out of its context*; would what happened in it then not be hope?—Think, for example, of the words which you perhaps utter in this space of time. They are no longer part of this language. And in different surroundings the institution of money doesn't exist either" (*PI* 584; italics added).

VII

A question of technique then—or, let us say, of style. But not of *mere* style, because we can no longer make an essential distinction between the phenomenality and the ideality of language. The question of deconstructive style is not that of its relation to truth but of its relation to the *discourse on* truth—that is, to the language of philosophy. In Wittgenstein and Derrida we have two styles, two relations to the discourse on truth, akin yet very different. In this book I emphasize the kinship; the differences are obvious, though this obviousness would bear much analysis. From the point of view of the present study, what matters most about the difference between Wittgenstein and Derrida is precisely the difference of style. Both styles are so original and powerful that it is easy for those who are drawn to deconstruction to come under their influence and ape their favorite terms and linguistic mannerisms. The present book will undoubtedly not have succeeded in escaping this influence. But there is nothing so inimical to the basic impulse of deconstruction as the adoption of a canonical style. To deconstruct philosophy is to wean ourselves from the canonical conceptual structures embodied in the vocabulary and style of philosophy; but if we replace these structures with a new, improved set, we are right back where we started. Deconstruction, in order to remain deconstruction, must be recursively applied to itself. This is difficult, perhaps impossible, to do unless we have alternative ways of going about it, alternative styles that can pull us in different directions.

So it is essential that Derrida and Wittgenstein not be *too* close together. A mesmerizing style, like a Medusa's head, will turn us to stone if we stare at it too long; we need a talisman to draw us away from it. But the talisman itself becomes Medusa when we turn to it, and the other then must pull us back. If in this study I try to bring Wittgenstein into an alliance with Derrida, this is ultimately in order to throw them against each other, to create a space of movement between their two styles where the fixation against which they warn us, but which they can cause, can be averted, and deconstruction can avoid becoming that "beautiful garment" of which Wittgenstein speaks, "that is transformed (coagulates, as it were) into worms and serpents if its wearer looks smugly [*selbstgefällig*] at himself in the mirror" (*Culture*, p. 22).

1 Meaning and Time

1 The Opening of Deconstruction in the Text of Phenomenology

Phenomenology, which can play the role of "tradition" for a European like Derrida, is in this country still an alien growth. In Europe, Husserl's phenomenology has been the great source from which have sprung a succession of major philosophical projects. Heidegger, Sartre, and Merleau-Ponty are only the most famous of Derrida's predecessors in the line of thinkers taking their departure from Husserl. In a European context, it makes sense that Derrida should treat Husserl as the culmination of classical philosophy, and phenomenology as the necessary point from which to move into a form of discourse that will no longer be philosophy, while yet having taken into account the full force of the laws of philosophical discourse. But in America Husserl has had no such central role, and the sense and force of Derrida's critique of phenomenology is necessarily lost on those who have never been much concerned with what Derrida criticizes.[1]

Deconstruction is not a system of concepts but a *textual labor*, a way of traversing the body of a text. Derrida's work on Husserl leaves "a track in the text" of Husserl, and the track cannot be traced without reference to the text in which it is marked. There is, Derrida argues, a "short-of" and a "beyond" of transcendental criticism, and to fail to traverse the text of Husserl is to risk falling back into the "naive objectivism" which Husserl rigorously criticized. Having traversed this text, we must retain the track of the journey; otherwise, "abandoned to the simple content of its conclusions, the ultra-transcendental text will so closely resemble the precritical text as to be indistinguishable from it" (*Gramma.*, p. 61). We must therefore begin this account of deconstruction with an account of the phenomenological text in which deconstruction is opened.

It should be understood, however, that Husserl's text is not here treated merely as a convenient foil for deconstruction. On the contrary, my own conviction is that Husserl's thought has great and enduring significance

31

and that recognition of this significance is bound to increase in America in the years to come. The central concerns of Husserl from the *Logical Investigations* to the *Crisis* were twofold: first, to establish that the objects of our knowledge are "transcendent" to the mental acts by which we know them—that is, not a "real" (*reell*) component of our psychological flow but ideal identities that could be repeated as identically the same by different subjects. But, second, Husserl was passionately concerned that man should not become a mere "technician," manipulating without "insight" the items of knowledge accumulated by his tradition. Husserl urged that in the process of knowledge accumulation we should constantly recover the generative or "constitutive" activity of thought that is required for the original institution of truths or fixing of insights in language, where they will be available for others. Language stores up insights for us, but saves us the trouble of actively bringing them into being; it is our ethical responsibility to quicken them with the constitutive activity of our own minds. Thus Husserl tells us in the *Crisis* that the meaning of scientific formulae is not in the relations of numbers but in a *task* given to scientific humanity (p. 41).

Husserl conceived of the task of the philosopher as enormously great. He thought the philosopher was "responsible for mankind" and philosophy was the entelechy of mankind become manifest to itself (*Crisis*, pp. 15–17). The phenomenological standpoint achieved through the "reduction," Husserl said, was a "complete personal transformation, comparable in the beginning to a religious conversion" (*Crisis*, p. 137). It is not the fashion in the Anglo-American world today to conceive of the philosopher in such terms; reading Husserl, and especially the *Crisis*, we come in contact with an archaic, even Greek, sense of the mission and dignity of philosophy. Indeed, Husserl saw himself as bringing to completion the task begun by Greek philosophy—and perhaps he was right.[2]

Precisely how are we to conceive of the relation between Husserl's philosophy of "presence" and Derrida's of *différance*? I do not think that it is a simple matter of choosing between them; and certainly Derrida always avoids such simple acceptances and rejections. Furthermore, I think it is unlikely that anyone who does not know what it means to desire to be awake to the meaning of his symbolic manipulations in the way Husserl teaches (e.g., *LI*, pp. 722–29) can grasp deconstruction in its strongest form. So the following account of Husserl's thought, though presented with an eye to the way it leads into deconstruction, ought not be taken as pretending to pass judgment on phenomenology. Deconstruction works a certain amount of violence on Husserl's text, but not in order to undo this text; rather, to wrest from it materials necessary to the construction of another text that functions according to different laws.

II

Philosophy aims at knowledge of what is true. This formula may be redundant, since knowledge by definition cannot be of what is false (though it may be of *the fact that* something is false). But still, knowledge is one thing and that which is known is another, and the question of how to forge an ironclad link between the two cannot be disposed of by a definition. *If* we have knowledge, then what we know is true; but everything hangs on that if, and the only way we have of checking it out is by examining the matter we seek to know. Now, however, when we go back and look at the thing itself over again to verify our previous judgment, all we get is a new set of judgments. The ideal of knowledge as *adaequatio* is precisely that knowledge must be of what *is*, in itself; knowledge cannot manufacture its objects according to whim but must adjust itself to the structure of what subsists independently of the cognitive act. The paradox is that what *is* independently of our experience only becomes accessible in *experience*, and the experience is not the same as the thing of which it is the experience. We believe that trees and rocks and so on exist when no one is sensing them, but we can have no experience of this unexperienced existence. We can never have the satisfaction of saying to the skeptic, "You see—there it is, even when you're not looking at it." So even the most resolute realist must admit that objects are by their very nature objects of knowledge only in the experience of subjects, and this is why "empiricism" so easily becomes a kind of idealism. *Empeiria*, "experience," may be experience *of objects*, but it is finally only *experience* of objects.

This is what Husserl called the "problem of transcendence." Husserl uses the word *transcendence* to refer to the objectivity of objects, their existence outside of the temporal flow of consciousness. In this sense, material objects as well as ideal objects such as mathematical truths are said to be "transcendent." "That I attain certainties, even compelling evidences, in my own domain of consciousness, . . . is understandable. But how can this business, going on wholly within the immanency of conscious life, acquire Objective significance? How can evidence (*clara et distincta perceptio*) claim to be more than a characteristic of consciousness within me?" (*CM*, pp. 82–83). For Husserl, the telos of rationality was objective knowledge, knowledge of a world, and he could not rest content with a mere subjective or even a purely logical self-evidence; but, on the other hand, he insisted upon self-evidence as the goal of phenomenological reflection. Phenomenology was to be an "absolutely transparent method," absolutely free from presuppositions, which would simply describe consciousness precisely as it is, and objects only as given to consciousness (*Ideas I*, p. 20). Yet it had somehow to preserve, within consciousness, the relation to an outside; within subjectivity, the relation to objectivity.

Husserl resolved the problem of this relation through the concept of "intentionality," the directedness of consciousness to the objects of which it is conscious. Even as there is no appearing of an object without an experience within which it appears, so there is no experience without an object of which it is the experience (that is, which the experience "intends"). The category of "objectivity" and that of "evidence" are thus, Husserl says, "perfect correlates": an objectivity is a unity of a specific kind which is precisely correlative to a possible experience of a corresponding kind (*Logic*, p. 161). It still remains true that objects appear only for experience, that "every externality . . . has its place from the very beginning in the pure internality of the ego" (*Logic*, p. 230), but what is given to consciousness is given "*as what* it is," with the specific "sense" (*Sinn*) or meaning which is appropriate to the type of objectivity that it is. And "if what is experienced has the sense '*transcendent*' *being*, then *it is the experiencing itself that constitutes this sense*" (*Logic*, p. 233; italics added). The "sense" of what we experience as an object out there (i.e., as "transcendent") is given within experience, but is given precisely as the sense "an object out there."

Thus what is "outside" (the "transcendent") is given as part of the "inside" (as "immanent"), yet not as an actual or real (*real*) material object, but as the *sense* (*Sinn*) "material object." This means that to attain the "phenomenological viewpoint" in which the problem of transcendence is resolved, we must leave behind the "natural standpoint" which science and the common man share. In the "natural standpoint" I posit, explicitly or implicitly, that the objects of which I am conscious really exist (and I sometimes raise questions about this existence, for example, concerning mistaken perceptions). Phenomenology, as a reflection upon this natural consciousness, seeks merely to describe what is evident, what is absolutely given within consciousness. Thus, phenomenological reflection suspends or "brackets" the question of existence, "puts out of action" the thesis or judgment that things exist, and reflects on the "experience as lived" by which the thesis is posited, yet without itself positing anything concerning the being of the objects of the experiences it reflects upon (*Ideas I*, pp. 96–100). The thesis that this or that is actually present to my perception belongs to the natural standpoint; from the phenomenological standpoint, the thesis remains the same, but it does not belong to phenomenological judgment as such; rather, it belongs to the experience-of-an-object which as a whole is the "object" to be described in phenomenological reflection. Thus, in the natural standpoint I judge that there is a tree before me; engaging then in the phenomenological "abstention" or *epokhe*, I do not make a judgment of existence, I only *view* this judgment as *part of the phenomenon* of consciousness to be described. Whether the tree is really there or not is indifferent; what remains, regardless of this, is the absolute fact that for the consciousness I am describing, a tree appears which is judged

by that consciousness to be really there (*Ideas I*, p. 244). The phenomenological *epokhe* is not a skeptical questioning of existence, not a "Cartesian
doubt," but a change of perspective which makes no use of the judgment
concerning existence, but only of the absolute being of the modality of
consciousness which makes such judgments.

We thus pass in phenomenological reflection from a simple distinction
between what is in consciousness and what is outside it into a much more
differentiated schema. The "sensualist" or "psychologistic" view against
which Husserl reacted saw the ideas of objects as entering consciousness in
the form of bundles of sensations, which then function within consciousness as images or representatives of the object. This sort of schema leads to
a split between an inner object which is really perceived and an outer object which is the source of the bundle of sensations but which itself is
only inferred rather than perceived. As Hume puts it, "nothing is ever
really present to the mind, besides its own perceptions" (*Treatise*, bk. 1,
chap. 2).[3] This sort of view is in one sense an "idealism" reducing real objects to their perceptual representatives in consciousness. But in another
sense it is really a sensualism or materialism, because the perceptual representatives which are the objects for consciousness are conceived as ready-
made packages of sensile stuff which impinge upon a passive consciousness. The "inner object" is really just another version of the outer object,
and nothing has been gained by the separation, which presents us with
two objects, one of which remains out there while the other is now in here,
a miniaturized version in my head.

As against this view, Husserl argued that there must be an interpretive
or constitutive *activity* of consciousness, aimed at a purely ideal objectivity,
if we are to have a truly accurate description of perceptual consciousness.
The distinction between "real" (*reell*), temporal contents of a particular
consciousness, and ideal or "irreal," and therefore intersubjectively available, contents is essential to such a description. The bundle of sensations
which I experience at this moment, as a "real content" of consciousness, is
a different bundle from what I experience tomorrow, or someone else experiences now, even if they are sensations occasioned by the same object
viewed from the same perspective. In order for my perception of this tree
to be the same as yours, or the same as my own of yesterday, there must be
an *ideal* identity between perceptions, since sensations, as real contents of
an individual consciousness at a particular moment, cannot be the same
sensations as those in someone else's consciousness. Sensations must be "apprehended" or "animated" by consciousness as having a particular "sense"
(*Sinn*).

> I see a thing, e.g. this box, but I do not see my sensations. I always
> see *one and the same box*, however *it* may be turned and tilted . . . each

turn yields a *new* 'content of consciousness' . . . though the same object is perceived. The experienced content, generally speaking, is not the perceived object. . . . different sensational contents are given . . . but . . . we apperceive or 'take' them 'in the same sense,' and . . . *to take them in this sense [die Auffassung nach diesem 'Sinne'] is an experienced character through which the 'being of the object for me' is first constituted.* (*LI*, pp. 565–66)[4]

Mere sense experience is, in this view, a "raw existence" requiring an intentional act to, "as it were, ensoul" it (*beseelen*) (*LI*, p. 567) and turn it into a conscious perception of an object.[5] Unlike the varying sense-experiences through which the object is given, the object perceived retains its identity as the same object, and this identity is what Husserl calls the "sense."

Thus, Husserl in the *Investigations* resolves the problem of immanence by distinguishing the object intended, which is transcendent, from the immanent sensory contents on the basis of which the object is intended. It is part of the *sense* of the "perceptual interpretation" of sensory contents that the perceptually intended object is an actual object out there. This sounds like an accommodation to naive realism, yet at the same time it is a new form of idealism. So long as the object is thought of as simply real, as a "ready-made" material object, it succumbs to the sensualist view according to which the object can simply be reproduced internally as an impression or internal image, thus as a second, subject or psychological, reality which replaces the first. In order to restore the objectivity of the object, its transcendence to subjectivity, Husserl argues that its identity must be ideal, must be an identity not of sensations but of meaning or sense. This means that the relation to a real object transcendent to subjectivity is guaranteed by understanding the real object through an ideally constituted identity. Only such an ideal objectivity is capable of being known or experienced as identically the same for different subjects, who cannot share identically the same real (*reell*) sensory contents (*Logic*, pp. 162–66).

In order to keep straight the relation between ideality and reality in Husserl's account, it is essential to keep in mind the distinction between the natural and phenomenological standpoints. In the natural standpoint, I see a tree before me; I perceive, not the inner representation of the tree, but the tree itself (on the basis of an experienced, but not itself perceived, "sensory content"). Now, shifting to the phenomenological reflection upon this natural consciousness, everything is preserved just as it is, but new elements of the scene come into view, are "thematized" as "objects." What I perceive is the tree, but when I reflect on my perceiving, on what is evident to the perceiving consciousness, what I "see" is the perceiving-of-the-tree—that is, the appearing of the tree to perception. This tree-as-appearing, or "perceived tree," is not a new, internal reality standing in place of the tree; it is simply the tree insofar as it actually appears for my perception. In the natural standpoint, my attention is absorbed in the object intended by my perception. But when I describe the character of the *perceiving* precisely as given to my reflection, this description has different characteristics than would the description of the *tree*. The most obvious difference is that, whereas the tree is susceptible of an infinite number of perspectival viewings, the tree as given to my perceiving—that is, as "noema," or correlate of consciousness—is the single perspective which is given to consciousness in one possible viewing. I look at this tree from a distance; then I approach closer; I take a nap under its branches; now I look up at these branches from underneath. At each moment I have a different perspectival apprehension of the tree, and this apprehension is not identical with the total tree. Yet *through* this perspective I perceive or "intend" the whole tree as it is capable of unfolding in an unlimited series of further perspectives. Now, the tree-as-appearing, or noema, unlike the "mental image" of representationalism, is not an object; it has no reality of its own. But the noema becomes an object *for the phenomenological reflection*, which is directed not towards objects but towards the modes in which consciousness is aware of objects. This reflection suspends or brackets the question of reality. The operation of bracketing, the phenomenological "reduction" of the material world, treats the mental act (noesis) as an absolute being without regard to questions of correspondence to empirical reality, and the noema, or object-as-perceived, as the correlate of this act. Whatever is present to consciousness, whether empirically it is an illusion or not, is susceptible to phenomenological investigation simply as being-for-consciousness.

Husserl considered the phenomenological reduction of the empirical or "natural" standpoint fundamental to his method. The phenomenological standpoint retains everything that is given to the natural standpoint, but views it in an entirely new way, as being-for-consciousness. Consequently, phenomenology is a form of "idealism," and has sometimes been accused of having become, with the reduction, nothing more than an "ordinary subjectivism."[6] But because the noema, or object-as-perceived, contains as part of its sense a reference to the objective world, phenomenology subtends both realism and idealism as they ordinarily have been conceived.

The crucial notion is that of the *irreality* of the noema. The noema is not a new something that comes between mind and world; its being is purely ideal, but not in the "Platonic" sense that it is a reality existing elsewhere (in a *topos ouranios*, or "heavenly place," as Husserl sarcastically says). It has being only in the sense that it has a definite and definable identity, and that this identity is capable of being reexperienced in any number of intentional acts and by any number of intentional subjects. The ideality of the noema is just the *repeatability as the same* of an objective identity or "sense." Hence, as Aron Gurwitsch says, the noesis-noema doctrine is not a theory but "a simply descriptive statement of an objectivating mental state, i.e., of a mental state through which the experiencing subject is confronted with an object."[7]

What is at stake in phenomenology is thus also at stake in projects seemingly far removed from phenomenology. Any project of truth, whether metaphysical, empiricist, or logicist, must be concerned with drawing the definite boundaries of (real or ideal) objects correlative with possible knowings, in such a way that these truths will be accessible to any rational subject in general. But that means that truths must be definite, unvarying, and "repeatable"; that is, their truth must be indefinitely capable of being brought to evidence again for a rational gaze.

The esoteric and seemingly metaphysical complexity of Husserl's language should not obscure the fundamental agreement between his aims and those of more familiar approaches. In particular, the notion of "irreality," far from being "metaphysical" in the sense of postulating a strange, other-dimensional realm of being, attempts nothing more than the rigorous formalization of a perfectly familiar fact, the mode of "being" of the *proposition* (*EJ*, p. 264). The concept of the proposition is central to modern philosophy, and a proposition has the peculiar characteristic that in order to be fully identical with itself, it cannot be identical with any of its spatiotemporal embodiments in signs.[8] The "thought" or "proposition" embodied in a statement or symbolic notation is, as Husserl says, a "free ideality" which is, in itself, neither in time nor in space, yet by virtue of being nowhere and notime is capable of being anywhere, anytime, repeatable as the same by any rational subject (*EJ*, p. 267). The nowhereness of the ideal object is its absolute possibility of presence. To say that it is "irreal" is simply to stress that though there is a repeatable identity of the proposition, there is no "proposition in itself" that *really exists* in any way even analogically like the real existence of objects, and especially not in a *topos ouranios*.

III

Husserl wanted not to theorize but to describe, to deny nothing that is undeniable and to assert nothing that was not evident.

Whether or not we agree that Husserl succeeds in living up to this ideal, the evolution of his thought shows that he pursued it tirelessly, and continued to revise, deepen, and expand his system in obedience to the demands of what he took to be evident. Despite its enormous complexity and frequently obscure manner of expression, Husserl's work is very striking in its balance and inclusiveness and even, properly understood, in its respect for common sense. The phenomenological viewpoint alters nothing in the natural standpoint which it brackets, and so a place must be made within the phenomenological system of description for everything that we already, as natural subjects, know. Husserl maintains an admirable balance between subjectivity and objectivity (the "two sides" toward which phenomenology is oriented; *Logic*, pp. 33–39, 151–75), between real objects and ideal objects, and between conceptual judgment and preconceptual experience.

For the purposes of this study, the most important of these balanced bipolarities is that between subject and object. As we have seen, objects are for Husserl experienced through ideal senses which are *repeatable as the same* in the repeated experience of any number of different subjects. Material objects are initially encountered in preconceptual or prepredicative experience, and in this experience they gradually take shape for us as tacitly known. This preconceptual encounter must subsequently be gone back over in a process that unfolds or makes conceptually explicit the complex of predicates which make up the object (*EJ*, pp. 205–9). Eventually, from the pregiven protoforms of mute experience we derive the highest or most general logical forms or forms of ideality, which are the forms of any possible world (among which is this actual world). This whole range of objects, from the tacitly encountered material object to the highest conceptual forms of ideality, is transcendent with respect to the multiplicity of mental acts which take them as objects.[9]

Husserl thus combats psychologistic "relativism" by demarcating the precise manner in which objectivities of all sorts are "intended" by particular acts of consciousness yet remain essentially independent of any such acts. This, then, is one of the two fundamental sides of phenomenological investigation. Now, however, having disengaged the realm of objective idealities from any psychologistic or relativistic interpretation, Husserl turns against a deeper-lying danger that arises if we ignore the ultimate sources of logical objectivity in transcendental subjectivity—the danger that the realm of logical self-evidence will itself be treated naively or unreflectively, that logical concepts and truths will now be treated as ready-made objects, even as in empiricist sensualism physical objects had been. The phenomenological investigation, as an investigation into the *sense* of experience, demands insight, demands the fully understanding glance of the wakeful cogito, into the senses it investigates. In this perspective, the ordinary logician or geometer is no better off than the naive sensualist: he takes his concepts and operations as self-evident without reflecting on the origins of this self-evidence, on the creative movement of insight by means

of which the self-evident form is first constituted. This means he can manipulate the accumulated or "sedimented" forms of logic or geometry as a
mechanical or "blind" technique. The ideal forms which are the geometer's
or logician's objects of knowledge have an origin and a history; they are
initially brought to light and then elaborated and accumulated by consciousness, and their full sense can be understood only when this process
of constitution has been clarified.

As understood by phenomenology, the intrinsic urge or tendency of
cognitive rationality is toward the fully conscious grasp of a fully evident
object (*Logic*, p. 160). This grasp, this fulfillment of the telos of cognitive
rationality, is achieved late in culture-history, as rationality develops from
its origins in Greek thought into the form of reflection called phenomenology. Phenomenology thus finds a world that is given to consciousness
clothed in the interpretations that have accumulated across this history,
and must get underneath this accumulation or "sedimentation" in order to
discover what the object is prior to being given form by some interpretation or other. Hence the phenomenological movement toward the telos of
cognitive fulfillment takes the form of a return to origins (*EJ*, pp. 41–51).
To take the world as it appears to unreflective experience, already shaped
by previous experience and by language and tradition, is to take it as a habitual world, as a world we can understand and manipulate only, as it were,
from the outside. Phenomenological insight demands that we peel off the
layers of interpretive form in which the world comes clothed for us, in order to return to the most primitive moments in which things spring into
being for consciousness. This is the only way we can arrive at a truly evident and presuppositionless description. In the absence of such a clarification, there is no telling what presuppositions might be admitted without
clarification and verification, nor what confusions, equivocations, and unnoticed "shiftings of intentionality" (*Logic*, p. 177) might underlie the
technical operations of the practitioner. For example, Husserl argues, if
the formal object or "anything whatever of logic" ultimately involves the
sense, "worldly being," then logic implicitly presupposes this sense as one
of its "fundamental concepts," and this sense must be clarified in a radical
investigation which seeks to clarify the sense of logic in its ultimate roots
(*Logic*, p. 229).

So for Husserl it is not enough that the autonomous objectivity and
transcendence of the forms intended by thought should be respected, because these forms are susceptible of a naive or technical interpretation
which lacks a fully evident, a truly radical, grounding. This grounding can
be attained only by a return to the subjectivity that originally constitutes
ideal objectivities. This constituting subjectivity is no longer the empirical
subjectivity of psychologism but *transcendental* subjectivity. In psychologi-

cal or "psychophysical" subjectivity, the world is "naively presupposed": it fails to reduce the psyche itself, fails consciously to suspend the presumption of its "relation to the organism and thus to something worldly" (*Logic*, pp. 253–55). The content, the findings, of a psychological investigation of the essential structures of intentionality would be the same as those of transcendental-phenomenological investigation, but their proper *sense* would be missed; they would be treated as "worldly" rather than transcendental-constitutive. Consequently, the transition to a thoroughly radical stance of critical reflection which, presupposing nothing, could rethink the origins of all cognition, would be blocked.

The transcendental-phenomenological reduction has been much criticized and widely rejected, even by followers of Husserl.[10] In this study I accept Iso Kern's evaluation of it according to its "ontological" form, which Kern takes to best exemplify Husserl's true and lasting intention. As achieved through the ontological way, the reduction is simply *the rigorous formalization of the concept of philosophical reflection as a thoroughly radical form of criticism*. The reduction, says Kern, is designed to "break through the limitations of natural objective cognition" which sees objects as "static, fixed, foreign things" in order to open out the depth character of the world as a dynamic achievement of consciousness. Thus the reduction is finally "nothing but a change of attitude." Kern cites Husserl's words: "To exclude the world means not to want to pass judgment on it straightway."[11]

If the world as a whole is intrinsically capable of being known (and this was for Husserl axiomatic), then it contains, in some implicit way, the protoforms out of which the forms of conceptual ideality may be developed. And in that case, the phenomenological reduction which suspends the question of the object-as-such in order to focus reflection on the noematic idealities (objects-as-known) and to unveil the transcendental subjectivity in which these idealities are constituted emerges as a way of unfolding the totality of the ideal possibilities which are given in the objective world, a way of allowing the fullness of possible consciousness to emerge as the mirror of the fullness of actual and possible being. Thus, transcendentally speaking, there is no "outside of consciousness," since any possible being has an objective sense that can be intentionally achieved by consciousness (*CM*, pp. 83–85). And the transcendental criticism of cognition achieved by phenomenological investigation is a radical clarification of this sense.

IV

From the early doctrine according to which consciousness "ensouls" or "interprets" a raw sense-datum to the later doctrine according to which all possible being is constituted in transcendental subjectivity, Husserl insists on the transformation of reflection upon objects into reflection upon the constitution of the sense of objects, thus upon the active achievement of consciousness in its knowledge of objects. The concept of "sense" as the preconceptual, language-anticipating meaning of the intuited object, is, as Dagfinn Føllesdal has argued, a "generalization of the notion of meaning,"[12] but this generalization is far from an assimilation of objects to language. On the contrary, as we will see, Husserl will forge the link between meaning and object by peeling off the layer of meaning from the sensuous substratum of language. The milieu of evidence with its poles of subjectivity and objectivity has no essential place for the physical phenomenon of language. Nevertheless, it was always clear to Husserl that language was the necessary medium of intersubjectivity (*Logic*, p. 188). "Verbal expression" fixes the ideal objectivities that are the objects of knowledge, and makes possible their accumulation in a communal tradition—for example, in the tradition of science or the tradition of philosophy that culminates in phenomenology.

So it would be inaccurate to say simply that Husserl considers "language" either essential or inessential. In one sense it is essential, in another not; there is a "living body" of language, transparent to intention, and a dead or opaque body. Husserl's treatment of language thus contains a tension that serves Derrida in his reading of Husserl as a mainspring for the deconstructive turn.

Husserl examines the dependency of ideality on language and tradition, and the problems that arise from this dependence, in the late essay called *The Origin of Geometry*. Because this essay brings out very sharply the necessity of "original reactivation" of ideal meaning by subjectivity, and the conflict between this necessity and the worldliness of the linguistic sign, Derrida made it the focus of his first book. Let us therefore briefly survey the central issues that Derrida raises concerning *The Origin of Geometry*, and then see how these issues are articulated in Husserl's earlier work.

Husserl argues in *The Origin of Geometry* that the original inventor of geometry (the "proto-geometer") must have engaged in a primal creative, spiritual act in which he "grasped" geometrical truth "with the consciousness of its original being-itself-there [*selbst-da*]" (*Origin*, p. 160). This original moment of insight was restricted to the "mental space" of the proto-geometer, and so was a real temporal event belonging to his empirical subjectivity; but the geometrical entity which he grasped was not psychological. It was in its essence something which exists supratemporally and for any rational subject in general. In order to escape from its "primary intrapersonal origin, where it is a structure within the conscious space of the first inventor's soul" and achieve its "ideal objectivity," geometrical

ideality had to be expressed in language or given, "so to speak, its linguistic living body [*Sprachleib*]" (p. 161). Now a second person, taking this
linguistic expression of the "original being-itself-there" which the proto-
geometer had experienced, could reproduce the creative activity of the in-
stitutor of the ideality and bring back to life for himself the very same
original self-evidence.

This activity of "original reproduction" is made possible for a historical
tradition by writing, which gives the linguistic expression of the ideality
a persisting existence. Derrida lays special emphasis on this moment in
Husserl's text (*Intro.*, pp. 76–78, 87–93). On one hand, writing is necessary in order for ideality to be freed from the contingency of any particular
empirical subject, so that it may remain permanently available, as a "vir-
tuality," even when, as Husserl says, "the inventor and his fellows are no
longer wakefully so related or even are no longer alive" (*Origin*, p. 164).
The originating consciousness achieves a fully wakeful moment of self-
evidence of an ideality; then it stores up this moment of wakefulness in
language. The originating consciousness can then go to sleep or die, but
the ideality which is a permanent possibility of wakefulness remains. On
the other hand, the ideality is not the same as the linguistic formula which
embodies it and makes it permanently available. The "being" and permanent availability of the ideal objectivity are different from, and *essentially*
independent of, their linguistic embodiments—even though linguistic embodiment in fact makes them possible. Because the linguistic formula is
only a receptacle for the ideal sense, it has to be transformed by the reader
back into the corresponding *activity* of meaning-constitution, an activity
which "reactivates" the primal self-givenness of the *selbst-da* in the mode of
full conscious presence which it had for its originator. But this necessity
for reactivation is impeded by the fact that we can read and in general operate with language on a level of habitual response, responding *passively* to
language in a way "dominated purely by association" (*Origin*, p. 165). So,
Derrida points out, embodiment in writing is necessary for ideality, yet at
the same time it is for Husserl a moment of crisis in which the embodied
meaning may be lost (*Intro.*, pp. 87–90; *S&P*, p. 81). The handing-down
of increasing accumulations of ideal meaning within a tradition is possible
only as these meanings are "sedimented" in language; yet, Husserl writes,
"It is easy to see that even in [ordinary] human life . . . the originally intuitive life which creates its originally self-evident structures through activities on the basis of sense-experience very quickly and in increasing measure
falls victim to the *seduction of language*. Greater and greater segments of
this life lapse into a kind of talking and reading that is dominated purely by
association" (*Origin*, p. 165). As we operate associatively with language,
failing to reproduce the original moments of insight in which meaning is

constituted, we fall into a dormancy or absentmindedness. Thus we make no contact with the primal unities which give authenticity and validity to thought, and thought becomes vulnerable to unnoticed incoherence.

The elements of this problematic of language are already present in the *Logical Investigations*, in the fundamental distinction Husserl draws between "empty" or "purely symbolic" thinking and the "fulfillment" of meaning, and in his analysis of the "sensuous" or "mere" sign and its transformation into the "meaningful" sign.

We have already seen that for Husserl sense perception involves an act of intellect by which an object is cognized or apperceived through an ideal object-identity or "sense" (*Sinn*). Being in the actual presence of an object and recognizing it as just the sort of object that it is, is the telos or fulfillment of the intentionality of thought, which "aims at its object, is as it were desirous of it" (*LI*, p. 726). "Meaning" is therefore, for Husserl, completed in knowledge, in the presence of an object intended before a consciousness that intends it, according to the intellectual form which is the shape of the intention and thus of the object as given to this intention. The "act of pure meaning," Husserl says, operates "like a goal-seeking intention," and when the object that was merely thought of "in symbol" is presented in intuition, "it is intuited as being precisely the determinate so-and-so that it was at first merely thought or meant to be" (*LI*, p. 694). The meaning intention is like the outline of the form in which the object is intended, and the intuition of the actual object then fits a perfectly corresponding filling into the empty outline. In the moment of object intuition, meaning and object are blended in unity, but this intentional or ideal blending of intention and intended in a single mental act is possible only on condition that the meaning-bearing linguistic sign drop out of the picture. "Signs are in fact not objects of our thought at all, even surrogatively; we rather live entirely in the consciousness of meaning" (*LI*, p. 304; cf. pp. 583–84).

Husserl repeatedly stresses the difference between the sensuous sign and the mental act that passes through this perceptual sign into the ideal meaning:

> What is involved in the descriptive difference between the physical sign-phenomenon and the meaning-intention which makes it into an expression, becomes most clear when we turn our attention to the sign *qua* sign, e.g. to the printed word as such. If we do this, we have an external percept (or external intuitive idea) just like any other, whose object loses its verbal character. (*LI*, p. 282)

It may also be the case that some sensible feature arouses interest on its own account, and that its verbal or other symbolic character is only then noted. . . . One and the same content has . . . altered its psychic habit: we are differently minded in respect of it, it no longer seems a mere sensuous mark on paper, the physical phenomenon counts as an *understood* sign. . . . It is in this sense-giving act-character . . . that meaning consists. (*LI*, pp. 302–3)

The sense-giving act by which marks become meaningful differs from the ensouling apprehension of sensational contents in perception of objects. I experience certain sense data from this tree, and on the basis of this sensational content I perceive the tree. There is an intrinsic relation between these sense data and the object perceived on their basis. But in the case of signs, the relation between the experience of the sign as sensuous phenomenon and the grasping of its meaning is arbitrary (*LI*, pp. 739, 741). So the sensuous sign has less connection with the realm of meaning than do ordinary material objects. Signs are indispensable vehicles of meaning, but meaning—at least, logical meaning, which is the essence of meaning—is not *bound* to signs in their sensuous particularity as signs, only to signs in general as the condition for fixing and communicating of meaning. That is, even logical meaning has to be given in signs, but the same meaning can be indifferently conveyed in different languages or notations or signifying media. Therefore meaning is in its essence, though not in fact, separate from or "free" of signs. The sign does not in principle present any opacity that could come between the merging of intention and object: when I say or think "this inkwell" while the inkwell is before me, meaning and object become one, and the signifying medium assumes a kind of pure transparency.

Nevertheless, thought and cognition are not the same: the object need not be given in order for me to think about it. Thought is meaningful only because in principle it points toward objects, but the interval between intention and fulfillment can extend indefinitely, and in this interval thought functions "emptily" or "signitively." Still, the "signitive intention," the intention that functions in the absence of the fulfilling intuition, is thought that plays, not among *signs*, but among the *meanings* of those signs (*LI*, pp. 710, 730–34).

V

The concept of a *signitive intention* is delicately balanced. Because it occurs in the absence of the object intended, it is "signitive"; but because it is directed not to signs but to their meanings, it moves in a realm of ideality which is not essentially conditioned by the contingency of the material sign. With the distinction between the meaning intention which functions signitively and the sense-perception or "intuition" that fulfills it, Husserl can retain both the freedom of thought, which must be able to function in the absence of the object it thinks about, and the teleological determination of the essence of thought, even when it is only signitive, as relation to an object.

Derrida calls these two sides of Husserl's project the "intuitionist" and the "formalist," and credits Husserl with an important breakthrough in the "formalist" moment of his analysis.[13] Husserl's trenchant and subtle analysis of intentionality yielded a decisive distinction between meaning and object meant, and this distinction led to his project in the Fourth Investigation of a "pure logical grammar," a grammar of the universal logical structures of language which would define a priori the conditions of possibility for linguistic meaningfulness. In the interval before fulfillment in sense perception, the pure forms of meaning unfold. "We can speak without knowing," Derrida comments (S&P, p. 89): "We know that the act of meaning, the act that confers Bedeutung (Bedeutungsintention), is always the aim of a relation with an object. But it is enough that this intention animates the body of a signifier for speech to take place. The fulfillment of the aim by an intuition is not indispensable. It belongs to the original structure of expression to be able to dispense with the full presence of the object aimed at by intuition" (S&P, p. 90). Thus I can intend a meaning "symbolically" which is not true and cannot be fulfilled; for example, "the circle is square." For Husserl, though this expression does not refer to an actual or even possible object, it still has meaning, because it obeys the same rules, has the same form, as expressions that can be fulfilled by objects. An expression like "Green is where," on the other hand, is mere nonsense; it lacks not only an object but even the form of meaning. Thus, in this formalist moment of his analysis, Husserl detaches a stratum of meaning from the stratum of object intuition, and shows how this stratum functions according to its own laws.

But, Derrida says, even though Husserl in his formalist moment describes "the emancipation of speech as nonknowing," as structurally independent of fulfilling intuition, he at the same time "effaces" this emancipation.

> In other words, the genuine and true meaning is the will to say the truth. This subtle shift incorporates the *eidos* into the *telos*, and language into knowledge. A speech could well be in conformity with its essence as speech when it was false; it nonetheless attains its entelechy when it is true. One can well *speak* in saying "The circle is square"; one speaks *well*, however, in saying that it is not. There is already sense in the first proposition, but we would be wrong to conclude from this

that sense *does not wait upon* truth. It does not await truth as expecting it; it only precedes truth as its anticipation. *In truth*, the telos which announces the fulfillment, promised for "later," has already and beforehand opened up sense as a relation with the object. (*S&P*, p. 98)

Meaning "waits upon" truth: it is determined beforehand, a priori, in its essence, as relation to an object, and "makes sense only insofar as its grammatical form tolerates the possibility of a relation with the object" (*S&P*, p. 99).

Derrida questions this teleological determination of the essence of meaning. "Following the logic and necessity" of Husserl's own distinctions, Derrida argues, "we might be tempted to maintain not only that meaning does not imply the intuition of the object but that it *essentially excludes it*" (*S&P*, p. 92; italics added). That is, the essence of meaning is precisely its ability to function in the absence of the object meant, simply by "animating the body of a signifier." On the other hand, once the object meant is present, we no longer see the unique and distinctive character of "meaning" as rigorously distinguishable from "object intuition." Derrida is thus trying to wrest the concept of meaning away from the moment of intuition in order to attach it *essentially* to the moment of signification. Since the concept of meaning is contested here, I will speak henceforth rather of signification to make clear the force of Derrida's claim. What is the essence of signification *as such*, thought short of its teleological determination as aimed at objective fulfillment? [14]

At this point it might be objected: "But surely the essence of a representation is to point toward that for which it stands." It is hard not to think of transparency to what is represented as the essence of representation. Derrida, in trying to think representation *as such*, the essence of standing-for short of what is stood-for, performs a conceptual operation that is, considered in isolation, neither valid nor invalid. It is a construction, a new conceptual operation, a new way of looking at things, comparable in a way to the new operation by which Husserl attained the phenomenological standpoint, and the question "is it valid?" must be suspended while we consider the full scope of the possibilities it opens. We are at a crossroads here, where a new set of pathways in language is made available to us. We can always choose not to take this route, but the character of the opening should at least be understood.

Derrida's deconstruction of Husserl's view of meaning and signification is not a refutation or a denial of that view. On the contrary, this deconstruction follows almost entirely the conceptual path traced by Husserl, reproducing, though with shifts of emphasis, the major steps Husserl had taken. The point is not to show that Husserl was wrong, or even that he contradicted himself. It is, rather, to show certain aspects of the articulation of his concepts, and of the threads by which one leads to another, and to bring to light the character of what Derrida calls the "ethico-theoretical" decisions which determine the precise shape that this articulation and this linkage take. Given the formalist moment of the analysis of meaning which we find in the *Investigations*, we could draw different conclusions about the nature of signification than Husserl does. But because Husserl predetermines his path according to the telos of fulfillment of signitive intention by something-itself, a subordinate valuation is prescribed for the moment of signification, and therefore a subordinate place in the linkage of moments of Husserl's discourse.

Since Husserl's ethico-theoretical decision determines *de jure* the value of the moment of the sign, to suspend the decision is to throw open the question of the place and value of the sign. And to make a different decision is to open new paths on which it is possible to continue, paths different from those chosen by Husserl. Treating language apart from fulfillment in knowledge, we can begin to explore its own originality, its peculiar character as a quasi-material medium, instead of throwing out of court from the very beginning everything in language which is not "essential" with reference to logico-objective meaning. Most obviously—though the matter is not so simple as this may suggest—it would be possible to pursue the path chosen by James Joyce. Husserl's path leads to the fixing of terminology in a univocality which would be transparent to the logical unities of ideal meaning. Joyce's, on the other hand, writes Derrida, would "repeat and take responsibility for equivocation itself, utilizing a language that could equalize the greatest possible synchrony with the greatest potential for buried, accumulated, and interwoven intentions within each linguistic atom, each vocable, each word, each simple proposition, in all worldly cultures and their most ingenious forms (mythology, religion, sciences, art, literature, politics, philosophy, and so forth)" (*Intro.*, p. 102). What is both original and problematic about Derrida's own project is that it does *not* pursue Joyce's path, but remains faithful to the problematic of that "univocity" that Derrida sees as underlying Joyce's equivocity, while yet opening out the univocal language in which he works, the language of philosophy, to that spread of meaning Joyce explored. That is what makes Derrida so difficult to read *well*, neither simply as poetry nor simply as philosophy (which in any case are undoubtedly weak ways of reading poetry and philosophy). There is nothing more difficult than trying to read something that violates the form we try to apply to it. It may be said of Derrida's work, as Wittgenstein wrote of his own, that "one cannot even compare the *genre* (*Art*)" it belongs to "with that of earlier works" (*Culture*, p. 67).

VI

Now, as against Husserl's model of presence, Derrida devises the model of the sign as structure of *differance*, as an in-principle "not this" and "not now" which evades the fully wakeful grasp of conscious reactivation and so opens the space of indefiniteness or nonessence. We have already seen that Husserl himself "describes the emancipation of speech as nonknowing." The question is whether the sensible contours of the sign are capable of being "reduced" in favor of the ideal meaning, as Husserl thinks it can. For Husserl, the essence of the sign is in the spiritual or mental act–character that makes the sensuous mark meaningful. Yet Husserl himself is aware that there is another level of ideality between the material substance of the sign and its meaning, the ideality of the signifier or "verbal corporeality" (*Logic*, p. 21). Derrida's argument is that this ideality of the signifier makes it impossible to split the sign into a worldly or material side and an ideal side, and that, consequently, existence of the sign cannot be bracketed in favor of its ideality.

We have seen that Husserl defines idealities in general as identities that present the standing possibility of repetition by a rational subject in general. The sign, too, is an ideality in this sense (*S&P*, p. 50). But the identity of the sign is that of a contingent existent, or, at most, as "type," of a set of allowable sensuous configurations that could be recognizable as "the same" sign. Yet this identity is not simply that of a real thing. The sign is not a terminus for thought, as a thing is, and could be said to have being only by analogy. Beyond this, there is the fact that the various sensuous configurations that can count as the same sign might have no "objective" identity with each other, so long as they retain the same relative function within the system of differences that constitutes the whole sign-system to which they belong. Thus one language can treat "l" and "r" as different phonemes while another treats them as the same. So the sign is neither quite ideal in the purity of ideality nor yet quite a material object. Now, there is nothing new or startling in these observations about the nature of the sign, yet they must be drawn out here because Derrida will make them do so much work. His conclusion is that the sign confounds the categories of ideality and materiality. This conclusion, all by itself, may not seem like much. But to make the nature of the sign the focus of thought would be to open out a meditation that is no longer that of classical metaphysics, which is no longer a meditation on the being of the thing. Because it is not conceivable "under the category of a thing in general"; it is "something other than a being—the sole 'thing' which, not being a thing, does not fall under the question 'what is . . . ?'" (*S&P*, p. 25). Because this essence or nonessence of the sign lacks both freedom and presence, Husserl wants to reduce signs in favor of their ideal significations, but because the sign remains in its essence a repeatable identity, Derrida holds that it belongs essentially to ideality and cannot be bracketed as the existence of ordinary materiality is bracketed.

But Derrida does not mean only to hold the sign apart as something distinct. Rather, he takes it as something like the limit point of the movement of idealization, from Plato to Husserl, and having shown how the wave breaks on this point, he proceeds to push back in the other direction and recapture the ground he has previously conceded. Having identified the distinctive structure of the sign as repetition of what is not fully present, Derrida comes back to reinterpret the fundamental structure of presence proper in its terms. That is, he reconceives all of experience on the model of signitive experience. "Repeatability," as the condition for the existence of all idealities, whether they are the "senses" of real or ideal objects, turns out to infect the entire domain of presence.

In order to accomplish this revision of the order of experience as conceived by Husserl, Derrida must show that the constitutive form of all ideality depends upon repetition, rather than repetition being made possible by a unified and unifying form of ideality, as Husserl would have it. At this point we rejoin the problematic of time we touched on in the introductory chapter, since Husserl in the period following the *Logical Investigations* came to see temporality as the matrix of all object constitution: "All Objectivation takes place in time-consciousness, and without a clarification of the identity of temporal position no clarification of the identity of an Object can be given" (*ITC*, p. 88). Because of his concern for the "self-givenness" or presence of objects to consciousness, Husserl concludes that consciousness depends upon the "primal impression" that an object makes on consciousness in an absolute "now." Only the moment of primal impression has full being; this moment is then immediately "shoved" back into a just-past Now and a new "now" takes its place as "in the living source-point of the now there . . . wells up ever fresh primal being" (p. 94). Husserl recognizes that the concept of a primal and irreducible Now is only an idealization, a limit-concept (p. 62); in addition to this concept of the Now "in the strictest sense," there is "a complete concept of the now" (p. 92) made up of the primal Now and, in addition, "retention" of a just-past Now, which itself retains a preceding Now and so on (pp. 51, 162); the complete Now also contains "protentions" or anticipations of the future. Time consciousness is a continuum, in which the ideal limit-notion of the pure Now "continually accommodates itself" to the not-now. However, even though this is true, the primordiality of the Now of perception is not compromised: "retention" is a "primary remembrance" of such a kind that what is seen in it is immediately *perceived* rather than re-presented. Primary remembrance brings the just-having-been to "primary, direct intuition," just as in perception proper, the Now is brought directly to intuition; this entire, composite Now is what "constitutes originarily" the objects of which we are conscious (p. 64). "Recollection," or remembering, in the usual, nonphenomenological sense of the term, does not give original or perceptual consciousness of what it represents, so Husserl calls it "secondary remembrance." Recollection is said to be "reproductive," or, in the neologism of the English translation, "representifying" (*wiedervergegenwärtigenden*), memory (p. 68), because it is discontinuous with the Now; it does not preserve the primordial presence of what is re-presented.

Husserl discusses time consciousness mainly in terms of objects that are themselves temporal, especially sounds and melodies; and melody illustrates well the necessity for positing the phenomenon of retention: "When . . . a melody sounds, the individual notes do not completely disappear when the stimulus or action of the nerve excited by them comes to an end. When the new note sounds, the one preceding it does not disappear without a trace; otherwise, we should be incapable of observing the relations between the notes which follow one another. We should have a note at every instant, . . . but never the idea [*Vorstellung*] of a melody" (*ITC*, p. 30). Thus "retention" is a phenomenologically descriptive concept that acknowledges the fact that perception in any given moment is informed immediately by the sense of what has immediately preceded it and is not a self-contained, isolated thing. Kant, we recall, faced the problem of the isolation of moments of consciousness and resolved it by reference to the concept of an object, but for Husserl the moments of "originary" consciousness are intrinsically linked in a continuous gradation (*ITC*, p. 70), and it is from this time-constituting continuity that the identity of objects is derived. "If in the whole phenomenon nothing remains unaltered, if it changes 'in every respect,' then even in this case there is always still enough to establish unity, namely, the indistinguishableness with which adjoining phases go over into one another and in so doing produce consciousness of unity" (p. 114; also pp. 144–45). Ultimately, what makes the consciousness of the unity of an object possible is "the formal structure of the flux" of time-constituting consciousness. Though every moment of consciousness is filled with new content, the form of this consciousness always remains the same: "a now is constituted through an impression and . . . to the impression is joined a train of retentions and a horizon of protentions" (p. 153).

For Derrida, the crucial question with respect to Husserl's analysis of time consciousness concerns the nature of retention. If the Now of impressional consciousness is constituted as such by its relation to a past Now that it retains, does it follow that retention belongs to perception in the primordial sense Husserl wants to affirm? It is true that there are clear descriptive differences between retention (primary remembrance) and recollection (secondary remembrance), but this does not by itself demonstrate that retention, as opposed to recollection, must therefore have the character of "perception," of immediate intuitive presence to consciousness of its "object." Husserl says that "consciousness is necessarily *consciousness* in each of its phases" (*ITC*, p. 162); it is this fullness of consciousness that Derrida challenges when he contests Husserl's judgment on the nature of retention. If primary remembrance did not belong to the primordial fullness of objective consciousness, it would contaminate the "originarity" of the origin: the primordial *presentation* of perception would be contaminated by re-presentation, by the intrusion of a content not itself belonging to originary presence. That the absolute, idealized Now of perception *must* be "accommodated" to the not-now of retention is certain, as Husserl's own analyses demonstrate; without retention "no content would be possible as lived experience" (*ITC*, p. 158). The question is whether "retained" contents are perceptually present. For Husserl they *must* be, because his whole system is worked out on the a priori assumption that all forms of mental representation must ultimately be referred back to primordial experiences of full perceptual presence. But this assumption is precisely what determines phenomenology as a philosophy of presence, and the deconstruction of phenomenology proceeds by treating retention as a non-fullness that infects perception. Thus, because there is no perception without retention, the "trace" of nonpresence emerges as essential to the constitution of perceptual presence. The originarity of the Now is seen as dependent upon the repetition of the not-now: "The ideality of the form . . . of presence itself implies that it be infinitely re-peatable, that its return, as a return of the same, is necessary *ad infinitum* and is inscribed in presence itself" (*S&P*, p. 67). The nonpresent not-now thus becomes the condition of possibility for the appearing of the phenomenon: "the presence of the present is derived from repetition and not the reverse," and this reversal of Husserl's "express intention" exploits what is "implied" in Husserl's accounts of signification and temporalization (*S&P*, p. 52). Consciousness is no longer conceived as full even in the Now of perception, and it becomes possible for Derrida to move in the direction of an accommodation to psychoanalysis, and specifically the notion of *Nachträglichkeit*, deferred constitution of a mental content that was never present consciously as such.

Beginning with the structure of the sign, then, Derrida reinterprets the structure of transcendental consciousness and of ideality in general on the same model, inverting the order of precedence so that the in-principle multiplicity of repeatable identity is the condition of the appearing of any present term. Apart from the entrenched habits of thought that are standard to us, it is difficult to see why Derrida's proposal should arouse the opposition it has. It is a striking inversion of the established formula, but quite soberly and rationally formulated and aimed at providing an alternate description of a set of phenomena. It is no less sober than the proposal that parallel lines might, for certain purposes and when handled according to an appropriate technique, be able to meet. Derrida says that repeatability splits the identity of the sign a priori (*Ltd Inc*, p. 190). Is the classical definition of essence in terms of unity and self-identity absolutely inviolable and given in the nature of things, or is it a conceptual structure devised for a certain purpose? Will we succumb to flux and babble if we allow an alternate formulation in terms of split identity and nonpresence?

Yet there is a difficult question concerning the legitimacy of the way language is being used here. To hold onto the classical concepts while stretching them to include what they were expressly designed to exclude, as Derrida does, is to risk nonsense. We must revise not only our concepts but our concept of concepts and our concept of language if we are to follow the logic of deconstruction; indeed, its logic is the logic of this revision. For Derrida as for Wittgenstein, deconstruction is not pure thought but allows itself to work in and be worked by the medium of language, and allows for the productivity of that medium. It is in order to open a space of philosophical legitimacy for that medium that Derrida refuses to let it be reduced and devises the concept of the divided essence.

The essentially divided essence has a trace structure. The trace is the retention within the same of the reference to an other which itself has never been present. The trace structure is the transcendental structure of experience; no this-here is given to experience except as its identity is marked by *differance*, by reference to a not-this and a not-now. The trace structure, as the structure of the Now and of the sign, is the possibility of experience and meaning. The possibility of a particular language is first the transcendental possibility of a trace in general (corresponding in deconstruction to the object-in-general of philosophy—which, let us recall, was no *actual object*). The trace in general is the pure form of signification. Not pure form as self-identity or self-presence, but as the form of openness to a nonpresence without which the present term could not have its positive content; call it the pure form of essential impurity.

VII

We must be very careful how we formulate the nature of the paths opened out by Derrida's critique. In particular, we must not summarize his criticism of Husserl in a way that confuses it with the views of orthodox "linguistic analysis," as represented for example by Ernst Tugendhat.[15] In his critique of Husserl, Tugendhat claims that "intersubjective communication in language" must function as our "universal system of reference," replacing the phenomenological focus on the relation of intentional acts to intentional objects.[16] For linguistic analysis, Tugendhat writes, "the primary unit of awareness is understanding the meaning of a sentence," and this understanding is itself to be clarified not in terms of an interpretive or constitutive subjectivity but in terms of intersubjective linguistic rules.[17] From the deconstructive point of view, Tugendhat's approach is just another way of repressing the linguistic sign, replacing its sublation into a subjective meaning by its sublation into a rule. Wittgenstein is commonly misread as sanctioning the rules-metaphysics of contemporary linguistic analysis which Tugendhat here invokes. The question of linguistic rules will occupy us further in the next chapter, where we will pursue a deconstructive reading of Wittgenstein. Here I can only alert the reader to the general theme of Tugendhat's reading and its distance from the deconstructive question of language.[18]

Neither is Derrida's critique of Husserl answered in the terms by which Donn Welton has answered Tugendhat. Welton demonstrates that Husserl eventually realized that "thinking is, at the very outset, linguistic and that language is necessarily intersubjective."[19] But Welton's view of language remains on the same ground as that of Tugendhat, as it must since no other view is possible *within philosophy*. According to Welton, the linguistic sense which dialectically interacts with the perceived object in the progressive constitution of new perspectives is an ideal sense "pared out" in the shape of "critical language" from "the heart of normal talk."[20] So the language which Welton claims Husserl came to see as essential is not at all the language in question for Derrida. In fact, Welton confirms what Derrida has emphasized about Husserl's view of language, that it defines the essence of language on the basis of a logico-objective core attained by a reduction of the "mere sign" or sign *as such*.

Now, the reduction of the sensible sign in favor of ideal meaning cannot be said without qualification to exclude the world in favor of ideality. On the contrary, as J. N. Mohanty says, for Husserl "even solitary monologue is about the world."[21] But which concept of the world are we talking about? For philosophy, the world divides into matter and form, and the world that is given to philosophy is the world as form, the correlate or matching double of rational consciousness. Matter as the unbounded, as the Aristotelian *prote hyle*, cannot be allowed. The realm of ideality, the logico-objective sphere, is reached by the working-over of the prereflective or "natural" world and of prereflective or ordinary language. This working-over results in a system of propositions which expresses the underlying form of the world; from ordinary language we precipitate out its logical system, and from the natural world its logical structure, and one is the correlate of the other (as in Wittgenstein's *Tractatus*).

From the perspective of the discourse on Truth, this logico-objective correlation is the condition of rationality and of rational speech, of the logos. The object is defined as self-identical unity, the world as the *in-principle* harmony of all possible object perceptions, and the essence of language as the ideal meaning-cores correlative with the harmonious world of object unities. Language and intersubjectivity are thus normed by the a priori possibility of harmonious object perception, by the possibility, Derrida writes, that "two *normal* men" can "stand together before the same natural existent" which would furnish "the ultimate arbitration for every misunderstanding" (*Intro.*, pp. 85–86).

So Mohanty has not quite grasped Derrida's meaning when he takes Derrida to be claiming that Husserl cuts off language from its "relation to the world" by his reduction of the sensuous sign. Husserl excludes, not the world (or intersubjectivity), but the world (and intersubjectivity) insofar as it has not been "worked over by Geist" (*S&P*, p. 35), insofar as it would not be the correlate of a possible noesis, and in this phenomenology is typical of philosophy in general. The phenomenological reduction does not get rid of materiality, but of the element of impurity, of indefiniteness, of nonessence in that materiality, so that the sense of the object-as-such, the intelligible object, may emerge. Essence is presence, or the in-principle (perhaps infinite and in fact unachievable) possibility of presence.[22] Matter as the unbounded is what in principle escapes presence as essence or as sense. Of course matter as the knowable object is another issue. So the question does not turn on matter but on the functions of pure availability, transparency, to noesis or, on the other hand, a certain in-principle opacity.

The reactivated presence of the ideal object is at the same time the fullness of rational consciousness as consciousness of this unified something-itself. Here there is, as it were, a permeation of the substance of the known by the substance or act of noesis. The ideal object is exhausted in its being by its correlation with a possible act of a wakeful rational consciousness; thus its substance is nothing but the substance of wakeful rational consciousness as *virtual* or *in principle*. Even if those who devised these propositions which are the embodiment of the ideality are asleep or dead, the wakeful moment which gave rise to the propositions is stored away in the propositions as the possibility of reawakened consciousness of the same.

This self-sameness of the thought, correlative with the self-sameness of the thinking, is modeled, from Aristotle to Kant and Husserl, on the unity and self-identity of the perceptual object thought as *form*.[23] Husserl writes: "*The primitive mode of the giving of something-itself is perception*. The being-with is for me, as percipient, my now-being-with: I myself with the perceived itself" (*Logic*, p. 158). This perceptual object is already a *dynamis* (potentiality) intrinsically destined to an *entelecheia* (actualization of full essence) (*EJ*, p. 29); it contains in an anticipatory mode the logical form which reflection will eventually extract from it.

The perceptual object is given only in perspectives; its full thingness cannot be given all at once to intuition. The full object is an unattainable limit-idea. Yet those aspects of the object which escape my cognition though outside my grasp are still continuous with what I already see. I know a priori that whatever lies beyond my view must be capable of unfolding harmoniously in a series of possible perceptions belonging to the unity of the same object. My particular anticipation of what I will find on the other side of this object I am looking at may be disappointed, but it will only be within a typical range of possibilities that the disappointment will come. This red ball may turn out to be green on the back side, but this modification maintains type (it occurs within the limits of the category "color") and occurs within the framework of fulfillment of other parts of the anticipation (*EJ*, pp. 35–37). It is still this same ball that I am looking at. Despite the disappointment, "a certain measure of continuous fulfillment is presupposed. Correlatively, a certain unity of objective sense must be upheld throughout the flux of successive appearances. It is only in this way that we have, in the process of a lived experience and its appearances, the unanimity of *one* consciousness" (*EJ*, p. 88).

The essence of a possible object of experience or object-in-general also binds the basic form of the terms of logic. When the logician writes "*S* is *p*," his terms, however "empty," must still represent the form of a *possible existent*, something which

> fits into the unity of experience, correlatively, into the unity of the world understood as the totality of objects of experience in general: therefore, not merely into the unity of what is actually experienced, but also of all imaginable experience. Thus it is an existent which, if it does not belong to the actual world, still belongs to a possible world. Accordingly, everything which can be arbitrarily chosen as the object of an activity of judgment, as a substrate, has a homogeneity, a com-

mon structure, and it is only because of this that judgments which have sense can be made at all. The object of judgment is bound by the fact that it is a something in general, i.e., something identical in the unity of our experience. (*EJ*, p. 39)

The form of experience is thus essentially predetermined by the form of unity. Husserl admits preverbal or preconceptual experience of the object as the substratum of the explicit forms of judgment, but this preverbality already has an implicitly logical form. So even though phenomenology presents the "inside" of subjectivity as inhabited by the "outside" of transcendent objectivities, the objects which are possible objects of rational experience have been assimilated to the mode of ideality which is the medium of cognitive subjectivity. This move is not at all peculiar to Husserl; his system is only a rigorous formalization of the principles of knowledge as universally defined by philosophy. For Husserl as for Aristotle, the thing *as such* is defined by the limits of its knowability. Philosophy, no matter how realistic, must purify matter of pure facticity, of any character of "exteriority" which would be *essentially* opaque to consciousness.

To think the sign as such, within the ideality of lived experience, is to begin to think an essential, irreducible exteriority within the subject. This "outside" or worldliness would be, not the exteriority of a material object, but the exteriority of nonessence, of what is not reducible to the act or correlate of wakeful consciousness. Not reducible, because essentially not self-identical or present as something-itself: the identity of the sign is "split *a priori.*" The ray of consciousness that intends the sign, or which is signitively structured, is essentially split by reference to what is nonpresent (both as "not here" and "not now").

For Husserl the signitive phase is transitory and is essentially destined to pass into the moment of the object itself. By calling this telos into question, and redefining the essence of the phase of signification, it becomes possible also to question the phase of the object. The door to this second revision is opened by the same movement that opens phenomenology and philosophy in general: if the thing itself and experience are defined reciprocally in terms of each other, then to question the essential form of experience is necessarily to question also the correlative concept of the thing. Notice: to question the *concept* of the "object itself" is not skepticism about *objects themselves.*

The question of objective reality would only be a red herring here, since from the perspective of deconstruction the strangeness and violence of the world and the otherness of other people, to say nothing of the "it" within the self, are domesticated by the discourse of truth with the help of the unified and knowable object. This object as construed by philosophy is a challenge but also a *reassurance*; so long as I aim at it, I know that my language will have the probity of its logico-objective telos and that my intention will be unified and self-identical.

VIII

Instead of thinking the essence of the sign by reference to the idealized model of object perception, Derrida thinks the sign as the trace of difference and then proceeds to interpret object perception on this model. "The thing itself is a sign," he writes in the *Grammatology*. The implications of this formula are precisely the opposite of what they are often taken to be. This is no reduction of things to language, no radical subjectivism, least of all a hermetic solipsism. On the contrary, it is a radical opening of the inside to what is not homogeneous with that inside understood as wakeful consciousness.

"The thing itself is a sign" does not mean "there isn't really any 'thing itself'"; nor does it mean "the thing is really all in your mind"; nor "there are really only words—we can't get outside of words." It means approximately this: "Let us consider the experience of what we call 'things themselves' as structured more like the experience of signs than like the experience of an idealized 'full presence.'"

The philosophical limit-idea of the thing itself should not be confused with the simple, unreflectively apprehended materiality of objects. The two do not stand or fall together, but can and ought to be separated. No doubt materiality is the primitive source of the philosophical idea of presence. The visual and tactile thereness of physical objects is the most blatant form of indisputable *thereness*, and for that reason it can function as a plausible substratum for *ideal* thereness. But we have already seen how mere matter has to be purified, "worked over by *Geist*," before it can be allied to the philosophical project. As Derrida analyzes the sign, it is an *impure ideality*, a membrane between world and subject that remains entangled in the web of worldliness while inhabiting the zone of ideality—worldliness not in its simple materiality, which is always capable of being allied to the project of presence or of being reduced, but in its essential non-self-identity, its incapacity to be teleologically defined by reference to the actual or in-principle possibility of fulfillment. And the cogito which thinks signitively is, correlatively, a nonunified cogito, not fully itself, therefore not fully wakeful—since wakefulness is the full self or presence, the actualized essence, of the cogito.[24]

Deconstruction has to work through the text of phenomenology and makes use of its results; thus it follows, up to a point, the radical movement of phenomenology by which the world is folded into transcendental experience as the essential possibility of experience of a world. Phenomenology in its furthest reach seeks to define the most fundamental or original structure of transcendental consciousness in which a world can be constituted as given to consciousness. Derrida provisionally accepts this movement. The phenomenological texts are there; a certain linguistic labor has been accomplished. The phenomenological reduction is a moment essential to the emergence of deconstruction because without it we would confuse the object itself with some determined *concept* of the object itself, say as defined by the positive sciences or in some realism or empiricism. The reduction opens the possibility of a radical reflection on the *sense* of the object as originally given to experience, and it is on the level of this radical reflection that deconstruction contests the phenomenological determination of this sense.

Working through phenomenology, then, we arrive at the concept of transcendental experience as the most general possibility of world experience. This possibility is then reinterpreted as a trace or sign structure. In the *Grammatology*, Derrida supplements his account of the trace structure in Husserl with Saussure's concept of the sign. The sign, says Saussure, is not a "positive term" but is constituted in its identity by its difference from the other terms in the system to which it belongs. The terms *a* and *b* are "radically incapable of reaching the level of consciousness—one is always conscious of only the *a/b* difference," and this is because language is a "form," not a "substance." [25] Here again we find the form of ideality as the trace of difference, or retention within the same of reference to a non-present other. The sign is constituted by a double difference, from itself (as essentially repeatable) and from other signs.

But Derrida radicalizes Saussure's concept of the differential form of language by assimilating it to Husserl's concept of ideality. A sensible existent, as such, in the world, cannot refer to or stand for something else; only *for consciousness* can something be a sign or representative. But this "for consciousness" must not be understood in the psychologistic sense whose inadequacies Husserl had revealed, but which Saussure still accepts. The sign is an "irreal" ideality, and the pure form of language as a system of differential trace structures can only appear in the "zone" of phenomenological "lived experience" (*Gramma.*, p. 65). On the other hand, by analyzing the structure of lived experience in terms of the Saussurean concept of significative value, Derrida fundamentally redirects the phenomenological discourse on which he draws. Signification appears only as lived ideality; yet it is not "presence," not self-identity there for conscious intuition. A sign is a structure of reference where difference, and not pure self-identity, appears *as such* (*Gramma.*, pp. 46–47). This "as such" contradicts the very notion of the "as such," because the sign as such is divided in its selfhood. Here, then, is a hinge between philosophy and deconstruction: to push the "as such" here is to push it over the edge.

During the Saussurean moment of the deconstructive critique of phenomenology, we say that signs reciprocally delimit each other within a total system, and that there is consequently no "original simplicity" but an "originary synthesis," the synthesis of reciprocal identifications within a system (*Gramma.*, p. 62). Decomposition is impossible, for the individual units (if a divided identity can still be called an "individual") cease to exist outside the system. On the other hand, the "total system" itself is only the system of relations of its terms. So the system exists only as it is "articulated," cut up or differentiated into units. The necessity of "articulation" is the necessity of a margin, a space of division between terms. If language were not articulated, divided, in this way, it would not be capable of syntax, of indefinitely numerous recombinations of its links in syntactic chains open to "all possible investments of sense" (*Gramma.*, p. 45). The link or *articulus* of the sign—first the phoneme or letter, then the word—must be "spaced," separated by an interval, from the other links. The necessity of the interval is essential; it is prescribed by the pure form of language, of articulation, prior to embodiment in a signifying medium. In speech, spacing shows up as the temporal separation of sounds in succession; in writing, as the visual interval between marks in sequence (*Gramma.*, p. 66). The constitutive margin that outlines from outside the discreteness of the sign is even less capable than the sign itself of sustaining the presence of consciousness. Phenomenological intuition is utterly baffled by this constitutive nothing. Spacing makes meaning possible, but cannot be consciously meant (*Gramma.*, p. 68).[26]

With concatenation, sequencing, the sign falls into time and space. So long as Derrida speaks of the sign by reference to the "total system" of signs, his remarks fall within the structuralist moment; but with the turn to "spacing" as constitutive of the sign we enter the moment of syntax, of succession in time and space. So long as we think in terms of a synchronic system, even if the *individual* sign is thought as a locus of differences, we can maintain presence as the presence of the *whole system*. This would be the restitution of transcendental being on a large scale. The celebrated structuralist "disappearance of the subject" in such a restitution would in fact be a classical metaphysical move. Purified of the limitations of an empirical subject, the total system of signs, or of signs and generative rules, would be the ideal correlate of a transcendental subject, as the a priori set of all possible meaning acts.

These themes—the split identity of the sign, signification as the trace of a difference, articulatory spacing—Derrida summarizes under the name of *writing*. "Writing" in the usual sense of the word is language physically detached from the subject who intends meaning, language that is material and intraworldly in a way that thought (and, to a lesser extent, speech) seems not to be. Derrida generalizes this ordinary sense of writing, holding on to the pure form of the concept prior to its realization in a signifying substance. The "only irreducible kernel of the concept of writing," he argues, is "the durable institution of a sign"—the persistent availability of a sign for an indefinite number of signifying acts in any possible signifying substance (*Gramma.*, p. 44). Prior to any "inscription" in the ordinary sense—with ink on paper, or by a furrow in stone, or even in a modified sense, say as magnetic traces on tape—there must be the pure form of "inscription"—that is, "durable institution" of a system of signs upon which any particular realization of the sign must draw. The transcendental concept of writing is thus nothing but the general possibility of the sign, and Derrida calls it "writing" to call attention to certain characteristics which have always been associated with the narrow concept of writing, but banished from the concept of the pure Logos. The Logos as essence of language has been thought as pure transparency to meaning, timeless and nonspatial, a pure thought rather than a sign. If thought has been the traditional image of pure meaning, writing is Derrida's image of the *signitive* essence of language, of speech and thought, of experience in general. "From the moment that there is meaning there are nothing but signs" (*Gramma.*, p. 50), and the sign must be structurally independent of the ensouling act of any present consciousness.[27] But this means that *within* my own experience, as the possibility of that experience, the "spacing" or partial nonpresence of writing is at work. I am not fully present to myself, not fully wakeful: "Arche-writing as spacing . . . marks *the dead time* within the presence of the living present" (*Gramma.*, p. 68). "I think, therefore I am" brings the fullness of self-presence to flower as the fullness of self-present thought; spacing within thought opens the relation to the unconscious and to death. Experience is *written*: on one hand, it makes a sense of its own, apart from the constitutive or ensouling intention of a wakeful consciousness; on the other hand, but for the same reason, the sense that it makes is equivocal, lacking in unity, and partially opaque.

IX

The point of all this is not, however, to set up a new metaphysics, a new explanation of how things *really are*. Deconstruction in its phase as critique of phenomenology proceeds by the rules of phenomenological discourse up to the moment of rupture. But the rupture would not be radical if all we were left with was a new foundational model installed in the zone of transcendental ideality. Rather, "differance" and "writing-in-general" are installed in that zone because that is the zone in which the concepts they are designed to contest are located. But once installed there, they redirect us away from the transparency of the zone of ideality into which the phenomenological reflection had temporarily raised us, and back into the written or "textual" milieu of experience which we had left behind. But the post-phenomenological investigation of the texture of experience now carries an alertness that it could not have had before going through that reflection. It would have been susceptible to uncritical assumptions of the sort that Husserl showed to be "sedimented" into our language and tradition. The turn to "writing" in deconstruction is not a simple return to the "natural standpoint" that precedes the phenomenological reduction; rather, Derrida says, it is a *reduction of the reduction*, a willed suspension of what we thought we knew that leaves the ray of consciousness stumped at the level of sign phenomena, unable to penetrate to the pure ideality of meaning. But this willed ignorance has to be justified by a critique of philosophy (whether critical or transcendental) that calls philosophy to account for that in its own conditions of possibility concerning which it has not been critical enough: "Attentiveness to the 'fact' of language in which a juridical thought lets itself be transcribed, in which juridicalness would like to be completely transparent, is a return to factuality as the de jure character of the de jure itself. It is a reduction of the reduction and opens the way to an infinite discursiveness" (*Intro.*, p. 70n).[28]

Now, as we redirect our gaze from the transcendental unities of pure meaning toward the equivocal surface of a writing, the zone of ideality itself begins to show up as a textual zone in the ordinary sense of text. The phenomenological reduction is a *linguistic effect* opened up by Husserl's text. This, at least, is how it begins to look to us as we find ourselves no longer able to view the purity of ideal objectivities, find ourselves instead looking at sequences of signs. And now we see how it is that "differance," as Derrida says, is "neither a word nor a concept" (*S&P*, p. 130). It is a *grammatical device*, a trace structure constructed as a baffle, to be installed in syntax so that it keeps the sign sequence from cohering in the ways dictated by the habitual norms of philosophical discourse. The habits of the philosophical use of language force the threads of its language to cohere at the juncture of the *tode ti*, "this-here (now)"; and *differance* as not-this and not-now keeps these threads apart. This baffle or shuttle thus holds open the texture of language against the pressure of the paternal tradition in such a way as to allow different kinds of texts to be interwoven. The space of nonintuition allows, for example, the Freudian discourse on the unconscious and the irrational to flow into the text of philosophy.

Derrida pushes very hard on the notion of the "as such" in order to open the space of nonintuition.[29] The "as such" or "in itself" is perhaps the founding concept of philosophy: it is from the beginning an indispensable tool for carving out the true objects of knowledge. Plato uses it to refine the medium of the eidos; the pure, self-identical eidos is the *auto eidos*, the eidos itself or as such.[30]

But the selfhood of the selfsame has always meant the ideal fullness of wakeful consciousness and the full presence of its objective correlate. How can we speak of "spacing" *as such*? Does the sign have an "as such"? The *auto eidos* is the fullness of visibility; how can there be an *auto sema*—a sign as such—an essence of contamination of visibility by opacity? Does it make sense to speak of "what is not itself, as such"? Undoubtedly it does not, so long as a certain conception of what will count as meaningful is in force. But it is this conception itself that is here being put in question.

2   Wittgenstein Deconstructs

I

The *Philosophical Investigations* is an intricate mixture of arguments, images, satire, dramatic mimicry, and how-to instructions, rather than a treatise. It is true that Wittgenstein, like Derrida, is often taken to have been engaged in correcting errors, but this impression arises from following out his *askesis* only up to a point. Up to the point at which Wittgenstein ceases to comment on his practice and begins only to *practice*, he gives the impression that he aims at pure clarity, at untangling confusion and "bringing rest" to the perplexed. The famous remark about letting the fly out of the fly bottle fits this pattern. Such remarks indicate the hope that Wittgenstein had for his method, and which he only reluctantly gave up. The preface to the *Investigations*, which we will consider more closely later, indicates as much.

But Wittgenstein's method inevitably turns against itself. On one hand, Wittgenstein wanted to loosen up crystallized patterns of philosophical language in order to force real thought, thought subject to the most radical perplexities, for which it would have no ready-made answers but would have to forge new language sequences. On the other hand, the philosophical patterns which supposedly forestall the necessity for real thought at the same time appear to him to be sources of endless perplexity and unrest because they do not correspond to the true complexity of the facts. So Wittgenstein's way, which is more difficult, the "bloody *hard* way," at the same time promises an end to the endless difficulty of philosophy.[1]

This, however, is only a preliminary movement. For once the difficult labor had resulted in satisfaction, the tension of its difficulty would collapse, and then once more there would be an end to hard thinking. So, thinking hard, Wittgenstein proceeds to think his way through the assured forms of ordinary speech and solid ground, in order once more, as he says in the "Remarks on Frazer," to "immerse himself in the water of doubt" and resume his productive labor.[2] Wittgenstein's doubt is not skepticism, but what Nietzsche calls "active forgetfulness," renewed perplexity about what he himself has already resolved, a loosening-up of the bonds of syntax of what he has already written in order to write anew. In the continued movement of his language, the reassuring forms of usage on which he has previously struck as though on bedrock become impediments to hard thinking, as the crystallized forms of philosophy had been. And the movement of deconstruction renews, in a new form, the restless perplexity which had formerly arisen from the supposed inadequacy of those forms.

This, then, is the "deconstructive" impulse in Wittgenstein which I want to trace, and it is, I believe, what he wanted to teach. Wittgenstein's "method" would be, unlike Husserl's, not one which could be repeated as *the same* by his followers, but one which would necessarily go new paths, "disseminating" as it went. Two ways of varying from Wittgenstein must carefully be distinguished here. The orthodox normalization of Wittgenstein begins by scorning as an "aberration" Wittgenstein's "revulsion at the thought of himself as a philosophical theorist" and treating his work as it does that of any other philosopher.[3] This kind of development of Wittgenstein's thought is independent in one way, but not at all what he meant when he said he wanted, not to save others the trouble of thinking, but to stimulate them to thoughts of their own. Writers who take this route do not repeat Wittgenstein, but they do repeat the formulas he deconstructed. They are thus this side rather than the other side of Wittgenstein; they have not traversed his text. The "true" "repetition" of Wittgenstein would catch, not his results, his arguments, his "models," but his deconstructive movement, not his words but his syntax, a syntax that continually varies and finds new directions.

In what follows, I will try to represent the movement of Wittgenstein's language in the first 242 remarks of the *Philosophical Investigations*. Much of what I say will be familiar to students of Wittgenstein, some not so familiar, and some will seem scarcely "serious." It will usually be possible to refute the deconstructive reading of a given remark with an orthodox philosophical interpretation. Nor is such orthodox interpretation simply wrong. There is always more than one thing going on in Wittgenstein's language, more forces than one transecting his words and images, and it is often possible to detach from this language a homogeneous and transparent layer of philosophical significance. I do not say such a procedure is invalid. Its possibility is given in the language; it is what Derrida calls the possibility of the "graft."[4] In fact, Wittgenstein's language invites being chopped up and carried away in pieces even more than most writers' language, because of the extent to which he has opened up its articulatory spaces. His investigations are broken into discrete "remarks" which, although they are woven into a sequence with the greatest care, retain an integrity or autonomy that allows them easily to be detached from this sequence.[5] What such a procedure cannot account for is the *style* of the language, its coherence as a zigzag movement, its dependence on metaphor, its use of irony, and so on. So the readings presented here should be taken in the context of this larger movement, this movement proper to the textual surface of the *Investigations*.

II

In what follows, it is necessary to keep in mind that Wittgenstein is not primarily making arguments or teaching new concepts, though much of what he writes certainly looks like those things; rather, he is instructing us in a skill, a method, a strategy.[6] Hence there will always be a double sense to each move he makes. On one hand, he will address a particular question or confusion and attempt to show how it is to be resolved. On the other hand, the attack on the problem will be an *example* of the operation of the skill or method that is being taught: "A method will now be shown by means of examples" (*es wird nun an Beispielen eine Methode gezeigt*) (*PI* 133). The method is difficult in the extreme to teach or to learn, because it is unlike any other method. It is an entirely new *kind* of method, and learning it requires breaking the linguistic habits of a lifetime and acquiring new ones. But the old habits make it almost impossible to understand what is being taught. It is difficult enough to grasp the arguments and concepts; to grasp them as examples of the operation of a skill, however, seems to require a prior understanding of the nature of the skill—otherwise how can we see them as *examples*? Examples of *what*? As we will see, a great part of the *Investigations*, while explicitly engaged in studying particular philosophical problems, will be an implicit probing of the problem of teaching and learning the method that is at work. A method without rules, without fixed boundaries—a blind and mute method, taught only by being practiced.

The first 242 remarks of the *Investigations* are concerned, let us say, with the machinery of language—with questions about the basic structure of naming, understanding a meaning, grasping a rule. Following remark 242 the discussion shifts to sensations and the questions become broader.[7] But this first part of the book is pretty sharply focused on the deconstruction of the fundamental picture of meaning as something mental and of a word as a unity corresponding to the unity of a mental act. In remark 38 Wittgenstein evokes a version of the primal scene of philosophy, in which naming appears as "so to speak, an occult process": "Naming appears as a *queer* connexion of a word with an object. —And you really get such a queer connexion when the philosopher tries to bring out *the* relation between name and thing by staring at an object in front of him and repeating a name or even the word 'this' innumerable times. . . . And *here* we may indeed fancy naming to be some remarkable act of mind [*merkwürdiger seelischer Akt*], as if it were a baptism of an object." I want to point out several themes struck in this remark which will recur repeatedly in Wittgenstein's (and our) discussion.

First, there is Wittgenstein's satirical turn: he will repeatedly present the philosopher as acting out an absurd or comical scene in his most intense moments of philosophical travail. Elsewhere we will see him looking out the corner of his eye at the mental object, or assuming a solemn facial expression in order to give his words a properly philosophical meaning, and so on. This is part of the generally "scenic" character of Wittgenstein's presentation: since he wants to investigate meaning as signification, as spatiotemporal and not as mental-instantaneous, he will continually evoke the *scene* of language as the locus of meaning. It is also part of the persuasion that Wittgenstein is working as teacher of a method: the tone of satire does combat with the language of philosophy in a different way from the arguments and examples. Wittgenstein presents a philosophical scene not only as misguided but as foolish or even ridiculous. This, one might say, is not the force of truth, but of "style"—and one might certainly be annoyed by it if one is not amused or convinced. Let us keep in mind, however, that Wittgenstein's prime exemplar of the philosophic urge for presence is himself. To a certain extent his satire is self-satire.

Second is his characterization of philosophic conceptions of mind and meaning as "occult" or "peculiar." These are Wittgenstein's terms for the "beyond" of language which philosophy postulates, the ideal realm where things like "meaning" are possible. Third, there is his use of figures to picture mental activities, here naming as a baptism. This is related to his satirical tone, but involves something more. For Wittgenstein is concerned not only or even primarily with philosophical problems, but with the *compulsion* which those problems exercise over us.[8] Hence part of his task is to find words to express the characteristic experiences associated with certain typical philosophical notions; here his language works like lyric poetry. If he can make his reader feel that this is *just* the experience associated with his own sense of his philosophical problem, then the persuasive force of the satire and of the new method in general is increased.

Scenic, satirical, figurative, this language is designed to exert pressure on the person thinking as well as on the problems thought about. This leads us then into the more specific themes struck in *PI* 38. A solitary scene, a philosopher in the immediate presence of an object, at which he stares—"und dabei unzähliche Male einen Namen wiederholt, oder auch das Wort 'dieses.'" I have called this a satirical characterization. It can also be read as a grim, obsessive scene, almost a scene of madness: a man addressing an object, saying "This! This!" over and over. Wittgenstein treats philosophy as a compulsive or obsessive activity, the domination of imagination by certain exemplary scenes of language use which force their impress upon language and perception and transform them into repetitions of these ideal or paradigmatic scenes. The "baptism" of an object described by Wittgenstein is such an exemplary scene. It is a version of the scene that lies behind Husserl's picture of primordial intuition, here reduced to an absurd nakedness, stripped of dignity—and of philosophical sophistication. As presented by Husserl, the scene is compelling, a scene of truth; as presented by the ironist it warns us away from itself. There is a war of language here, and there is no simple adjudication of competing claims.

Finally, *PI* 38 evokes the compulsion of the word "This." This word has what seems an absolutely unique role in the language: it is spoken in the presence of, seems to be absolutely transparent to, the object. It is as though with this word, language transcends its separation from things and makes contact with them. "Strange to say," says Wittgenstein earlier in the same remark, "the word 'this' has been called the only *genuine* name [*eigentliche Name*]; so that anything else we call a name was only one in an inexact, approximate sense."

This word "this" will play an important role in Wittgenstein's discussion. I am inclined to call it the hinge on which his deconstruction turns. For, on the one hand, "this" is the word that accompanies the pointing gesture (*hinweisende Gebärde*) in the presence of the object and the "ostensive definition" (*hinweisende Erklärung*) which is the centerpiece of the conception of language against which Wittgenstein is working. And, on the other hand, it will be the word that Wittgenstein uses in his writing as a way of pointing to words that he is using, citing, in quotation marks, as samples (*Mustern*) of language. It will turn out that the boundary between object and word cannot be drawn; that the act of pointing is inscribed in a syntax[9] and that a word can function as a thing.

III

The background of Wittgenstein's concern with the "baptism of the object" is his own attempt in the *Tractatus* to present a conception of language as immediately in touch with reality. Wittgenstein in the *Tractatus* supposed that names had meaning because they were immediately correlated with simple individual objects or things which constituted the unalterable form of reality. "Propositions" were concatenations of such names which "pictured" a possible configuration of such objects; they had sense because they had "absorbed" the "form" of the objects whose names they concatenated; and the sense of the proposition, its correlation with objects, was immediately available to simple inspection.[10] A proposition, as a "logical picture," was an immediate representation of the unalterable form of reality.

2.026   There must be objects, if the world is to have unalterable form.

2.0271   Objects are what is unalterable and subsistent; their config-uration is what is changing and unstable.

2.15   The fact that the elements of a picture are related to one another in a determinate way represents that things are re-lated to one another in the same way.

2.1514   The pictorial relationship consists of the correlations of the picture's elements with things.

2.1515   These correlations are, as it were, the feelers with which the picture touches reality.[11]

In the *Tractatus*, then, Wittgenstein had conceived of the meaningful-ness of language as founded on a direct and rather mysterious connection between names and things. In the *Investigations* he reopens the question of this connection in his discussion of the problem of "ostensive defini-tion"—what I will call the problem of the scene of naming. Speaking the name of a thing in the physical presence of that thing, or pointing to it and saying "this," seems to provide an unimpeachable model of the relation between language and "reality." The problem with *names* is that they can always be spoken in the absence of the thing named, but it seems as though "the demonstrative 'this' can never be without a bearer. It might be said: 'so long as there is a *this*, the word "this" has a meaning too.'"

When we point to an object and say the name, or say "this," it seems as though something instantaneous happens, the filling of a word with mean-ing by means of an objectively grounded mental act. So there are two es-sential components here: the presence of the object, and the mental experi-ence of meaning or intending just that object by this word. Wittgenstein's reply to this is that "an ostensive definition [*hinweisende Definition*] can be variously interpreted in *every* case" (*PI* 28). Whenever I point to an object and say a word, the act is meaningless except insofar as "the place is already prepared" (*PI* 31) for this word; that is, insofar as there exists a language within which such specific language games as naming or saying "This!" make sense. Pointing at an object and uttering a sound could be a com-mand, or it could be calling attention to the shape or color or shade of color or the number of the object or objects. Or, depending on the circumstances, it could be calling attention to the difference between this object and some other.

So it is always possible to ask "What?" when someone points and makes a sound, even if we imagine a perfectly bare room with only one object in it to be pointed to—unless we also suppose a preparation for the pointing, suppose that we already know what is to be demonstrated here. The act of pointing and the naming or saying "this" do not accomplish anything by themselves, but only fit as it were a syntactic slot.

And it doesn't help to get rid of the words and point silently, because the silent gesture is even more exposed to ambiguity than the gesture and word combined.

It is very difficult to keep in mind that when we say "thing," it is not just an accident that we utter a word, use a sign. We feel that when we say "thing" or "this," even though we are using a sign, the sign is of little account, actually a distraction from what it is a sign for. We feel as though it is accidental that we have to use a sign: we want to indicate the thing in its thingness, and would like to do it without using a sign, but we can't. For it is clear enough that we can point to things for any number of purposes, in our ordinary use of language; but these uses are, from a philosophical point of view, mute. They do not establish the philosophical boundary line between word and thing. That is, it is unclear how the ordinary pointing of language for ordinary purposes is to be transformed into, or seen as a case of, pointing not to a thing as distinguished from other things ("No, not *that* one, *this* one"), but to a thing *as thing*. For when you try to point to a thing as thing, all I see is you pointing to a thing. You point, for example, at this book, and I ask you, "Why are you pointing at that book?" for there seems to be no occasion for this pointing. "Do you want me to hand it to you?" I ask. And now perhaps you say, "No, no, I'm just trying to get you to look at the book and see that it is an *object*, something different from mere *words*." But I was never in danger of mistaking a book for a word. Words are what we find *in* books. Nevertheless, *object* and *book* are *words* too. So what you're really saying is that we use words like *object* differently from the way we use words like *word*. And now to free yourself from being reduced to mere words again you simply point silently, perhaps assuming a very solemn and significant facial expression as you do. But what is it you are pointing at? What makes this act of pointing into a gesture toward the "beyond" of language, and not simply a purposeless pointing at this book? The only thing which could (if anything could) would be the explanation which you could give, and you disavow the explanation because it is only words.

So we hover between the explanation and the act of pointing, which seem to supplement each other's deficiencies, and so long as we do not look too closely, we give ourselves the impression that we are here indicating the beyond of language—when all we are doing is *making signs*. And there is no sign whose signification is "that which is beyond signification." Isn't this so in principle, by the very meaning of the concept of the sign? How could it even occur to us to think that it is possible to *signify what lies beyond signification?* [12]

Wittgenstein insists, in what seems a very literal-minded way, on not allowing any shadow of imprecision to remain in the expression of the philosophical urge. Only its imprecision can allow this urge to seem plausible, an imprecision which feeds on itself, for it prescribes that language is necessarily inadequate—and anyhow inessential—and then proceeds to posit the grounds for this prescription in language which is inadequate to the positing but which is excusable for its inadequacy because it is necessarily inadequate—and anyhow inessential—to the positing. That which seems to be posited is justified by its being posited as preposited. Hence all we need to establish it is a gesture in its direction—since it is already established prior to our establishing it and is what grounds our establishing of it. But Wittgenstein argues that all we have here is an impression of positing, a pretending to posit which never gets so far as an actual positing, since it only *seems* to make sense.

The case is no better if I try to use the evidence of "internal" experience. Say I try to demonstrate to myself that there are experiences as such, beyond signs. I shut my eyes tight and concentrate on the sensation of my tense eyelid muscles. I am careful to keep my mind empty of words. Ecco! There it is, a pure sensation. And now? Now I can say nothing about it, for if I do, it becomes a sign in the language game. But I can also think nothing of it, for that would make it part of the language game as well. Furthermore, I cannot even experience the private demonstration of the sensation *as* a private demonstration of a sensation, for even that would constitute the sensation as a sign. It would then have been a "sample" of wordless sensation; it would *signify* "wordless sensation." I do not have to think the words "this experience signifies a wordless sensation" for this to be so—for if this is a demonstration of a "wordless sensation," then it is *part of the structure of the experience* that the sensation *signifies* "wordless sensation." The very concept of such a demonstration is incoherent and self-contradictory, "so in the end when one is doing philosophy one gets to the point where one would like just to emit an inarticulate sound" (*PI* 261). And even *then* one would not be free of the net of syntax, for "such a sound is an expression only as it occurs in a language-game, which should now be described."

"Just as a move in chess doesn't consist simply in moving a piece in such-and-such a way on the board—nor yet in one's thoughts and feelings as one makes the move: but in the circumstances [*Umstände*] that we call 'playing a game of chess'" (*PI* 33), so pointing and naming, and understanding such gestures, are not meaningful as such, nor by virtue of some mental act or process that accompanies them. Rather, they are inscribed in a sequence and derive their meaning from a "before" and an "after." There are "characteristic experiences" which accompany our acts of pointing and intending, but these may also be absent. And whether these experiences are present or absent, the *meaning* of the gesture would remain independent of them: "It would still depend on the circumstances—that is, on what happened before and after the pointing" (*so käme es doch auf die Umstände an—d.h., auf das, was vor und nach dem Zeigen geschieht*) (*PI* 35).

What is afoot here in Wittgenstein is what Derrida in his discussion of Husserl's formalism calls "the emancipation of speech as nonknowing," the casting-out of meaning from the instantaneity of a mental act into the spatial and temporal sequencing of a medium which is not dominated or permeated by a *Geist* that makes it mean. Language is a scenic writing, a syntax which means only from the sequence of its moments; and the subject is displaced into the moments of this writing, his meaning exiled from himself into the before and after of the *Umstände*.

To demonstrate this, Wittgenstein has to deconstruct the idea of the "mental object" or "mental picture" and the idea of "understanding" as a mental event.

The "mental picture" (*Bild im Geiste*) is intended to explain the unity of the meaning of a name. For example, I see samples of leaves or of the color green and eventually learn to apply the words *leaf* or *green* correctly. Now it seems as though I must have in my mind a generalized picture or sample (*'allgemeine' Muster*)—"Say a schematic leaf, or a sample of *pure* green" (*PI* 73). Very well, says Wittgenstein, let us suppose you have such a mental sample—now how are you going to *apply* it? Is this sample of "pure green" a sample of everything greenish—or only of what is pure green? And what is the shape of this sample? Rectangular? Then why wouldn't it be a sample of a green rectangle? Is it irregular in shape? Then why isn't it a sample of irregularity of shape? The discursive point is that there is no way of giving a precise characterization of the mental sample, that no matter how it is described it will be subject to the same ambiguity as a mere *physical* sample would. And in that case, we could replace the mental sample with an actual physical sample, since the question of whether we have learned the meaning of the word *green* is entirely answered by the way we *use* the word. If we use it as other people do, then we have learned the meaning of the word, whether we have a mental picture or not.[13]

But there is, in addition to the discursive point, a habit of thought or of writing displayed in this remark—the extreme literalness we noted earlier. When we gesture in the direction of mental occurrences, Wittgenstein wants a very literal description of what we are talking about. Where *we* feel that there is something important here which we mustn't allow incidental difficulties of expression to distract us from, but must press on to the subtle fact—it as though *Wittgenstein's* thought keeps adhering to contiguous surfaces, getting stuck to the particularities of objects. A *rectangular* mental color sample? Surely it is just the nature of mental pictures that they don't have to act like actual things! We can see here something of what Findlay considers to be a "schizophrenic" quality in Wittgenstein's writing,[14] what looks like an inability to pursue an abstract thought consistently because the thought keeps getting distracted by incidental features of physical surfaces. We will return to this subject later; for the moment let us simply note that what I am here calling "extreme literalness" is another aspect of the scenic and figurative bent of Wittgenstein's style—that is, it is all part of a tendency to confine thought within the limits of the *imageable*, the *Bildlichkeit* of language.

Returning to the discursive point: Wittgenstein's argument is that a picture—even a mental picture—cannot determine its own meaning but that its meaning will be determined by its use or application, its insertion into a certain sequence. Inserted into *this* sequence, the sample will be a sample of one thing; inserted into *that*, of another. And the application occurs *im Laufe der Zeit* (in the course of time) (*PI* 141). But, on the other hand, couldn't the *application* of the picture flash before our mind's eye at the same time as the picture does? Wittgenstein describes this as the experience of "knowing how to go on," and explores it in connection with learning how to develop an arithmetical or algebraic series. Notice that this sort of understanding is related to understanding the meaning of a word but is the understanding of the character of a sequence of terms rather than of a single term. Yet here too it appears as though there could be an instantaneous mental occurrence which would be the experience of grasping or understanding. We think of the experience of understanding as an essence separate from the actual performing of a derivation: the writing down of these numbers is not "understanding"; understanding is what makes it possible for me to write them correctly. Wittgenstein suggests that here one is thinking of understanding by analogy with an algebraic formula or something similar. "But this is where we were before. The point is, we can think of more than *one* application of an algebraic formula; and every type of application can in turn be formulated algebraically" (*PI* 146). A formula, like the schema of "pure green" or the pointing gesture, does not have its meaning immanent within it: it must still be *applied*, unfolded in time and space. A formula can occur to us, flash upon our minds, so that we feel "Now I understand!" and then we might get stuck, find that we cannot go on after all. And the feeling that we had might be just the same experience that we would have had if we *had* been able to go on. But in either case, we do not say someone "understands" because he has an experience but because he shows that he can *do* something. This shows that "understand" does not refer to a mental occurrence, but is intertwined with a sequence of events.

IV

There is a profound tension in Wittgenstein's language connected with this business of how we understand a meaningful or ordered or learnable and teachable activity. On one hand, Wittgenstein in challenging the notion that understanding is something mental points us toward practices in their social context, what has come to be summed up in the too-convenient phrase "forms of life" which commentators on Wittgenstein continually cite. Wittgenstein shows over and over that any sign (or formula or mental picture) taken in isolation can be *interpreted*, that it contains no essence within it that dictates how we must necessarily understand it. Even this sign:

Why should we not read this as pointing in the direction of the shaft rather than of the head? he asks (*BB*, p. 33). Yet the point of these demonstrations seems to be that in fact we do *not* interpret signs when we use them under *normal* conditions. "What this shews is that there is a way of grasping a rule which is *not* an *interpretation*, but which is exhibited in what we call 'obeying [*folgen*] the rule' and 'going against it'" (*PI* 201). Along this axis of Wittgenstein's discourse, then, there is, even as with the "elementary propositions" of the *Tractatus*, an end to interpretation. We *could* take this word, this formula, this command, this signpost, differently than we do, if we did not have the context of a custom, a practice; but since we do have such a context, there is no need to interpret at all: we simply understand the sign.

> If I have exhausted the justification I have reached bedrock, and my spade is turned. Then I am inclined [*geneigt*] to say: "This is simply what I do." (*PI* 217)

> When I obey a rule, I do not choose. I obey the rule *blindly*. (*PI* 219).

> The sign-post is in order—if, under normal circumstances, it fulfils its purpose. (*PI* 87)

Along this axis, Wittgenstein's project is a "normalization" of philosophical language, a return to "real life," a dissolving of fruitless and misguided speculation by a recognition of how things really are. "What *we* do is to bring words back from their metaphysical to their everyday use" (*PI* 116). This recognition involves a certain heroic recognition of limits to our understanding; but we *know* what those limits are. And in return, we get to move from the slippery ice of metaphysics back to the "rough ground" of actuality where there is friction and we can walk (*PI* 107).

It is possible to do a sophisticated reading of Wittgenstein's project this way, as a philosophic *nostos*, bringing language "home" (*Heimat*) (*PI* 116) once again. Charles Altieri has offered such a reading as a counter to Derrida's presumed Continental skepticism. His reading is well-informed, consistent, and, as far as it goes, accurate. Yet we perceive the limits of this reading when we find Altieri calling "forms of life" the "irreducible ontological base" of Wittgenstein's investigations.[15] Is there any more thoroughly *metaphysical* concept than this? Is not in this way the entire discourse that Altieri claims Wittgenstein to have superseded reinstated at the heart of Wittgenstein's writing? Altieri's instructive and necessary reading shows just how difficult it is to cut that last thread, that umbilicus, to the classical conceptuality; a mere thread, but one which sustains the body of the new discourse and which it seems impossible to do without.

But along another axis this entire reading is destabilized. If Wittgenstein's arguments seem to establish a new ground of security, on the other hand remember that Wittgenstein is not primarily making arguments but teaching a linguistic skill, a *method: es wird nun an Beispielen eine Methode gezeigt*. This method is a way of writing, a style, a sense of the material substance of language, of its possibilities of combination and recombination. Hence it is not transitionally, subordinate to the establishment of a "normality" of "forms of life" (within which questions do not arise as to the interpretation of signs), that all his surreal destabilization of even the most "natural" of signs arises: the method that Wittgenstein is teaching is precisely the method of destabilization.

Wittgenstein's method is critical. It is a way of attacking another style of language, the traditional style of philosophy. This traditional style is characterized by the pursuit of stable unities, "essences" which can be at the base or foundation of "the world," which can have "ontological primacy." Wittgenstein's own "objects" in the *Tractatus* were such a foundation. Now, in order to fracture these unities, Wittgenstein develops a style of writing which is radically errant, which unlids all the accidence concealed by "normal" uses of words in order to show how many different routes it would be possible to take from any given point in the discourse— routes which we had simply not thought of because we were bemused by normality.

For there is a profound complicity between normality, between "ordinary language," and philosophy.

Philosophy has been a certain kind of "speculation," a certain way of looking at things, at language. Under the compulsion of the philosophical urge "we feel as if we had to *penetrate* phenomena" (*die Erscheinungen durchschauen*) (*PI* 90). This penetrating vision would see something ideal, a logical structure beneath appearances the seeing of which would be the fulfillment of vision. This logical structure would be "the a priori order of the world: that is, the order of *possibilities*. . . . no empirical cloudiness or uncertainty can be allowed to affect it—It must rather be of the purest crystal" (*PI* 97). But we cannot see it; the required order conflicts with what we do see, we feel as though we are dealing with "extreme subtleties," as though we had "to repair a torn spider's web with our fingers" (*PI* 106). "'*The essence is hidden from us*' [*Das Wesen ist uns verborgen*]: this is the form our problem now assumes" (*PI* 92). And the solution seems to be to focus the gaze "absolutely sharply" upon this fact in question (*PI* 113).

Now, says Wittgenstein, the only way to escape from the intolerable contradictions involved in such a project is to turn around the whole perspective from which we look at things (*PI* 108). We are not concerned with anything hidden, because everything already "lies open to view" (*PI* 126). Instead of penetrating vision, what we want is to command a clear view (*übersehen*) (*PI* 122).[16] It is true that in a sense there is something "hidden," but not because it lies beneath the surface: rather, it is because it is right on the surface, in plain sight (like Poe's purloined letter). "The aspects of things that are most important for us are hidden because of their simplicity and familiarity. (One is unable to notice something—because it is always before one's eyes.)" (*PI* 129).

So far, it seems as though the entire problem arises from the compulsion to see the hidden object ("our inability to turn our eyes from this picture") (*PI* 352), from a corrupted vision that needs to become innocent once more and simply see what actually *is*. (And here is the point at which it seems as though Wittgenstein is simply putting forth his own pet candidate for "ontological primacy.") But what is it that gives rise to the illusions of essence, of hidden unities beneath the variegated play of phenomena? There are two sources, one of them our language about language, the other ordinary language itself. On one hand, one is unable to see "how propositions really work" because "the forms that we use in expressing ourselves about propositions and thought stand in his way" (*PI* 93); but on the other, it is because we miss "distinctions which our *ordinary forms* of language easily make us overlook" (*PI* 132; italics added). Anscombe translates "ordinary" for *gewöhnlichen*; I would like to call attention to its connection with *wohnen*, its sense as "dwelling in" or "being at home" with something, to bring out the fact that it is the normality, the at-homeness of

ordinary language—to which we are supposedly to be returned by Wittgenstein—that creates the blindness, the unconsciousness of distinctions.
(Notice also that "overlook" here is in German *übersehen*, the same word
that in *PI* 122 Wittgenstein uses to mean "having a clear view." Ordinary
language makes us overlook what we will have to carefully look over—in
ordinary language.) Philosophical disquiet arises when "a simile that has
been absorbed into the forms of our language produces a false appearance"
and makes us think something must be so even though it seems as though
it couldn't be. For example, we know what "studying" or "finding out"
about something is like—say, studying the workings of a machine or the
anatomy of the body. So we propose to "study" or "find out about" thinking, about the mind. And now things become very puzzling indeed; we
find ourselves deeply confused about the "mechanism" here and must propose a very peculiar, an "occult" mechanism (cf. *PI* 308). We use the same
words, the same form of expression, to describe two projects, and we are
misled into seeing them as more alike than they really are. ("Where our
language suggests a body [*Körper*] and there is none: there, we should like
to say, is a *spirit* [*Geist*]" [*PI* 36].) Or a man, knowing a sentence like "On
many occasions I have in Chicago been deceived," might be led to frame the
plausibly similar-sounding sentence, "On many occasions I have in dreams
been deceived," and so bequeath an inexhaustible puzzle to philosophy.[17]

So it is that *surface features* of language suggest the misleading analogies
which give rise to philosophical disquiet. This is very clear in one of the
later remarks which the editors suggest have not undergone final revision:

> In the use of words one might distinguish 'surface grammar' from
> 'depth grammar.' What immediately impresses itself upon us about the
> use of a word is the way it is used in the construction of the sentence,
> the part of its use—one might say—that can be taken in by the ear.
> —And now compare the depth grammar, say of the word "to mean,"
> with what its surface grammar would lead us to suspect. No wonder
> we find it difficult to know our way about. (*PI* 664)

Whereas Wittgenstein has been characterizing his investigation as directed
at what is already in plain sight, at "the spatial and temporal phenomenon of language" (*PI* 108), here he seems to be talking about something
hidden.

Wittgenstein in fact presents "ordinary language" in a double aspect, as
Penelope and as Circe, as the home to which language has to be returned
and as the seduction of the play of surfaces. The pictures which enslave the
gaze lie in *language*, and language seems to repeat them to us inexorably
(*unerbittlich*) (*PI* 115). Philosophy is "a battle against the bewitchment of
our intelligence by means of language" (*PI* 109).

Is this how it goes, then? We have an impure ordinary language, one that gives rise to philosophical illusions, and also one that has been purified of its seductiveness by the purification of the speculation of which it is the object? And would that then be the underlying, the true reality of language? Could anything be more traditional in philosophy than such a project? It sounds very nearly Platonic, the achievement of a vision that is not deceived by perspective but knows how to measure what it sees by looking through the play of appearance.

But in Wittgenstein's account the illusions are not of sense but of *penetrating vision*. It is unities, stable forms, essences, that are illusory, and accidence, errancy, contingency, that are actual. The eye that sees truly is the eye that knows, not how to penetrate, but how to follow the play of surfaces, and what Wittgenstein calls "depth grammar" is not something that lies beneath appearance but in the subtle articulation of appearance, of the material of language.

So the philosophical urge to see essences and mental entities is fed by certain actual features of ordinary language. Philosophical problems mirror those features of the surface of language (or "of language," since there is nothing from which a surface could be distinguished) that are in accord with the urge to *durchschauen*, to penetrate with vision. Other features— distinctions, differences—are missed; the eye is "blinded to them by the ideal" (*PI* 100). It is these differences where we are inclined to see identities that Wittgenstein wants to teach us to see, to write—areas of language that have remained unthought, unconscious. *This unconsciousness is normal*; it is normality.

> It is only in normal cases that the use of a word is clearly prescribed; we know, are in no doubt, what to say in this or that case. The more abnormal the case, the more doubtful it becomes what we are to say. (*PI* 142)

> I obey the rule *blindly*. (*PI* 219)

> It always tells us the same, and we do what it tells us. (*PI* 223)

> The rule can only seem to me to produce all its consequences in advance if I draw them as a *matter of course* [*selbstverständlich*]. As much as it is a matter of course for me to call this colour "blue." (*PI* 238)

This last remark draws explicitly the analogy between "following a rule" and the normal use of a word. Theorists of "forms of life" generally emphasize the social, intersubjective character of rules and meanings, the concreteness of custom and practice as opposed to the solitariness and abstraction of metaphysical theorizing (the "private language" debate, the problem of "other minds"), but the above remarks point to the *automatism* which is an essential aspect of normality. When I use language normally, according to custom, I use it without thinking: and it is just this that makes it possible for the philosophical illusions to arise. *Normality is the necessary background against which it would be possible to think the essence.*

V

When we think meaning in terms of the essence, we treat a sign (word, picture, algebraic formula) as the locus or container of a present or immanent meaning. We think that of course the mere sign out in the world is too coarse, too material (*zu grob, materiell*) (*PI* 120) to have meaning immanent within it, but that the *subtle sign,* the instantaneous mental representation of the sign (*die Vorstellung in gegenwärtigen Augenblick*) (*PI* 105), could. And the material sign simply stands for this instantaneity of self-identical and self-present meaning. It is only in a certain setting, in terms of certain circumstances, that signs mean what they mean; yet the circumstances seem to be only the inessential background against which we think the essence. (This is the illusion embodied in the idea of "This!")

Wittgenstein examines this problem through the example of chess. Suppose we have taught someone the rules of chess and shown him all the pieces except the king (*PI* 31). Now we say, "This is the king," and show it to him. Here we have the impression that the king stands before us complete in his kinghood; but we get this impression only because we already know how to do something with the piece, which in turn implies knowing what to do with the other pieces as well. Similarly, I must already know the "overall role" of a word in language before I can so much as ask for the name of something: for example, I cannot ask what that color is called unless I already know the use of color words (*PI* 30). And of course knowing how color words are used implies knowing how to do many other things with language as well.

The point Wittgenstein is making here is related to, but must not be confused with, Saussure's point, also made with the help of chess, that the sign has no "positive content," only a relational value arising from reciprocal demarcations among an entire system of terms, "where elements hold each other in equilibrium in accordance with fixed rules."[18] Wittgenstein is sometimes mistakenly taken to sanction in the *Investigations* just such a view of language as a "rule-governed activity." Wittgenstein's method is strongly at odds with, was in fact developed as a critique of, a similar view. The concept of "following a rule," far from being an answer to the question of how we know how to use a word, is the central problem of the *Investigations.*[19] Wittgenstein rejects the idea of a system of rules underlying the diversity of uses in favor of looking carefully at those uses to see how they are in fact ordered. He is interested, not in atemporal formulas that can assimilate new cases to their pattern, but in *the patterns that actual words and actions present to us as spatiotemporal phenomena.*

Although Wittgenstein agrees with Saussure in treating the "value" of words as relational, he goes a different way in treating these "relations" as *syntactic* rather than as systematic, that is, as functions of the concatenation of elements. The "overall role" of a word is thus not to be thought of as its place as defined within an abstract, synchronic system but as the qualitative or "physiognomic" character of the sensuous-appearing word as it emerges from the panoply of its syntactic settings. The value or meaning of each appearance of a sign arises in part from this "physiognomy" of the sign as gathered from its past appearances, and for the rest, from the circumstances (*Umstände*) of a given appearance—that is, from what happens "before and after" (*was vor und nach geschieht*) (*PI* 35). This means that in a particular case the meaning of a sign is always dispersed across the sequence of elements that constitute the sign situation.

Because Wittgenstein's investigation of meaning is oriented to these actual sign sequences in use, his analysis of the chess game is really only a preliminary. When we know that the king is this piece, and that such and such can be done with the king, we are not yet investigating meaning. The "rules" tell us only what the "constituent parts" of a game are, what the minimal armature of its concepts is, out of which signifying sequences can be constructed. The realm of "constitutive rules" is for Wittgenstein too impoverished to count as part of "meaning." This part of language must be presupposed when we use language and thus gives the impression of harboring the most basic and undeniable truths, when in fact we have not yet gotten to the point at which we can speak truths or falsehoods. For example, Wittgenstein, reflecting on his own previous misconception, remarks that it looks as though the test of whether something is a "proposition" is whether the concept "true" fits it or not. Here the "concept of truth" seems like a cogwheel that can engage with something, and whatever it can engage with would then be a proposition. "But this is a bad picture. It is as if one were to say 'The king in chess is *the* piece that one can check.' But this can mean no more than that in our game of chess we only check the king" (*PI* 136). Notice the precise distinction Wittgenstein makes here. What looks like a property of the king is being translated into a remark about *how we do something.* That we check only the king is part of what we mean by *king,* or is part of how we use that piece; and the use of the word *king* or of the piece is intertwined with the use of the word *check* (or the operation of checking). Similarly, the use of "proposition" is intertwined with the use of "true"; they are both part of the same "concept" or "language game." The super-connection remarked between "true" and "proposition" turns out to be simply the connection between the terms that set up this language game. Philosophers sometimes treat this "grammatical" connection which Wittgenstein describes as a new form of a priori, and perhaps in some sense it is, but Wittgenstein is interested in chasing down this a priori, not to make it an essential foundation, but to neutralize it, to "bracket" it off from the main arena of his investigations as a level at which we have not yet gotten to the *use*.[20] The fact that we say "true" in connection with "proposition" is no more significant in itself than the fact that we say *k* before *l* when we say the alphabet: "In *that* sense 'true' and 'false' could be said to fit propositions; and a child might be taught to distinguish between propositions and other expressions by being told 'Ask yourself if you can say "is true" after it. If these words fit, it's a proposition'" (*PI* 137).

We have usual or customary (*gewöhnlich*) ways of thinking about things —say, about words and meanings, or about thinking itself—and these ways come to seem natural to us, a matter of course. We no longer see or hear the "before" and "after" of the occurrence of a word: it seems to carry its meaning with it, a portable, intrinsic sense like a halo or atmosphere. Wittgenstein wants to displace our attention onto the surroundings of the sign in order to break the mesmerism of this repetitive normality. As an illustration of this, I want now to adapt remarks 139–41 to a simpler example, one which will be easier to diagram. Wittgenstein uses a cube; I will use a square. Supposing that I hear the word *square*, how do I understand it, know how to use it? Perhaps a picture of a square comes into my mind. Now it seems as though all I have to do is see whether something *fits* this picture or not, and then I will either call this something a square or not. For instance, if I see a triangle, this won't fit the picture.

But, asks Wittgenstein, in what sense does the triangle not fit the picture? That is, what dictates that we should take this square just this way and not some other? For we could imagine a "method of projection" such that the triangle would fit. For example:

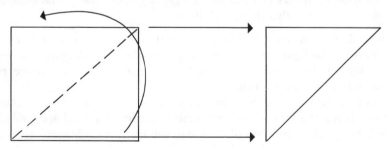

Wittgenstein comments: "What was the effect of my argument? It called our attention to (reminded us of) the fact that there are other processes, besides the one we originally thought of, which we should sometimes be prepared to call 'applying the picture of a [square].' So our 'belief that the picture forced a particular application upon us' consisted in the fact that *only the one case and no other occurred to us*" (*PI* 140; italics added). And the reason that the picture makes us expect a certain use, that leads us to think that it contains and dictates just this use, is that "people in general apply *this* picture like *this*" (*PI* 141). This is the *normal* case.

Wittgenstein's emphasis on *Verwendung* (use) and his rejection of the "holiday" of language as used by philosophy (*PI* 38) has obscured the extent to which his *own* use of language is a *Ver-wendung*, a per-verting or turning of language from its normal use in which it is *unerbittlich*, inflexible, or *atropos*. In Part II of the *Investigations* Wittgenstein discusses his technique in connection with "seeing *as*" and noticing an "aspect."[21] "There are here hugely many interrelated phenomena and possible concepts," he writes (p. 199), and these possibilities, to which we are normally blind, dawn upon us when we remove a word or picture from its normal surroundings and put it into new ones. An arbitrary cipher, for instance, will reveal various "aspects"—will look like a childish script, a letter in a foreign alphabet, or a calligraphic flourish—"according to the fiction I surround it with" (*nach der Erdichtung, mit der ich es umgebe*) (p. 210).

Take as an example the aspects of a triangle. This triangle

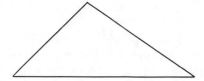

can be seen as a triangular hole, as a solid, as a geometrical drawing; as standing on its base, as hanging from its apex; as a mountain, as a wedge, as an arrow or pointer, as an overturned object which is meant to stand on the shorter side of the right angle, as a half parallelogram, and as various other things. (P. 200)

The only limit to the possibilities of insertion of this sign into different contexts is the limits of our *Erdichtung*, our ability to imagine new surroundings within which more of the "hugely many . . . possible concepts" would dawn as aspects of the sign.

The concept of "family resemblances" should be understood in these terms. It is not a formal or formalizable concept; we should not now ask for some precise definition of what is meant by a "resemblance." Indeed, the concept of a resemblance itself would be infected by Wittgenstein's deconstruction and would itself break up into a series of different—though related—uses. Terms like "similarity" and "family resemblance" are introduced as images which help to think relation, sequence, ordering, in a new way, allowing for more variation between terms, more "play" (*Spielraum*) in their linkage. Above all, the image of "family resemblances" is not to be taken as a new master concept, but as one in a series of helpful illustrations, along with the image of the toolbox, the locomotive with many different switches, the chess game, and so on. Remember that a picture cannot dictate its own use; what must be learned is the syntax ("grammar") within which a picture finds its application. (Of course nothing is more common in the reading of Wittgenstein than to borrow his pictures and discard his syntax.) Wittgenstein himself drops the image of family resemblances almost as soon as he brings it up, switching, within the very same remark, to another image which seems to be an illustration of his illustration, the image of the thread: the different uses of "the same" concept, such as that of "number," are related to each other like the fibers of a thread: "And we extend our concept of number as in spinning a thread we twist fibre on fibre. And the strength of the thread does not reside in the fact that some one fibre runs through its whole length, but in the overlapping of many fibres" (*PI* 67).

The aim of all these images—tools, chess pieces, likenesses, switches, fibers—is to suggest the articulation of concepts into discrete (though related) segments, each of which has a variety of possibilities of movement, that is, of use or application, depending on the character of the surroundings within which it occurs. "A multitude of familiar paths leads off from these words in every direction" (*PI* 525, repeated in 534).

Now, in order that this articulation might not disintegrate into chaotic multiplicity, we have to take for granted the automatism of language use, our unreflective mastery of the "normal" uses of words. But we then move to deconstruct the unity which these normal uses give the illusion of having, the decomposable unity that suggests the existence of an "essence" of meaning. The deconstruction takes its orientation from the philosophical problems: it looks at the mirroring of language which they give and then rearranges the language in a way directed at the dispelling of the philosophical picture. Where features have been abstracted from the characteristic scenes of language, we take these features and resituate them in such scenes.

This is an activity that is as varied as language itself. A "scene" as I am using the term might be as little as a phrase or as much as a whole culture. Obviously, Wittgenstein can only "sketch" scenes toward the latter end of the scale, and his examples tend toward the former end. The point is not the satisfaction of some static formal requirement—for there are no clear boundaries to the notion of *Umstände*—but the bringing out of *differences*, practice in sharpening the eye and the pen for nuances of language. And sometimes only a phrase is needed for this, or two words set side by side. For instance, compare these two exclamations (adapted from *PI* 27):

Water!
Fire!

Imagine the scenes within which such exclamations occur, and the differences in the way the words are being used. They have the same grammatical form, but we set them side by side in order to "hear" the differences which may be concealed by the "sameness" of form.

Other times, a much more extended exploration is required. For example, Wittgenstein explores the meaning of the word *reading*. We are inclined to think that *reading* refers to, or names, a certain mental process. Now we look more closely at this unity which seems to constitute the essence of "reading." What actually happens when we read? Can we define the essential factor in reading? Is it "deriving the repetitions from the originals"? But then what is *deriving*? We no more know the essence of deriving than we do that of reading; the definition is a perfectly good one, but it doesn't get us any farther if deriving is just as various as reading. Well, say then that in reading the sounds are *systematically* derived from the marks we see. But it is also possible to systematically derive the *wrong* sounds from the marks we see. Is that still reading? Further, there is no clear boundary between systematic derivation, a systematic mistake, and randomness. What about the "experience" of reading—doesn't that determine what reading is? But we can have this experience in a dream, or under the influence of a drug, when we are looking at meaningless characters or characters in a language we don't know—and in those cases, experience or no experience, we would say this was not reading. There is no characteristic intrinsic to a specific moment of reading which makes it into reading; for any given moment, as such, could be an accident (*PI* 157). It is only of the activity as a whole that we say it is reading—and the activity as a whole is infected by what is not reading. Reading is, for example, intertwined with "reciting from memory."

> There is a continuous series of transitional cases between that in which a person repeats from memory what he is supposed to be reading, and that in which he spells out every word without being helped at all by guessing from the context or knowing by heart.
>
> Try this experiment: say the numbers from 1 to 12. Now look at the dial of your watch and *read* them. —What was it that you called "reading" in the latter case? That is to say: what did you do, to make it into *reading*? (*PI* 161)

What we call "reading" is an assemblage of characteristics which in each separate case of reading will be variously reconstituted, and in these different reassemblings there will always be the infection of characteristics of what does not correspond to what we want to think of as really, essentially *reading*. (It is as though these characteristics had a dual membership in two mutually exclusive sets.)

Our normal use of the word leads us to think that there is some single mental tincture that colors all the characteristics of the activity. In particular, the use of print and standardized spelling give an impression of uniformity (*Gleichförmigkeit*) to the act of reading. The visual image of the word and its sound are deeply imprinted (*eingeprägt*) in our sensibilities; as a result of constant repetition they become like the faces of intimates, and we feel uneasy when there is some change in the visual image—as in spelling controversies. This is the usual thing, the normal thing—*gewöhnlich*. This is the automatism of custom (*PI* 167).

Now Wittgenstein makes us aware of these characteristic and unthought aspects of reading, by evoking the abnormal.

> Read the letter A. —Now, how did the sound come? — . . . Now write a small Roman a. —How did the movement of the hand come as you wrote? . . . Now look at the mark ⊘ and let a sound occur to you as you do so; utter it. (*PI* 166)

> Read a sentence.—And now look at the following line
>
> &8§≠   §≠?β   +%   8!'§*
>
> and say a sentence as you do so. (*PI* 169)

Wittgenstein asks us to notice the differences between these experiences, the way, for example, the eye passes without resistance over printed lines as opposed to the way it passes over arbitrary marks.

Again, the discursive point which can be detached from all this is that metaphysical questions are confused and may be forgotten, that ordinary language is in order as it is, and that all we need do is see how this language normally works. But on the way to normality we fall into a disintegration of the coherent forms of that normality and into a perverse activity of invention, of fictionalization, *Erdichtung*, whose aim is the creation of new contexts that can suggest differences and help us to think the unthought of ordinary language.

This activity is aesthetic,[22] a conclusion already implied when I said that Wittgenstein trains the eye to follow the play of surfaces. We have now seen that if there is no essence, no unity, to the meaning of a word, all we can do is adduce instances of its use and describe the characteristics of the instance. Among these characteristics we can include gestures and facial expressions and also fine shades of experience which we have access to only through introspection. The difference between inner and outer doesn't matter. It is all unfolded into the scene of language. And it is all inessential—though, generally speaking, "characteristic." All we have is the grammar of the accidental transformations of related assemblages of inessentials. It sounds incoherent, chaotic: but it was in just such scenes as these that we learned to speak.[23] And, knowing how to speak, or write, we now have the susceptibility to the forms of language which enables us to arrange them, to set them before ourselves, in some form that will satisfy the requirements of a particular sort of viewing. Philosophy, done this way, is like a form of poetry or collage, word-collage, language treated from outside as preexistent material with which constructions having a certain configuration can be devised: I must use language as I find it, already there, and this means "I can adduce only exterior facts (*nur Äusserliches*)" (*PI* 120) about it.[24]

VI

We have seen that Wittgenstein rejects the idea of a subtle sign (mental representation of the sign) which would not be subject to the limitations of an actual physical sign. The mental sign or picture would be just as much or just as little open to interpretation as the corresponding physical representation. But this means that the "queer medium" of "mind" drops out of consideration entirely. Wittgenstein writes in the *Blue Book*: "As we are not interested in where the processes of thinking, calculating, take place, we can for our purpose imagine the calculations being done entirely on paper. We are not concerned with the difference: internal, external" (p. 13). This is an extraordinarily simple and yet audacious, even revolutionary, move. It is, I think, precisely parallel with that of Derrida when he replaces the phenomenological "voice" (silent, internal) with the concept of "writing." In a sense the whole of the *Investigations* follows upon this instigating move, but the first 242 remarks are especially marked by it. In the earlier sections, the "writing" of the sign takes the form of the use of tables and *samples* (*Mustern*). In *PI* 1 we read: "Now think of the following use of language: I send someone shopping. I give him a slip marked 'five red apples.' He takes the slip to the shopkeeper, who opens the drawer marked 'apples'; then he looks up the word 'red' in a table and finds a colour sample opposite it . . . [etc.]." Wittgenstein is trying here and elsewhere to build up a clear picture of how we operate with signs, beginning from very simple cases. Treating signs as visible material things removes the "occult" aspects from his examination and makes it scenic. But there is one more crucial complication in his procedure. I quote the remark in question in full:

> What about the colour samples [*Farbmustern*] that A shews to B: are they part of the *language*? Well, it is as you please. They do not belong among the words; yet when I say to someone: "Pronounce the word 'the,'" you will count the second "the" as part of the sentence. Yet it has a role just like that of a colour-sample in language-game (8); that is, it is a sample [*Muster*] of what the other is meant to say.
>
> It is most natural, and causes least confusion, to reckon the samples among the instruments [*Werkzeuge*] of the language.
>
> ((Remark on the reflexive pronoun "*this* sentence.")) (*PI* 16)

On the one hand, Wittgenstein here assimilates things (the samples) to words as "instruments" of the language. On the other—and here is the point I want to emphasize—he indicates the special nature of *citation* in his investigations. That is, when language is folded back into itself by the agency of quotation marks, it will count as a sample of language. As a sample, it will be a *piece of material* like any other, introduced into the language game in order to call attention to some property or other or to some use of that material, and "this" will be used as a way of pointing within the written text to the infolding or citation of language.

In a sense, this folding-back of language into itself is the replacement *by a form of writing* of what has been called "reflection" in traditional philosophy. Consider, for example, the famous presumptive "doctrine" which is often abbreviated as "meaning is use." What Wittgenstein actually wrote was: "For a *large* class of cases—though not for all—in which we employ the word 'meaning' it can be defined thus: the meaning of a word is its use in the language" (*PI* 43). Leaving aside the opening qualification concerning the scope of the remark, Wittgenstein here is careful *not* to say simply "meaning is use," but that the definition of the *word* "meaning" could be put this way. Wittgenstein is not concerned with "the meaning of meaning" but with "the meaning of 'meaning'"—not with meaning *as such* (indeed, such a notion is inconceivable in Wittgenstein's language) but with the use of the word *meaning*.

Put it this way. We are inclined to think that meaning is a sort of *thing*, as a word is, but that it is also different from a word. "Here the word, there the meaning. The money, and the cow that you can buy with it" (*PI* 120). But this "thing" seems to be of an exceedingly slippery sort, requiring the medium of "mind," etc. Now Wittgenstein unfolds language into its before and after, and finds that when this is done, there is no metaphysical mystery about meaning. That is, when the scene of language is unfolded, the word *meaning* appears there as one word among others, and there is nothing left over besides this appearance. Wittgenstein's perhaps unfortunate remark seems to present us with a begged question, for he seems to be saying, "If we look at the *use* of 'meaning,' we see that it applies to the *use* of words"; the definition seems to have been pre-applied to *meaning* itself. *Meaning* seems to have a very special role; it seems to dominate the set rather than to be just another member, and Wittgenstein seems to be trying to make the term a member of its own set. But Wittgenstein is saying that the term *meaning* is just another member of the set "language," although it does play a special role because it is language about language. This "reflexive" character of the term is what gives rise to the illusion that it has a different or higher character than other terms, whereas Wittgenstein shows that it may be treated in the same way as any other: it is written, it plays certain roles in certain scenes. We could say: "If we look at the role *meaning* plays in our language games, we will see that this role is to call attention to the roles the other words are playing." The reflection on language occurs not from outside but from within the scene of language. Citation is the means by which language becomes the object of language, without thereby acquiring depth distinct from a surface but only a new articulation of the surface. Wittgenstein's remark on the treatment of *philosophy* is also applicable to *meaning*: "One might think: if philosophy speaks of the use of the word 'philosophy' there must be a second-order philosophy. But it is not so: it is, rather, like the case of orthography, which deals with the word 'orthography' among others without then being second-order" (*PI* 121). Wittgenstein can find here no better way to describe the in-folding of language in his way of doing philosophy than that of a style of inscription, of writing as the making of marks—the purely material stratum of writing, detached from consideration of meaning. (Cf. *Culture*, p. 8: "I should like to start with the original data of philosophy, written and spoken sentences, with books as it were.")

Wittgenstein's style in the *Investigations* is deeply involved in the kind of liberation of language as material substance from the domination of meaning which we associate with modern poetry: the concern with visual and auditory characteristics of words, with seemingly incidental connections of sound between words, with the use of metaphor as an irreducible mode of expression. We get some insight into the sensual character of Wittgenstein's thought from this manuscript remark:

⟨I⟩ just took some apples out of a paper bag where they had been lying for a long time. I had to cut half off many of them and throw it away. Afterwards when I was copying out a sentence I had written, the second half of which was bad, I at once saw it as a half-rotten apple. And that's how it always is with me. Everything that comes my way becomes a picture for me of what I am thinking about at the time. (Is there something feminine about this way of thinking?) (*Culture*, p. 31)

One cannot learn the mode of fictionalization, of invention of alternatives of syntax, which is the deconstructive activity taught by the *Investigations*, unless one learns to recognize the enormous variety of material resources of language and the excess of these resources over what can ever be permeated or dominated by the meaning intention of the user of language.

We have already seen the attention Wittgenstein pays to the nuances of our perception of print, and his presentation of meaningless marks as signlike phenomena. As transitional cases between these two, Wittgenstein discusses writing in unfamiliar scripts or in a foreign language. The effect of all this is to stimulate a consciousness of writing as a physical imprint, as a particular configuration or series of shapes. His use of color tables and arrow schemas to interpret tables are further sign phenomena which, because nonverbal, help to blur the distinction between language and non-language, leaving us instead with a sense of a continuous spectrum of indicative or meaning-suggesting *marks*, ranging from doodles and decorative patterns to the most familiar language. Wittgenstein defamiliarizes language and heightens the sense of signs as *ciphers*—which, however, rather than calling for *decipherment* call for *syntaxis*, sequencing or arrangement. Language passes into doodles and pictures in one direction and into something like music in another:[25]

> It would be possible to imagine a people who had something not quite unlike a language: a play of sounds, without vocabulary or grammar. (*PI* 528)

> "But what would the meaning of the sounds be in such a case?" — What is it in music? Though I don't at all wish to say that this language of a play of sounds [*klanglichen Gebärden*—literally, "sound-gestures"] would have to be compared to music. (*PI* 529)

There is here no question of a Rousseauian inarticulateness of melody;[26] rather, Wittgenstein is suggesting something else in order to create new verbal contexts which can open up our sense of the material resources for signification which language possesses. The investigation of meaning continually veers as aspects of a phenomenon suggest analogies and then the analogies suggest further aspects of their own, which also call for investigation. Wittgenstein compares the sight of familiar words to the sight of familiar faces, and this reminds him that we also speak of "reading" or "understanding" a facial expression, and then "understanding" and "expression" lead to a consideration of how we use these words in connection with paintings and music.[27] There are no "essences" here behind the words, only the paths traced by the words themselves, paths that continually slide from one context to another; and all we can do is follow them.

The *Investigations* begins as an inquiry into "meaning," and this leads to the intertwined concepts of "understanding," "thinking," "grasping a rule," "being guided," "giving orders," "teaching and learning," and so on. But because the concept of the subtle medium of mind is rejected, no demarcation is made between words as a more nearly spiritual medium and gestures, pictures, and inarticulate sounds as sublinguistic. Instead, the scene of language is unfolded as a rebus with an indefinite potential for an indefinite number of kinds of signifying sequences.

There is no telling, and few philosophers have had interest in figuring out, how much Wittgenstein learned from Freud about the rebus character of signification.[28] Rush Rhees says that Wittgenstein read Freud from 1919 on, and in the mid-forties spoke of himself as "a disciple of Freud" (*L&C*, pp. 49–50). There are clear resonances between Wittgenstein's discussion in the *Investigations* of the suggestiveness of languagelike marks and the following comment from his "Conversations on Freud":

> There seems to be something in dream images that has a certain resemblance to the signs of a language. As a series of marks on paper or on sand might have. There might be no mark which we recognized as a conventional sign in any alphabet we knew, and yet we might have a strong feeling that they must be a language of some sort: that they mean something. There is a cathedral in Moscow with five spires. On each of these there is a different sort of curving configuration. One gets the strong impression that these different shapes and arrangements must mean something. (*L&C*, p. 45)

Here Wittgenstein's sense of scene as writing is very marked, a sense dependent upon an acute susceptibility to the influence of form and configuration. (This is the way in which his exploration of language becomes aesthetic.)

But Wittgenstein, like Derrida, believes that Freud ultimately remains caught within a traditional philosophical schema. For Wittgenstein, this is because Freud wants to recuperate all the materials of the dream for the category of "meaning." Wittgenstein wants to leave open the possibility of meaning-indicating phenomena which only *indicate* (i.e., suggest) meaning without actually meaning anything, so that all we can do is follow out the character of their indicativeness as far as it goes. (This is again the aesthetic susceptibility at odds with the meaning intention.) More important,

Wittgenstein argues that there is a history and a specific material character to the medium of symbolization which exceeds and escapes the control of even unconscious intention:

> Suppose we were to regard a dream as a kind of game which the dreamer played. . . . There might be a game in which paper figures were put together to form a story, or at any rate were somehow assembled. The materials might be collected and stored in a scrap-book, full of pictures and anecdotes. The child might then take various bits from the scrap-book to put into the construction; and he might take a considerable picture because it had something in it which he wanted and he might just include the rest because it was there. (*L&C*, pp. 49–50)

Though Wittgenstein is speaking here of the character of dream symbolism, the remark is highly illuminating with respect to the way he treats language in the *Investigations*, as a given which he can treat only externally and rearrange, not penetrate but only *present*. If we now look again at the famous sentence whose standard translation is "Philosophy is a battle against the bewitchment of our intelligence by means of language," we can give it a fuller reading. The key word is "means," a translation of the German *Mittel*, which can also be rendered in three other ways: "remedy," "medium," and "wealth" or "resources." So we could translate, "battle against bewitchment . . . through the *remedy* of language"—and this would be an accurate account of Wittgenstein's method; in fact, Anscombe's translation and this one hold at once, because, as we have seen, language is what bewitches but language is what we must remain within in order to cure the bewitchment. The other two possibilities can also be paired. "Medium" suggests, more than does "means," the consistency of language as material, as spatial and temporal (*räumlichen und zeitlichen*), and it is this material character of language which constitutes its *wealth*, its *resources* over and above its subservience as mere *means*. This wealth, this profusion of appearances which cannot simply be effaced in the service of the meaning intention, is what bewitches the intellect, but it is also what we have to learn to see and hear, for it is the source of the possibility of new analogies, new possibilities of syntax.[29] The remedy for the illusions that arise from the excessive wealth of language is the transit through the material medium of language, an endless transit, exile in the endless accidence of language. The promise of a return to the homeland of language is never fulfilled.

We enter into this exile by means of citation and the demonstrative pronoun *this*. The primal scene of philosophy, a man pointing to an object, is replaced in Wittgenstein's text by the demonstrative pronoun pointing to a word or expression—as in the phrase "this sentence" (above, *PI* 16). The linguistic texture of the German text more openly marks certain connections here than does the English. In English we use the phrase "pointing gesture," "ostensive definition," and "demonstrative pronoun," but in German "pointing," "ostensive," and "demonstrative" are all *hinweisen*, "to point" or "to show." Apart from tradition, we could revive the scenic connection of these three phrases in English by rendering all three with the word *pointing*. But in fact the English term *demonstrative* points us back to a Latin root that enables us to put together an even more comprehensive tissue of linguistic background. (The important thing here is not etymology; certainly Wittgenstein himself never dips into word history for his resources. What matters is the way signifiers in various languages alert us to different areas of the semantic field of a concept or set of concepts, and to the ways in which these areas may be connected with each other. Wittgenstein himself shows us in the "Remarks on Frazer" how we may use historical connecting links ahistorically "in order to sharpen our eye for a formal connection." [30])

Demonstrative of course comes from Latin *monstrare*, which, like *hinweisen*, means "to point or show." But Wittgenstein's word for "sample," *Muster*, is also derived from *monstrare*, and means "the thing pointed to or shown." So *monstrare* connects *Muster* with the scene within which the self-showing-forth of the object is classically conceived, and reminds us also of the ultimate Presence, Ur-thing, ultimate showing: the "monstrance" is the "vessel in which the consecrated Host is exposed for the veneration of the faithful." (But from *monstrare* we also get *monstrum*, that which is pointed to as excess, as deviation, not as Ur- but as Un-.) So far we are staying close to the scene of showing or monstrance as the presence of a "this!" But in English the word *muster* has the sense of assembling a group, specifically for a formal military inspection, and also for the act of critical examination which one would give to such a group. The Greek word for ordering or arranging troops is *suntassō*, from which we get *syntax*. So we now pass by means of *monstrare* from the singular showing forth of presence to the arranging in sequence of what is to be looked at—"muster" as syntax, and "muster" as review, *übersehen* of what has been arranged. (Liddell and Scott cite Xenophon on the use of *theōreō* with the sense of "to inspect or review soldiers.") "The problems are solved, not by giving new information, but by arranging [*Zusammenstellung*—literally, "syntaxis"] what we have always known" (*PI* 109). The essence becomes surveyable by rearrangement (*durch Ordnen übersichtlich*) (*PI* 92); we get a "perspicuous representation" (*übersichtliche Darstellung*) (*PI* 122), one whose configuration is open to a vision which sees its surface or outside.

This syntax or muster is strategic, polemical. It is the means of a certain warfare, a war of language, war against the language of philosophy. Syntax is tactics; *tactics* comes from *tassō*, from which *suntassō* is compounded. (For the Greeks, the primary sense of "ordering" is preparation for war.) So Wittgenstein's writing is speculative, theoretic, *übersichtlich*, with respect to *syntaxis* rather than monstrance; and it is also monstrous, deviant, unorthodox.

This discussion of etymological and semantic resonances—or puns—is not idle or arbitrary. These are concepts and themes which bring us (indirectly, allusively) to some of the most difficult questions raised by deconstruction. Derrida, discussing his deconstructive device "differance" in the essay by that name, writes:

> In marking out differance, everything is a matter of strategy and risk [*stratégique et aventureux*]. It is a question of strategy because no transcendent truth present outside the sphere of writing can theologically command the totality of this field. It is hazardous because this strategy is not simply one in the sense that we say that strategy orients the tactics according to a final aim, a *telos* or the theme of a domination, a mastery or an ultimate reappropriation of movement and field. In the end, it is a strategy without finality. We might call it blind tactics [*tactique aveugle*]. (*S&P*, p. 135)

These remarks, I believe, apply as well to Wittgenstein's writing as to Derrida's—in fact, I would say that Wittgenstein's work has never been so well characterized as it is by these remarks.

VII

"Blind tactics." How can there be such a thing? How can there be a grammar of an endless accidence? Aristotle writes in Book VI of the *Metaphysics* that "there is no science of the accidental, since all science is of what is always or generally so," and yet it appears that deconstruction is in fact a "science of the accidental." Is it only a play on words to suggest, as Derrida does, that the possibility of accidents is always part of the essence? Is not *language itself* the science of the accidental, the endlessly shifting calculus whose play is the co-incidence of chance and necessity?

Here we stand on the verge of another metaphysical hypostasis, that of capitalizing and transcendentalizing language itself, and of presenting deconstruction as a rapt receptivity or hearkening to the voice of language. And now we must remind ourselves of the double aspect of language, as appearance that hides and as appearance that shows its play. So a certain alertness is required, as well as a certain receptivity. We must allow ourselves to be guided by the accidence of language, but in order to do this we must supplement the guiding power of language with a technique, a method. The uses of words are intertwined and shade off into one another like the fibers of a thread; and these new uses that the deconstructor devises—uses of words like *game, family resemblance, use,* or *differance* and *supplement*—these are twisted onto the old uses in a similar way. In such a way the threads are extended and the web of the deconstructive text is woven. In the text or textile of the *Investigations* many of the fibers which are worked into it are fictive (cf. p. 206: *Eine Erfindung in sie gewoben*), but that is just the nature of this web. "The strength of the thread comes from the overlapping of the fibers." What matters is not that *these* uses of words be serious or factual, but that they be woven into the threads of the *other* uses (some of which will themselves be fictive or unserious). There is an endless intertwining of strands, and the skill that must be learned is the skill of this intertwining, for the pattern of the weave is continually changing. Hence we have the most limited movement, like that of a blind man feeling his way with his stick, of a weaving that is constrained by the accidental at every turn. How much constrained? What counts as a "turn"? Exactly what is the particularity of the particular; what counts as particular enough, as opposed to the generality of philosophy? These are questions that cannot be answered in this form; they have the form of the language which is being unraveled so that its threads may be rewoven. We can say that there is a certain texture to weaving, which shows itself only in the weaving and can be learned only from it. (*Es wird nun an Beispielen eine Methode gezeigt.*)

And now we can see how "ordinary language" can be used in the critique of philosophy. (I seem to have shifted from the manly activities of the *strategos* to the classically female activity. Perhaps if we recall that nets are used in war and hunting, or if we think of the spider, we can bring the two together.) For it is a mystery how ordinary language and philosophy can ever be confronted with each other. As Wittgenstein notes in *On Certainty*, one cannot say to the radical skeptic, holding out one's hand, "I know that this is a hand." In the first place, this ceases to be ordinary language when it is presented as a refutation of idealism; and, in the second place, if such a sentence continued to be meaningful in the way that ordinary language is meaningful, then it would have no effect at all on the philosophical thesis. In Wittgenstein's writing, this is not how the strategy works. Instead, we follow the intertwining of the threads of language from one register into another. We see how the texture is broken (by comparison with the preferred texture) at this point and that point. "See, this is shoddy weaving."

But if Wittgenstein compares philosophical language to "an engine idling" (*PI* 132) or to going "on holiday" (*PI* 38) instead of doing *work,* we have to keep in mind that he does not exclude fictive or unserious applications from what he considers to be "use." We could, for example, imagine a name for a tool which has never been used in a certain language game, and this name could be given a place in that game—perhaps as "a sort of joke" (*eine Art Belustigung*) (*PI* 42).

In fact, we could say that the connections between different uses of the same word, the connections whose system or nonsystem Wittgenstein calls "grammar," are nothing but a joke. Word uses are related by "family resemblance," and a family resemblance is a form of homonym or pun or rhyme.[31] All of these are names for the coincidence of the phenomenal form of signs whose meanings differ. Wittgenstein tells us that meaning is not an ideal unity, nor an inward spiritual activity. We have to look at how words function (*PI* 340), and when we look, we do not penetrate to an ideality: we remain within a phenomenal scene. The trouble with thinking of meaning as a kind of essence is that it leaves out too much of what Wittgenstein wants to call meaning; in order to learn to handle language in the way Wittgenstein does, we must become alert to the entire *physiognomy* of the scene of language use and of each of the elements within it.

> Look at a stone and imagine it having sensations. —One says to oneself: How could one so much as get the idea of ascribing a *sensation* to a *thing*? One might as well ascribe it to a number! —And now look at a wriggling fly and at once these difficulties vanish and pain seems able to get a foothold here, where before everything was, so to speak, too smooth for it.
>
> And so, too, a corpse seems to us quite inaccessible to pain. —Our attitude to what is alive and to what is dead, is not the same. All our reactions are different. (*PI* 284)

Notice that Wittgenstein does not speak of "pain language" hooking onto an appropriate object, but simply "pain." The whole scene—words, emotional responses, visual images—is on one plane as we feel around for the pieces that belong together, that will "rhyme." "Pain" does not rhyme with "stone." We must learn to sharpen our ears, our eyes—for that matter, our noses—for the surfaces of signifying substance: "How do I find the 'right' word? . . . Without doubt it is sometimes as if I were comparing them by fine differences of smell" (p. 218). Even kinesthetic acuteness is needed: "Think of the recognition of *facial expressions*. . . . Think, too, how one can imitate a man's face without seeing one's own in a mirror" (*PI* 285). As a word slides from one set of surroundings to another, it undergoes subtle shifts of function ("meaning") in response to variations in the surroundings, and if we keep our attention fixed on the unchanging element in the meaning, we miss these shifts. This is no mere literary play, for the confusions and category mistakes of philosophy that Wittgenstein exposes arise from failures to perceive just such shifts. But neither is the skill purely negative: it is not just a way of showing that what seems to make sense (to "fit" or "rhyme") does not, but also of showing how we *can* make sense of what at first sight appears not to. The point is not that words just do have certain allowable uses built in and our job is to see that these uses are not violated; rather, we do not know in advance which uses will work out and which will not, and the question is whether we can bridge the gap between old and new uses, passing over by intermediate grada- tions (*Zwischenglieder*) (*PI* 122). Wittgenstein's preferred mode of clari- fication is by means of arrangement of instances in such a way that they pass over into each other in a "continuous series of transitional cases" (*Übergänge*) (*PI* 161). This form of "perspicuous presentation" draws out and elucidates the concept of family resemblances, for a family is just the sort of group that could be arranged in a sequence by which we pass gradually from one extreme facial type to another through intermediate gradations. This form of account replaces explanation in terms of category and essence, for instead of discrete classes with a boundary of identity be- tween them, we now have a spread of particulars varying from each other in accidental ways along a continuum until at last there has been "essential" change without a boundary of essence ever having been crossed. There is a profound convergence here between Wittgenstein and Darwin, who was, I believe, the first to formalize this principle of what I propose to call *transi- tive essences*.

Darwin's greatest conceptual breakthrough was his perception that there was no essential difference between species and varieties, that vari- eties were "incipient species" in process of accumulating minute differ- entiae that had no specific standing but which in time would add up, by nonspecific gradations, to "good and true species." But these variations that were accumulated by natural selection were initially *individual* varia- tions, so individuals are incipient varieties.

> Certainly no clear line of demarcation has as yet been drawn be- tween species and sub-species—that is, the forms which in the opin- ion of some naturalists come very near to, but do not quite arrive at, the rank of species: or again, between sub-species and well-marked varieties, or between lesser varieties and individual differences. These differences blend into each other by an insensible series; and a series impresses the mind with the idea of an actual passage.
>
> Hence I look at individual differences, though of small interest to the systematist, as of the highest importance for us, as being the first steps toward such slight varieties as are barely thought worth record-

ing in works of natural history. And I look at varieties which are in any degree more distinct and permanent as steps toward more strongly-marked and permanent varieties; and at the latter, as leading to sub-species, and then to species. . . .

From these remarks it will be seen that I look at the term species as one arbitrarily given, for the sake of convenience, to a set of individuals closely resembling each other, and that it does not differ essentially from the term variety, which is given to less distinct and more fluctuating forms. The term variety, again, in comparison with mere individual differences, is also applied arbitrarily, for convenience's sake. (*Origin of Species*, chap. 2)

Darwin's remarks interest us here not because of their pertinence to biological fact, but purely for the conceptual structure they define. Of course Darwin is talking about genetic sequences and Wittgenstein is concerned only with *revealing* sequences, but the principle of transition by intermediate gradations is the same. (Actually, Darwin himself made use of nongenetic sequences to make evolution plausible, as in his argument for how the eye might have evolved.) The minute change that occurs from one gradation to the next contains an increment of essential or specific change: the transition to a new category has already begun in the slightest individual variation. Yet it is only when we take terms some distance apart in the series that we can see category differences, and there never was a definite specifiable moment when the transition occurred. The class boundaries are an artifact arising from the suppression of the continuum. Perhaps John Locke was wrong when he suggested that such a suppression operates in our classifications of natural kinds, but when applied to the domain of meaning this argument is not susceptible to the scientific objections that can be made concerning natural kinds. Perhaps there are real essences of *things*, but *words* can have only nominal essences.

To think a continuous series of transitional cases is to think the cases not as unitary and self-identical but as assemblages of characters that may be variously reassembled. In a way every character is essential, as part of the physiognomy of the case, and in a way none is essential because each is only an essence gradation. What I am calling a transitive essence is thus an identity that is a term in an identity continuum and has no distinct or unique essence boundary to separate it from the immediately surrounding terms. Because a transitive essence contains, as part of its own identity, characters that are spread across terms farther along the continuum as part of *their* identity, it is transitive—is already, within itself, part of the way along toward the essence or physiognomy of something distinct from it.

Wittgenstein is very badly served when he is understood as a policeman who enforces community standards in language use. He is concerned with a technique that by its very nature makes language open to new signifying chains, chains that are connected with old uses but that vary away from them. The new uses may be strikingly different from the old ones; the only question is whether we can find the intermediate links, the continuous transition along contiguous terms, that will connect the new use with the old ones.[32] There is no formal criterion that constitutes continuousness; this is where the nose for small differences comes in. And when he can find the connecting links, Wittgenstein is willing to allow meanings other people might not. For example, he ponders these sentences:

A new-born child has no teeth.
A goose has no teeth.
A rose has no teeth.

The last example, he says, "one would like to say," is "obviously true." "It is even surer than that a goose has none. —And yet it is none so clear. For where should a rose's teeth have been? The goose has none in its jaw. And neither, of course, has it any in its wings; but no one means that when he says it has no teeth." But Wittgenstein does not reject the last sentence as nonsense; what he wants is the connective tissue that will weave it into the language. For one *could* say that a rose *has teeth*: "Why, suppose one were to say: the cow chews its food and then dungs the rose with it, so the rose has teeth in the mouth of a beast. This would not be absurd, because one has no notion in advance where to look for teeth in a rose" (pp. 221–22).

The ability to feel the intertwining of the threads of language is sharpened by a tactical yielding to temptation or inclination. Stanley Cavell, noting the frequency with which Wittgenstein uses phrases like "I want to say" and "Here the urge is strong" (and also, though Cavell, oddly, does not mention them, "We are tempted [*versucht*] to say" or "I am inclined [*geneigt*] to say"), concludes that "the voice of temptation and the voice of correctness are the antagonists in Wittgenstein's dialogues."[33] In fact, though, it is only by continually exposing ourselves to the temptations of language that we can make our own way in these investigations. That is, we do not know in advance what the accidence of a word's applications will be. "Let the use of words teach you their meaning" (p. 220), Wittgenstein writes: we must use a word first, and then see where it has led us. Frequently, the temptations of language will, as Cavell notes, lead to the unities of philosophy which Wittgenstein wants to fracture and scatter, but even these are an essential part of the investigations. The investigations are oriented to these unities; their tactics are guided by the aim of undoing them. But the analogies and fictions and suggestive new forms of expression which open up the possibilities of syntax Wittgenstein is after also come from yielding to inclination:

> I should like to say "What the picture tells me is itself." [Here Wittgenstein is trying to formulate the sense in which we can speak of a picture's expressing something.] (*PI* 523)

> Then has "understanding" two different meanings here?—I would rather say that these kinds of use of "understanding" make up its meaning, make up my *concept* of understanding.
>
> For I *want* to apply the word "understanding" to all this. [Here he is treating his impulse to use the word in different ways as the thread by which to follow the errancy of the use, rejecting the chopping up of the thread into discrete categories labeled "different meanings."] (*PI* 532)

And, strikingly:

> Given the two ideas 'fat' and 'lean,' would you be rather inclined [*geneigt*] to say that Wednesday was fat and Tuesday lean or vice versa? (I incline decisively toward the former.) Now have "fat" and "lean" some different meaning here from their usual one? —They have a different use. —So ought I really to have used different words? Certainly not that. —I want to use *these* words (with their familiar meanings) *here*. —Now, I say nothing about the causes of this phenomenon. . . . Whatever the explanation, —the inclination is there. (p. 216)

There is no "voice of correctness" to chastise this inclination; it is in this way that the use of words is extended, that new uses are twisted onto old ones and that the possibilities of movement of language are discovered. The trouble with the inclinations that lead to the ideal, to what Wittgenstein calls "super-expressions," is not that they are inclinations, but that they create language forms that then cut off the process which made them possible; they are, as it were, terminal inclinations. Philosophy—arising from puns, analogies, fictions—condemns these vagaries as accidental and tries to purify its language of them.

It is misleading to speak of a voice of correctness, of rectitude, orthodoxy, or the straight line—even though there is a method, a *technē*, hence also prescriptions and proscriptions—because it is precisely the straight line which this method makes impossible. Wittgenstein writes in his Preface:

> After several unsuccessful attempts to weld my results together into . . . a whole, I realized that I should never succeed. . . . my thoughts were

soon crippled if I tried to force them on in any single direction against their natural inclination [*natürliche Neigung*]. —And this was, of course, connected with the very nature of the investigation. For this compels us to travel over a wide field of thought criss-cross in every direction [*kreuz und quer, nach allen Richtungen hin zu durchreisen*].

Wittgenstein's own thoughts are like the refractory pupils he describes who naturally go off in directions of their own, against the intention of those who have given them an order. No remark of Wittgenstein's has been more fascinating to his interpreters than *Philosophical Investigations* 185, in which he introduced us to the pupil with the deviant understanding of the +2 rule:

We teach him to write down . . . series of cardinal numbers and get him to the point of writing down series of the form

$$0, n, 2n, 3n, \text{etc.}$$

at an order of the form "$+n$"; so at the order "$+1$" he writes down the series of natural numbers. —Let us suppose we have done exercises and given him tests up to 1000.

Now we get the pupil to continue a series (say $+2$) beyond 1000— and he writes 1000, 1004, 1008, 1012.

We say to him: "Look what you've done!" —He doesn't understand. We say: "You were meant to add *two*: look how you began the series!" . . . suppose he pointed to the series and said: "But I went on in the same way."—It would now be no use to say: "But can't you see. . . . ?" —and repeat the old examples and explanations. —In such a case we might say, perhaps: It comes natural to this person to understand our order with our explanations as *we* should understand the order: "Add 2 up to 1000, 4 up to 2000, 6 up to 3000 and so on."

It is very striking how quick commentators on this passage (Stroud, Bogen, Kripke) have been to decide that Wittgenstein's deviants are "different sorts of beings from us, beings which we could not understand and with which we could not enter into meaningful communication."[34] This readiness to read them out of the human community arises from the "forms of life" argument, that we share certain judgments and natural reactions and that this is what makes meaning and rule-following in general possible.

But these writers fail to distinguish the different levels on which our "forms of life" are constituted, and take insufficient account of the looseness of the tie between culturally constituted practices and their "natural" substratum. Kripke remarks that it is part of our "form of life" to find it "natural" to follow the rule for addition in the way we do; but this sense of "natural" just means "that's how we're used to doing it around here," not "this is universally natural to all humankind." Wittgenstein does emphasize the underlying "natural" regularities in human behavior, but there is an important distinction between our "natural" tendency, say, to cry when we feel pain, and our "natural" tendency to understand mathematical formulas in given ways: the latter is "natural" to us only because we have been trained to do it this way. (Undoubtedly universal regularities underlie this training, but no one has yet explained exactly what they are or how they are connected to the way one would "naturally" follow the +2 rule in a particular way.) Wittgenstein says that someone who cannot understand why someone else does not see the application of the rule in the way he does is "under the compulsion" of that rule. Kripke cites this remark in support of his own point that we can't understand the deviant, but Wittgenstein's point is not that we can't because the deviant's behavior is unnatural or intrinsically unintelligible, but rather, that we can't because our minds are closed to some other way of doing it as a consequence of our being so utterly under the spell of our usual way.[35] The important distinction is not between two intelligent human beings, both of whom receive the same training, one of whom grasps the rule in a natural, intelligible way, the other in an unintelligible, deviant way; but between one person who is already initiated into a practice and sees it as natural, and another who is not yet initiated into it. What looks natural or even automatic from the initiate's point of view may look not at all natural from the novice's. The way Kripke and others interpret Wittgenstein on this point leads to the view of his thought as conservative, even constricting; but Wittgenstein's own characteristic act of imagination was precisely to imagine the liminal moments of rule learning during which it is *not yet natural* to go on in the standard way and something new might be done. Wittgenstein's concern was as much with the possibility of the new as with the importance of the established forms of life.

The deviant responds naturally in a way that differs from our own: he *sees* things differently. For him a new aspect has dawned and a path may be opening where there was none before. It has been pointed out that Wittgenstein never develops in very great detail the ramifications of his suggested strange forms of rule-following, and that this shows they aren't really intelligible. Yet it is an important fact about the emergence of the new that when it is really new it will look bizarre to the old point of view. We cannot know at the time of emergence of an individual variation if it will turn out to make sense or not. An individual variation is an incipient possible form of life or revision of some branch of an existent form of life, and may or may not pan out. We have so far only a possibility given, which "now will have to be filled in. But Wittgenstein is only concerned to make us more receptive to the liminal moment when possible sense may look as yet like errant nonsense."

We are even farther away from Wittgenstein if we think, with Specht, Tugendhat, and others, that the meaning of words is constituted by "rules of usage." The concept of a rule does not explain anything in the *Investigations*; it is what has to be explained. The word *rule* is itself subject to the same conditions for meaningfulness that other words are, and it too has a vague and shifting family of meanings. "And is there not also the case where we play and—make up the rules as we go along? And there is even one where we alter them—as we go along" (*PI* 83). Philosophers have not liked to emphasize remarks like this one; for them, these are peripheral rather than paradigmatic cases—as though the fraying they cause at the edges of the text can be stopped from unraveling it all if it is just ignored. If we say that rules determine meaning, must we not say rules determine the meaning of the word *rule*? But then what are we saying? Either we are launched upon an infinite regress, or we run the risk of multiple and shifting rules for *rule*. Wittgenstein says that explanation must stop somewhere, and stops with *use*, but rules theorists have proceeded to put "rules" in the privileged place, transcendentally controlling the use, that "meaning" formerly held. For Wittgenstein, rules provide no explanation; we can only describe scenes of language use, and these scenes will be what the rule amounts to. If we formulate a rule to sum up a group of uses, this will not be something more fundamental than the uses, a soul which inhabits them, but a formula adapted to a specific purpose. A rule describes a use; it does not "constitute" or "determine" it, is not a new form of logical necessity or a priori. It perhaps does not even name what it is we learn when we learn an activity:

> You must remember that there may be such a language-game as 'continuing a series of digits' in which no rule, no expression of a rule is ever given, but learning happens *only* through examples. So that the idea that every step should be justified by a something—a sort of pattern—in our mind, would be quite alien to these people. (*Z* 295)

> How queer: It looks as if a physical (mechanical) form of guidance could misfire and let in something unforeseen, but not a rule! As if a rule were, so to speak, the only reliable form of guidance. But what does guidance not allowing a movement, and a rule's not allowing it, consist in? —How does one know the one and how the other? (*Z* 296)

> We say: "If you really follow the rule in multiplying, it *must* come out the same." Now, when this is only the slightly hysterical style of uni-

versity talk, we have no need to be particularly interested. It is however the expression of an attitude towards the technique of multiplying, which comes out everywhere in our lives. *The emphasis of the 'must' corresponds only to the inexorability of this attitude, not merely towards the technique of calculating, but also towards innumerable related practices.* (*Z* 299; italics added)

For just where one says, "But don't you *see* . . . ?" the rule is no use, it is what is explained, not what does the explaining. (*Z* 302)

"He grasps the rule intuitively." —But why the rule? Why not how he is to continue? (*Z* 303)

Because Wittgenstein sees no transcendental form in orderly activities, he can argue that it would *always be possible to deviate* from the "normal" sequence and yet for the deviation to be "following a rule." This is one of Wittgenstein's initially strangest-seeming claims, especially because he makes it in terms of what would seem to be the clearest and most unquestionable sort of rule-governed proceeding, the deriving of mathematical series. The point which he makes about mathematics would apply *a fortiori* to less abstract, structured, and explicitly rule-bound operations, such as those involving natural languages. On Wittgenstein's account, it is as though an activity were inhabited by a multiplicity of souls, and any one of them could at some stage take over and guide the sequence in its own direction. Learning the "normal" sequence would be to discipline this anarchy of souls, to establish a unified, a monarchical polity among them (as in the *Republic*).

Whether we say that the same thing or something different is happening is not determined by the nature of things. We could say that continuing by twos is the same, or that it is different, as we could say of continuing by fours—depending on how we framed our rule. The sameness of what is repeated, since it is not the sameness or inexorability of an essence, is a merely actual sameness; that is, a sameness that merely *happens to be*, or that *happens to* the elements or characters in a sequence as a function of their sequentiality. The soul of the sequence does not already, in advance, permeate the characters and give them their identity with each other before they are ever put in sequence. It is not insignificant that Wittgenstein in the *Investigations* so carefully avoids using terms like "necessary" or "analytic" or "a priori" to describe the nature of "grammar." He detests any kind of what he calls "super-expression" (*PI* 97, 192), the "super-hardness" of logical and transcendental expressions so dear to the hearts of philosophers (cf. *RFM*, pp. 119–21).

So in the *Investigations* we are concerned not with a question of rules but with a question of method. The question of method is inseparable from the question of how we use language, because it is a method for following the threads of language use. Wittgenstein pursues as the most illuminating those scenes of language use in which someone is being instructed how to play a particular language game (cf. *BB*, p. 1). It is as though here the structure of the language game becomes molten, loses the aspect of crystallized order which it may appear to have for someone who already knows it. One who already "knows the rules" follows the rule blindly, as a matter of course, and perhaps does not see that things could be otherwise, that one could do things differently, that "a multitude of familiar paths leads out from these words in every direction." But for the learner, no such automatism is in place. It is as such a learner that Wittgenstein attempts to teach us to approach language. But the reading of the *Investigations* is itself a scene of instruction in a method, and subject to the kinds of questions which are raised *within* the *Investigations* concerning how this happens. Hence, his discussions of different sorts of language practices and how they are taught implicitly probe the question of what sort of method Wittgenstein's is and how it can be taught. The *Investigations* are themselves the demonstration, the showing or example, of the method they are designed to teach. Are they a "paradigm," do they establish, like the standard meter at Paris, the "rule" of the practice they teach? Are they a rigid rule, or are they more like the rubber ruler of which Wittgenstein speaks in the *Remarks on the Foundations of Mathematics*? Does their example always "tell us the same"? Does it have "implicit rules"? Could we state them? Is not Wittgenstein's teaching of his method itself an *Abrichtung*, a training which cannot speak its own sense—even though it is a linguistic practice?

Wittgenstein's method is no sort of method—has no "sort" that it belongs to. All possible methods are possible signifying sequences, revealing arrangements of the accidents of the signifying material; but Wittgenstein's method is a technique for following the accidence that generates the components of signifying sequences of whatever kind. Hence the *Investigations* considers many different kinds of method, and none of these is like the method of the *Investigations*, but all of them are aspects of this method. Not because it is a higher method, the ultimate *Aufhebung* of method, but because they are woven into the text, they are the examples (*Beispiele*) which make up this series of language games (*Sprachspiele*), a language game consisting of and taught by examples. "Here giving examples is not an *indirect* means of explaining—in default of a better. For any general definition can be misunderstood too" (*PI* 71).

The examples of method woven into the *Investigations* range from calculating and deriving algebraic series, to transcribing marks and continuing an ornamental pattern, to making impressionistic pictures and interpreting facial expressions. Towards the latter end of the scale, of course, we can no longer strictly speak of method—but there is a graduated series by which we pass from one end of the scale to the other, and no clear boundary can be drawn between what is method and what is not, or what is a rule and what is not. At one extreme, we obey the rule blindly, are carried forward by the automatism of habit. But

> Let us imagine a rule intimating to me [*gebe mir ein*] which way I am to obey it; that is, as my eye travels along the line, a voice within me says: "*This* way!" —What is the difference between this process of obeying a kind of inspiration and that of obeying [*folgen*] a rule? For they are surely not the same. In the case of inspiration I *await* direction. I shall not be able to teach anyone else my 'technique' of following the line. Unless, indeed, I teach him some way of hearkening, some kind of receptivity. *But then, of course, I cannot require him to follow the line in the same way I do.* (*PI* 232; italics added)

This remark, I think, cuts close to the heart of the *Investigations*. For Wittgenstein is not teaching rules—and he is not teaching a method of inspiration, either. But neither is his method entirely unlike these (cf. *Culture*, p. 24: "Philosophy ought really to be written as a *poetic composition*"). For it involves a yielding to the automatism of language—a use of words blindly, in the way we are inclined to use them without thinking and without justification. This is like "following a rule" because we do it as a matter of course, without awaiting inspiration. But this yielding is methodical, tactical, cultivated as a way of multiplying possibilities, of creating alternatives. I follow a path without question—unless I come to a crossroads. A word's meaning is like a rule, but only up to a point. For this "rule" continually undergoes shifts as I move from fiber to fiber in the thread, from link to link in the continuous series of its uses. So I have to learn to "hearken" to the shifts that my "rule" keeps making. I must be aware of all the different ways in which it is possible to be guided:

> You are in a playing field with your eyes bandaged, and someone leads you by the hand, sometimes left, sometimes right; you have constantly to be ready for the tug of his hand, and must also take care not to stumble when he gives an unexpected tug.
> Or again: someone leads you by the hand where you are unwilling to go, by force.
> Or: you are guided by a partner in a dance; you make yourself as receptive as possible, in order to guess his intention and obey the slightest pressure.

Or: someone takes you for a walk; you are having a conversation; you go wherever he does.

Or: you walk along a field-track, simply following it. (*PI* 172)

Or:

Make some arbitrary doodle on a bit of paper. —And now make a copy next to it, let yourself be guided by it. (*PI* 175)

Wittgenstein's own experience of writing was a species of "being led by the hand"—that is, his own hand led his thoughts: "I really do think with my pen, because my head often knows nothing about what my hand is writing" (*Culture*, p. 17).

Wittgenstein's use of the example of the chess game has limited the imaginations of many of his readers in their attempts to understand his conception of language. But even a chess game, in Wittgenstein's way of thinking of it, has multiple possibilities of use as a tool for thinking with. We can, for example, imagine the game as having no stated rules, but as being learned by observation of others playing (cf. *PI* 54); or we can imagine it played without a board and pieces, but with yelling and stamping of feet corresponding to our present moves (*PI* 200). More important— "one would like to say"—a game has "not only rules, but also a *point* [*Witz*]." And knowing how to play a game or being master of a technique does not involve simply knowing rules (*if* it involves rules at all; cf. *BB*, pp. 12–13), but knowing what all these rules are *for*, what the *game* is. Even in chess, the rules give only a minimal determinate structure or armature for the movement of the pieces. (In the *Blue Book* Wittgenstein suggests that we could call this the "freedom" of the pieces; it would be worthwhile to rethink the whole question of rules on the basis of this hint.) Yet there is also the pattern of the integration of these moves into the larger structure which has not yet come into existence, the game which is played. And this more comprehensive structure, this *Witz* of the game, calls not for "obeying" rules but for *strategy*.[36] When a player makes a "mistake" in chess it is not usually that the player, say, moves a pawn like a rook.

So the method of the *Investigations* is like chess, and not like chess (and so is chess). It is also like dancing and calculating and hearkening to inspiration—and like making an arbitrary doodle and then copying it. And there is a *Witz* to all this, hence tactics, strategy.

Philosophy is not refuted. There is no "precise moment of deconstruction" (as Rodolphe Gasché has claimed)[37] but only an endless intertwining of the threads of the deconstructive text with those of the classical text and of "ordinary language." Deconstruction is a simultaneous unraveling and reweaving of "Ariadne's threads of discourse" (Bouwsma's phrase, in his essay on the *Blue Book*) in the labyrinth of language. ("Language is a labyrinth of paths. You approach from *one* side and know your way about; you approach the same place from another side and no longer know your way about" [*PI* 203].)

By twisting fibers together we get a thread; by weaving threads together we get a text; by unraveling the text into its threads and the threads into their fibers we get deconstruction, which is at the same time itself a fabric woven according to the variable pattern of the unweaving of the deconstructed fabric.

Now in this essay I have woven together portions of Wittgenstein's text and portions of that of Derrida. Most of the words have been Wittgenstein's, but I have been continually guided by the patterns of Derrida's text. I have tried to show how such a weaving is done, how one must feel for the material of the fibers and threads. When doing philosophy, Wittgenstein writes, we feel as though we are pursuing the most extreme subtleties, as though we were trying to repair a torn spider's web (*Spinnenetz*) with our fingers. The web of language is not subtle beyond experience, but it is as subtle as experience. And we are not called upon to repair it, but only to continue to weave it—which always means to reweave it. We cannot do this with our fingers; we must learn the spider's touch. There is a certain automatism or mechanism (we could call it instinct, though this word too needs to be rewritten), but also play (*Spielraum*) in the joints of this mechanism (*PI* 194), and endless games with its instruments (*Werkzeuge*) and pieces (*Spielfiguren*). (The multiplication of metaphors is essential to the cunning of this method.)

Deconstruction is not, as Richard Rorty has suggested, "parasitic" on the text of philosophy,[38] for in the first place, the threads of the deconstructed text are made of the fibers of a language which is not the unique possession of that text but the common medium (*Mittel*) of ordinary speech, philosophy, and deconstruction; and, in the second place, the deconstructive text is indefinitely open to the intrusion of aspects, accidents, underground communications, and punning resonances, which had been excluded from the philosophical text, into its discourse.

On the other hand, if the threads of philosophy are displaced from their old configuration, if they are denied the place they formerly held in the new text, it is not because they are *false*—not because there is some new essence of truth which they fall short of.

Philosophy is not senseless in the sense that sense is something settled that is missing from it—"it is not as it were its sense that is senseless. But a combination of words is being excluded from the language, withdrawn from circulation" (*PI* 500). And not entirely withdrawn, either, for "sense-less" sentences are interwoven with the recommended combinations of words, though a boundary is drawn between them. But if I draw a boundary, "that is not yet to say what I am drawing it for": it could be "part of a game [*Spiel*] and the players be supposed, say, to jump over the boundary" (*PI* 499).

2   The Law of Identity and the Law of Deconstruction

3 "Now I'll deceive him"

The ideal object of philosophy must be essentially independent of the presence of any empirical subject in order to be "there" (nowhere, everywhere) in principle for viewing by any rational subject, anytime. This moment of the disappearance of the subject is transitional, on the way to his reappearance in full wakefulness as clear and distinct perception of that ideality. But Derrida, while taking advantage of the disappearance of the empirical subject, arrests the movement toward fulfillment in order to focus on the moment of signification, the moment during which the availability of the knowable undergoes storing-up in signs. And, I have argued, Wittgenstein's practice takes place in this zone of mere signification.

In proportion as signification points forward, toward the possibility that we can all know the same thing, it points toward harmonious intersubjectivity. Anglo-American linguistic philosophy, while it avoids any such notion as Husserl's "object intuition," is compatible with Husserl in maintaining the determination of language as the in-principle possibility of harmonious intersubjectivity. There are rules according to which language operates, these rules are communal, and they constitute meaning as the same for anyone who obeys them.

Deconstruction, as practiced by Derrida or by Wittgenstein, questions the presence of any ideal selfsameness, either in the subject, the object, the meaning, the words, or the rules. Language remains, for them, a common thing, because essentially independent of anyone's own proper intention to make it mean. Yet this commonness, because it lacks a basis in ideal selfsameness, by no means predestines intersubjectivity to consensus.[1]

The word, like Iago's purse, is just what can be mine, yours, anybody's. This occurrence of this expression, in my mouth, now, is "mine," but so far as it is, it is nothing—a mere sound, a physical event. So far as it is *language*, however, it is not mine; you can carry it away. But if meaning is contextual, a function of the syntax in which it occurs, my words cannot mean identically the same in your mouth or in your mind that they mean in mine.[2] In proportion as *my* meaning is capable of becoming *your* meaning, it has to be detachable from me, from what Derrida calls its origin in my present intention: the sign is essentially a structure "which is not exhausted in the present of its inscription [or utterance]" (*Margins*, p. 317). This "instituted," perduring, or "written" character of the sign (whether spoken or written) goes even further:

> It belongs to the sign to be legible, even if the moment of its produc-
> tion is irremediably lost, and even if I do not know what its alleged
> author-scriptor meant consciously and intentionally at the moment he
> wrote it, that is abandoned it to its essential drifting. . . . [B]y virtue
> of its essential iterability[,] one can always lift a written syntagma
> from the interlocking chain in which it is caught or given without
> making it lose every possibility of functioning, if not every possibility
> of "communicating," precisely. (*Margins*, p. 317)

Described in this way, the intersubjectivity of language—its capacity to function as a vehicle for the repetition of the same by different subjects—is, ironically, at the same time its capacity to be torn away by reader or hearer from what it meant to its issuer, so that it continues to mean something, but not *identically* what it meant to its writer or utterer. Derrida calls this kind of repetition-with-a-difference "iteration," and the insertion of signs into new contexts, "grafting."

Speech-act theory relies heavily on the notion of "context," and this use is sometimes thought to be vaguely compatible with Wittgenstein's method, but the two are in fact very far apart. In his essay on Austin and his controversy with John Searle in the pages of *Glyph*, Derrida has set forth views on context that are just such as could be derived from or applied to Wittgenstein and therefore reveal just where in its foundations speech-act theory differs from Wittgensteinian (as well as Derridean) deconstruction. And since Derrida's remarks here are so appropriate to Wittgenstein, they show in a particularly clear way how his technical vocabulary, on its face so alien to Wittgenstein's mode of discourse, can be used to supplement it.

Derrida has taken some interest in speech-act theory; he has even written that he considers himself "in many respects quite close to Austin, both interested in and indebted to his problematic" (*Ltd Inc*, p. 172). Derrida finds of special interest Austin's notion of "illocutionary force," in part for reasons paralleling his interest in Husserl's "formalism": both Austin and Husserl separate off the problem of reference from the problem of the formal structure of meaning, and therefore to some extent separate the problem of meaning from the metaphysics of entity. But whereas for Husserl the formal structure of meaning ("pure logical grammar") remains tied to the form of objects, Austin's analysis of utterances as "performatives" seems to Derrida to be "nothing less than Nietzschean" (*Margins*, p. 187) in its turn away from the category of substance in the direction of force. Beginning with such speech acts as promising and christening that clearly do not refer to objects or preexistent states of affairs but bring them into being, Austin concludes by deciding that even straightforward declarative statements are performative. "'I state that'" is "exactly on a level" with "'I argue that,'" "'I suggest that,'" or "'I bet that'";[3] it tells us how the sentence is to be taken, what its "illocutionary force" is. Once we take statements as performatives, we see that, like other performatives, they must be analyzed in terms of the full context of utterance, and we must take into account all the situational constraints that determine whether the speech act has been properly performed or not (in Austin's terms, whether it is "happy" or "unhappy"). Austin argues that, just as I must be in a position to give something before I can give it, or to christen a baby before I can christen it, so I must be in a position to know something before I can "state" it. If I speak about what will happen in the future or what is going on in someone's head, I am, according to Austin, not really making a statement; my speech act has the explicit form of a statement, but considering "the speech-situation as a whole," I am really guessing. Similarly, if I "state" that "the cat is on the mat" but do not believe that the cat is in fact on the mat, this purported statement too is "unhappy" because "insincere" (one of the forms of performative "infelicity").

Now, this is a radical move on Austin's part: he is making truth depend, not on the simple existence of a referent, but on the whole speech-act context: "It is essential to realize that 'true' and 'false,' like 'free' and 'unfree,' do not stand for anything simple at all; but only for a general dimension of being a right or proper thing to say as opposed to a wrong thing, in these circumstances, to this audience, for these purposes and with these intentions" (*Words*, p. 145). But this argument is the opposite of a weakening of the concept of truth or the demand for truth; Austin's whole enterprise has a strong ethical underpinning, and he is here arguing that our responsibility to truth cannot be so easily satisfied as simple notions of meaning and reference might lead us to think.

Austin's entire analysis gravitates toward the models of the contract and the promise. Despite his careful survey of the great variety of types of speech acts, his most general concept of a speech act is normed by the category of the "commissive," which includes promising, contracting, covenanting, and giving one's word. When Austin argues that statements are really performatives, he reminds us that statements *commit* us to future behavior as do promises and contracts (*Words*, pp. 137, 139). When he compares the category of commissives with his other four categories of performatives, he finds that all the other categories share in the "commissive" dimension (*Words*, pp. 158–59). And of course the whole discussion of speech acts had been launched in the first chapter with the example of Hippolytus, who makes an oath in bad faith ("my tongue swore to, but my heart did not"), not understanding, or refusing to understand, that his speech act committed him regardless of his mental reservation. Austin reminds us, as against Hippolytus, and launching us on the track of illocutionary force, that "accuracy and morality alike are on the side of the plain saying that *our word is our bond*" (*Words*, p. 10).

It is important to keep in mind the ethical underpinnings of Austin's project because what seems most questionable about Derrida's critique of Austin is precisely that it seems to evade the plain moral force of the plain saying that Austin cites. The subtlety of Derrida's critique may well seem overly subtle, and something plain may seem to be lost in its oversubtlety. Therefore, as we now turn to an examination of Derrida's analysis of speech-act theory, we will not let ourselves at any point wander too far from this ethical question.

II

"Communication" has classically been conceived as the transferring or "transporting" of a ready-made or "already constituted" meaning. Derrida thinks Austin moves toward a more radical conception of communication, in which it is "an original movement" and "produces or transforms a situation." Thus, for Derrida the interest of Austin's approach is in his emphasis on the "force" that causes a situation to come into being (*Margins*, pp. 321–22).

However, Derrida appears to overplay the "Nietzschean" implications of Austin's theory. Though "illocutionary force" does produce a new state of affairs rather than reporting on a preexisting one, Austin's use of the term "force" would seem to be an accident of English usage. When we ask, "What is the force of that remark?" we could paraphrase the question as "How is it meant?" or "How does he intend it?" without loss. It would be less misleading to speak of illocutionary *form* than force, for what we understand when we understand the illocutionary force of a remark is its category: we grasp what kind of performative has been used, what class it belongs to.

But if that is the case, it only means that Austin is less close to Derrida than Derrida seems to think, and that Derrida's criticism of Austin is all the more relevant. This criticism is that, despite his radicalism, Austin remains tied to presuppositions which are fundamentally the same as those of the Continental metaphysical tradition, and specifically of phenomenology (*Ltd Inc*, pp. 172–73, 193). These presuppositions center on the value that is given to the "conscious presence of the speakers or receivers who participate in the effecting of a performative, their conscious and intentional presence in the totality of the operation," which "implies teleologically that no *remainder* escapes the present totalization . . . no irreducible polysemia, that is no 'dissemination' escaping the horizon of the unity of meaning" (*Margins*, p. 322).

Let us see precisely what Derrida is getting at here. We have already seen that Hippolytus is committed to his oath by the force or form of the speech act he commits, regardless of his intention as he spoke. So we will need a closer look at the structure of Austin's analysis to see where the justification is for Derrida's claim.

In his second lecture, Austin lays down the system of "necessary conditions" for the "happy" execution of a speech act. Conditions of the first category specify the ritual or conventional *form* that must be satisfied: A_1, the form exists; A_2, the persons involved are formally qualified. Conditions of the second category specify that the form must be correctly (B_1) and completely (B_2) *activated*. Once these conditions have been satisfied, the speech act has in fact come into existence; we can say that such and such a speech act has been performed. What, then, is the role of conditions of the third category? Austin labels them with the Greek letter Γ to indicate that they are of a different type than the first two, and says that they involve the "implementing" or "consummating" of the act. The status of conditions Γ seems to me peculiar; the act has in fact been completed, but not "consummated." Yet, however peculiar their status, Austin does not consider them marginal or accessory conditions; on the contrary. These are what we could call the "commitment" conditions: we must be sincere where sincerity is called for (Γ_1); and we must fulfill our commitment in our subsequent conduct (Γ_2). When conditions A and B are satisfied, we have only the dead shell of a ritual; conditions Γ are its *energeia* or *entelecheia* (as we could translate into formal Aristotelian terms Austin's "consummation").

Looking back over this scheme, we see how tightly knit it is. All of these conditions must be satisfied for the speech act not only to come into being but to come into full or, as Austin will have it, "happy" being. If I have an intention but do not say the right words, my act is unhappy; if I say the right words but have the wrong intention, again my act is unhappy. If I say the right words with the right intention but I am not formally qualified to say them, the same. And so on. It is all part of what Austin calls the "total context."

This notion of a total context is for Derrida too "totalizing" because it is in principle incapable of being total. His argument is that a context is "never absolutely determinable," or rather, that "its determination is never certain or saturated" (*Margins*, p. 310). Austin supposes that we can or ought to be able to determine all the relevant structural members that outline the self-identical form of the speech act against the indefinite matter of the total context (using "total" here to include everything against which Austin's total context must be defined, out of which it must be carved). Thus he returns repeatedly to the questions of ambiguity, equivocation, vagueness—in general, the problem of *inexplicitness* (e.g., pp. 33, 36, 61, 70, 73, 76–77). When we have no explicit formula for a speech act, or fail to use it, we do not know exactly which speech act it *is*. "To say 'I shall' may be to promise, or to express an intention, or to forecast my future" (*Words*, p. 77). The movement toward explicitness in the telos of Austin's investigation, and he implies that it is part of the telos of the history of natural language itself as it moves away from its "primitive stages" (*Words*, p. 73). The boundary of definition, the form of the illocutionary act as "what precise action it is" (*Words*, p. 61), must emerge in the clarity of its outline out of the indeterminate mass of possible meanings.

But need it be any precise illocutionary act at all? In fact, Austin's own analysis plays at the very edges of the kind of idealization that he invokes. His categories have blurred edges, and he often reminds us of the way they overlap and slide into each other (e.g., pp. 16, 21, 23, 31, 79). He repeatedly finds that a given performative will participate in various categories at the same time, so that even if we know that "I shall" in a given case is a promise, a promise need not fit neatly into a single category of illocutionary force.[4] Austin is halfway between Aristotle and Wittgenstein, and his categories are halfway between essences and family resemblances ("*families* of related and overlapping speech acts" [p. 150]). So is Derrida justified in trying to indict Austin of an attempt to determine *absolutely* and *exhaustively* the form of the context?

In order to understand the force of Derrida's argument we must understand his emphasis on the notion of "teleological determination." Derrida is interested in the most general constraints that determine the form of Austin's inquiry, and the clue to these constraints is given not so much by what they include as what they leave out. Austin's inquiry is, as Derrida says, "patient, open, aporetic, in constant transformation" (*Margins*, p. 322), yet it is always guided by its aim at a normative or ideal structure, the ideal form of the successful performative in which I mean what I say, the correct illocutionary form is correctly and completely activated, you understand it, and the sequel is faithfully fulfilled.[5] But in order to organize the inquiry under the guidance of this normative or teleological definition, we have to make massive exclusions right at the outset. Austin excludes certain kinds of "ill, which infect all utterances" from his inquiry—"parasitic" uses that do not occur in "ordinary circumstances," such as words spoken "by an actor on the stage, or . . . introduced in a poem, or spoken in soliloquy." These uses, says Austin, are not serious (*Words*, pp. 21–22). For a speaker to use language seriously is then, as Derrida reads Austin, for the speaker to be fully and consciously present to the meaning and force of his words, such that there is a precise coincidence of the form of the intention and the form of the utterance. John Searle, in his reply to Derrida's essay on Austin, confirms this analysis: "Of course in serious literal speech the sentences are precisely the realizations of the intentions: there need be no *gulf* at all between the illocutionary intention and its expression. The sentences are, so to speak, fungible intentions."[6] In nonserious speech, on the other hand, there would be a gap between intention and expression; I would not stand four-square behind my words as I do when I speak seriously.

We begin to see, then, what Derrida means when he says that for Austin the conscious intention of the speaker is "a determining focal point of the context" and must consequently be "totally present and actually transparent for itself and others" (*Margins*, p. 327). This does not mean that intention *creates* the context; there remains the difference between the objective forms that make the intention possible and the intention that activates these forms. Thus, if I say "I state that" when I'm in no position to state, regardless of how fully I intend to state, according to Austin it isn't a statement. We could deduce from this that it wasn't properly the *intention* I took it to be either; how could it be? I *thought* I was making a statement, yet it was no statement at all, but, say, a surmise. My intention is unfulfilled, is not fully itself, if the form in which it expresses itself turns out to be other than what the intention took it to be. I thought I was stating, but I was deceived. The form of the utterance can only be "saturated" by intention if the form of the intention is precisely adjusted to it. So I must know when it is proper for me to emit this utterance. If I command or state when it is improper for me to do so, this is an accident or a mistake—a failure of consciousness. The "total" context continues to function as the norm in terms of which such mistakes and accidents are defined, and that norm is projected as ideally determinate in the form that it would have for an ideal consciousness, one that knew precisely what's what—meanings, necessary conditions, and its own intention. Of course Austin does not say that the "total context" is the one that is there for an ideal consciousness; he simply idealizes and presents the idealization as something given in ordinary speech and discoverable by empirical investigation. It is precisely the brunt of the deconstructive critique to show the idealizing, totalizing form of this empirical inquiry.[7]

The telos of serious, literal speech is the ideal of perfect correspondence between mental act and linguistic formula, in which logos as speech act gives the true form or essence of logos as psychic act. But precisely how are we to establish this correspondence? The locution "serious, literal speech" is elliptical, a sort of figure in which the predicate "serious" that properly belongs to intention is displaced onto the language that expresses the intention. This figure of speech then begs the crucial question as to the precise relation between language and what it expresses. As Derrida points out, "No criterion that is simply *inherent* in the manifest utterance is capable of distinguishing an utterance when it is serious from the same utterance when it is not" (*Ltd Inc*, p. 208). Wittgenstein makes the same point even more forcefully: "'My intention was no less certain as it was than it would have been if I had said, "Now I'll deceive him."'—But if you had said the words, would you necessarily have meant them quite seriously? (Thus the most explicit expression of intention is by itself insufficient evidence of intention.)" (*PI* 641). The guarantee of the self-identity of intention as ideality must be the self-identity of its linguistic formula, which gives the boundary of definiteness, the determination of the ideal form. But the walls of this boundary are themselves confirmed in the firmness of their determinacy by their definite correlation with an intention that is definite as such, self-identical in its seriousness. The correlation between the definiteness of the intention and the definiteness of the verbal formula can be guaranteed only by the indwelling within the formula of the seriousness of the intention, and this in turn seems to be definable formally in terms of explicitness. Fully explicit language would be language which set forth the true self-identical form of a unitary intention. Yet explicitness is not an autonomous formal character of language, but can be read only in relation to the postulated spirit of seriousness which is assumed to inhabit an utterance. The phrase "explicit expression of intention" presents a picture of a definite something that can be expressed in the truth of its outline, like a seal in wax, yet the form of expression which we see (the verbal formula) has nothing in its form as such that would guarantee such a correspondence. The "most explicit" form may be serious—or it may not.

Notice that to argue this way is not to argue that there is no such thing as a serious intention or serious speech. Discourse like Austin's trades on ordinary language while using it in ways that are covertly metaphysical, and criticizing or rejecting such adaptations of ordinary language must not be taken for a rejection of ordinary language itself. Serious, literal speech functions as a theoretical concept in Austin's analysis, enabling him to define a normative structure that then in certain cases will authorize him to legislate against ordinary uses of language. When Austin tells us that we can state only what we are in a position to know, he informs us that certain ordinary ways of speaking of stating are excluded by his idealization. "You *cannot* now state how many people there are in the next room; if you say 'There are fifty people in the next room,' I can only regard you as guessing or conjecturing (just as sometimes you are not ordering me, which would be inconceivable, but possibly asking me to rather impolitely, so here you are 'hazarding a guess' rather oddly)" (*Words*, p. 138). In such cases we might *say* that we state or order, and we might think it too, but we are really doing something else; on Austin's analysis, the form of what we are doing is in such cases not truly named in ordinary usage, and we require his theoretical rectification to understand the true or underlying form of the speech act.

So Derrida is not denying the possibility of seriousness; he is arguing against a philosophical picture that makes use of these concepts for its own purposes. This picture is fundamentally that of what Wittgenstein calls the "queer medium" of mind in which *form* as self-identity and presence circulates between intention and word. Not that Austin or Searle explicitly invokes this picture, but it characterizes the grammar of their concepts. Their discourse takes its direction by aiming at the ideal of adequation or precise correspondence without residue of noesis and logos, and this transparency of thought to itself is only possible when the *différance* of signification is distilled into the substance of the ideal—that is, form.

Yet the difference between what Derrida is arguing and this concept of adequation remains subtle. Derrida does not deny intention or the possibility of communicating an intended meaning; what he denies is the possibility of *saturation* of language by intention, the possibility that meaning can be absolutely *full* in the sense of the precise correspondence we have been discussing. This denial may not seem like much; it may seem as though Derrida is putting too fine a point upon the matter. Can't we just shrug and say, oh, all right—we aren't Platonists around here, and nobody ever intended to say that there's an absolutely perfect sort of fit between intention and expression; let's just say that for all practical purposes, in serious, literal speech we mean just what we say. Yet this margin of difference, no matter how small, is all Derrida is looking for. Once this margin is admitted, the question becomes, what are we to do with it? If we are intent on establishing normal cases and normative descriptions, we will disregard this negligible margin. But if the difference is always and necessarily present, does it not acquire essential status, and must we not then, instead of shrugging it off, inquire into what this essential predicate implies for the nature of speech acts?

Derrida's move here is in the style of the classical moralists, and has the same motivation. He is looking for the flaw, the element of impurity, the *memento mori*, no matter how barely visible, that keeps anything from closing the final gap separating it from the perfection of the ideal. The Greek atomists understood this principle very well, arguing that anything in which there is an admixture of space, no matter how slight, gives an opening to the forces of decomposition, and that consequently, for a thing to be undecomposable it must be absolutely full, so densely compacted that no margin at all remains for the entry of disruptive force. This almost negligible doorway to death is symbolized as well in the story of Achilles' mortality. We could also consider such modern examples as the slight bruise that kills Ivan Ilyich and the birthmark of Hawthorne's story by that name.

Thus Derrida's insistence on the margin of opacity to presence that is inscribed in the essential structure of the sign is no formalist quibble. We begin from the fact that the sign is essentially structured in such a way as to make up for some measure of absence. It is true that we can speak to ourselves, but we can do even that only because language is structurally open to the understanding of other human beings: "There is no code . . . that is structurally secret" (*Margins*, p. 315). In holding that a code must in principle be capable of being understood by someone other than the originator of the code, Derrida is arguing along lines parallel to Wittgenstein's argument against the possibility of a "private language." For Wittgenstein as for Derrida, a language or "code" must be such that it can be learned and practiced by someone else; Derrida's way of putting this is to say that signs or marks must be capable of being "repeated" or "iterated" by "any possible user in general" (*Margins*, p. 315). But if the intrinsic structure of a code is public in principle, this means that the code is in its essence independent of the presence of any determined or empirical subject in particular. This is why Derrida speaks of signification in general as "writing" in his special sense. "Writing" is precisely the persistent functioning of signs beyond the disappearance of the subject from whom they issue forth; and all signs, whether written or spoken, because they are capable of being repeated by some indeterminate other, are structurally "written" in this sense (*Margins*, p. 316).

Derrida notes that in classical accounts of writing, such as Condillac's, writing is seen as a means of communicating with someone who is absent, but that absence is always seen as a modification of presence—as the presence somewhere else, farther away, of the absent one (*Margins*, pp. 312–13). What is not brought into the analysis is the possibility of a radical break in presence, the "death" (Derrida puts it in quotation marks) or "possibility of the 'death' of the addressee, inscribed in the structure of the mark" (*Margins*, p. 316). Derrida puts death in quotation marks because he speaks of death, as of writing, in a generalized sense. Death in general is the absence of the fullness of intentional consciousness. It is called death in order to mark absence as something other than an attenuation of presence—as something like an *absolute* absence. Defining absence in this way then allows Derrida to define less apparently radical forms of absence— such as absentmindedness or the wandering of attention (*Ltd Inc*, pp. 185– 86)—as forms of death. Once again, this is the pursuit of the *memento mori* that Derrida finds contaminating all thought of presence—a thought which is ultimately the thought of life as fullness of consciousness. So long as we think the margin that keeps consciousness from full self-presence as an accident or modification of consciousness, we think it as Augustine thinks evil, as the retraction of a fullness that remains essentially full. Only when absence is thought in its essence as absolute and irrecuperable nega- tion of presence do we begin to think death within presence.

The now of writing is split by the absence that makes writing necessary, the absence of the whole subject, the absence of memory that comes a mo- ment later, or the absence that is the impossibility of conscious intention's ever being full and present to itself. The later moment of absence splits the moment of its origin as its condition of possibility: there can be no writ- ing, no real *signification*, where there is full presence of consciousness— say, in the mind of God. We can imagine God making letters of flame in his own mind, and yet, so long as these letters remain absolutely consub- stantial in fact and in principle with the fullness of the thought that thinks them, they are really only thought; only in so far as they could detach themselves from this thought, become a virtual or sleeping thought— what Derrida calls "inscription"—would they be writing. But in that case there would be in them that margin of difference that would keep them from absolute identity with the thought that gave rise to them.

> At the very moment when someone would like to say or to write, "On the twentieth . . . etc.," the very factor that will permit the mark (be it psychic, oral, graphic) to function beyond this moment—namely the possibility of its being repeated *another* time—breaches, divides, ex- propriates the "ideal" plenitude or self-presence of intention, of mean- ing (to say) and, *a fortiori*, of all adequation between meaning and saying. Iterability alters, contaminating parasitically what it identifies and enables to repeat "itself"; it leaves us no choice but to mean (to say) something that is (always, already, also) other than what we mean (to say). (*Ltd Inc*, p. 200)

Yet this structural detachability of the sign from our intention is at the same time the possibility of its being "repeated" by someone else. Derrida calls this repeatability "iterability" to bring out the factor in repetition of becoming *other* (*iter-*, "again," probably related to Sanskrit *itera*, "other"). In iteration the identity that is repeated is at the same time essentially al- tered: "Iterability alters" (*Ltd Inc*, p. 200). Once we have admitted the sign's margin of structural opacity to intention, we admit that when the sign is repeated in a new context, its sense will be determined as at least marginally different by its new context. Derrida, like Wittgenstein, believes that signs are "intrinsically determined by context," that they have no inviolable core of self-identical meaning that we can intend as identically the same when we repeat them in different contexts. "Context is always, and always has been, at work *within* the place, and not only *around* it" (*Ltd Inc*, p. 198). Since the context is not "exhaustively determinable," there is no drawing limits to the extent that it can transform the sign; all we know is that there must be a "minimal remainder" (*restance*) that enables us to recognize the sign well enough for it to continue functioning as a sign. At the same time that different occurrences of a sign are recognizably the same, however, they are also different because new contexts bring out new aspects of their meaning possibilities. This difference cannot be limited as an accident or inessential difference because there is no unitary essence to meaning that could limit to inessentiality the inroads of context. The word, like a face, is a set of characters. None are essential or all are essential. A word is what I called, in the chapter on Wittgenstein, a transitive essence. We have a continuum of variants, and each variation is both sub-essential and yet a gradation of essential change. This opens the possibility of the "nonmasterable dissemination" of meaning of which Derrida speaks in the "White Mythology" (*Margins*, p. 248).

Yet this is not an arbitrary or undisciplinable phenomenon; we know a good deal about how to activate and delimit the range of a word's functions within a skillfully or artfully constructed syntax. Not that we can ever *fully* control this range of activation; on the contrary, we know a priori that we cannot, that this range will endlessly extend beyond our conscious intention. But the absence of one determinable or knowable limit does not mean that anything and everything is possible anytime and every time; rather, the range of future activation of meaning will occur in future contexts, and each context will bring out corresponding aspects of meaning. "This does not suppose that the mark is valid outside its context, but on the contrary that there are only contexts without any center of absolute anchoring" (*Margins*, p. 320).

Because Derrida argues a discrepancy between intention and utterance, he seems to reintroduce the mentalism that Wittgenstein opposed. Searle's argument that the words of a sentence are themselves a "fungible intention" seems like a more advanced view than Derrida's. But for Wittgenstein there is no self-identical mental reality that blends in unity with "expressions" of this reality. Our mental experiences in connection with intention are on the same level as our utterances and actions: they are all "intention-phenomena." Searle, however, asserts the nondistinction of intention and utterance, not in order to do away with the ideality of intention, but rather, in order to saturate the utterance with the self-identity of this ideality. Derrida's maneuver is designed to undo this absolute subordination of utterance to ideality in order to read intention itself as differing-deferred. Thus his strategy, though following a different route, is in agreement with Wittgenstein's, because once mental reality is stripped of its special ideal character and interpreted as differential, "the difference, inner-outer, doesn't matter."

It should now be clear how Derrida is able, in appealing to the iterability of a code and its reliance on context, to speak of both "the disruption, in the last analysis, of the authority of the code as a finite system of rules; [and] the radical destruction, by the same token, of every context as a protocol of a code" (*Margins*, p. 316). The iterability of a code ruptures its authority because it makes it essentially permeable to the deformations of context and yet makes it independent of the power of any given context to determine its meaning once and for all, because the sign carries an irreducible structure that will not let itself be absorbed into a present intention that would fix it in relation to an intentionally totalizable present context.

III

Austin recognizes that performatives are always liable to infelicities, but he does not, as Derrida does, examine this possibility "as an essential predicate or *law*" (*Margins*, p. 324). Austin treats as accidental the possibility that a performative might always partially or totally fail to fulfill its (teleologically defined) function. But for Derrida, if impurity is always possible, then that possibility is in some sense a "necessary possibility" and belongs to the essence of the performative (*Margins*, p. 324). Searle, attempting to establish the normality of adequation between intention and expression, unconsciously phrases his reply in terms that confirm Derrida's argument with striking precision: "To the extent that the author says what he means the text is the expression of his intentions. It is always possible that he may not have said what he meant or that the text may have become corrupt in some way; but exactly parallel conditions apply to spoken discourse" (*Reply*, p. 202).

We could have no better example than this of the closeness and distance between philosophy and deconstruction. Derrida will assent fully to these two sentences, and yet his weighting, his emphasis, will be the inverse of Searle's. The issue between them concerns the force of the "to the extent that." There is no doubt that *to the extent that* I say what I mean, my utterance expresses my intention; but this is tautologous. The question still remains, to what extent *can* I say what I mean? Searle mentions the possibil-

ity of corruption only to elide it in favor of the ideal case; Derrida meditates
on the law of corruptibility: "A corruption that is 'always possible' cannot
be a mere extrinsic accident supervening on a structure that is original and
pure, one that can be purged of what thus happens to it. . . . This *possibility*
constitutes part of the *necessary* traits of the supposedly ideal structure. . . .
What must be included in the description . . . is not merely the factual reality of corruption and of alteration, but corrupt*ability*" (*Ltd Inc*, p. 218).
Derrida goes on to say that it would be better not to use the word *corruptibility* because it implies "pathological disfunction." Pathology implies ab-
normality, deviation from intrinsic nature, and so far as the word *corruptibility* is tied to such a notion it keeps us from conceiving its effects as
essential, as part of the "inside."

Derrida lays considerable stress on the use of terms like *nonserious*, *parasite*, *etiolation*, and *corruption* by Austin and Searle. He sees in such language an ethical condemnation of ironic, metaphoric, and fictive language,
a condemnation that is implicitly metaphysical:

> Metaphysics in its most traditional form reigns over the Austinian heri-
> tage. . . . Two indications bear witness to this: 1. The hierarchical axiol-
> ogy, the ethical-ontological distinctions which do not merely set up
> value-oppositions clustered around an ideal and unfindable limit, but
> moreover *subordinate* these values to each other (normal/abnormal,
> standard/parasite, fulfilled/void, serious/non-serious, literal/non-literal,
> briefly: positive/negative and ideal/non-ideal). . . . 2. The enterprise of
> returning "strategically," ideally, to an origin or to a "priority" held to
> be simple, intact, normal, pure, standard, self-identical, in order *then* to
> think in terms of derivation, complication, deterioration, accident, etc.
> All metaphysicians, from Plato to Rousseau, Descartes to Husserl, have
> proceeded in this way, conceiving good to be before evil, the positive
> before the negative, the pure before the impure, the simple before the
> complex, the essential before the accidental, the imitated before the im-
> itation, etc. And this is not just *one* metaphysical gesture among others,
> it is *the* metaphysical exigency, that which has been the most constant,
> most profound and most potent. (*Ltd Inc*, p. 236)

Searle objects to Derrida's arguing that Austin's language "involves
some kind of moral judgment." "Such parasitism is a relation of logical dependence; it does not imply any moral judgment," Searle argues.[8] But the
question is whether Austin or Searle or anybody can *say* "parasite" or
"nonserious" or "corruption" and *mean* no moral judgment by it. How we
decide this question depends on how we decide the major issue, the issue
of whether the sign structurally exceeds the intention and to some ineradi-
cable degree goes its own way. Are we not in some way committing our-

selves when we choose to use these terms? Can my tongue say "parasite" while my mind withholds moral judgment? Perhaps it could, in the cases Searle cites from mathematics, though as Derrida asks, "What logician . . . would have dared to say: B depends logically on A, therefore B is parasitic, nonserious, abnormal, etc.?" (*Ltd Inc*, p. 235). But given the "ancient quarrel between poetry and philosophy," can we really believe the philosopher when he says he implies no value judgment in calling poetry nonserious? What illumination does Austin think he is casting when he informs us that "Walt Whitman does not seriously incite the eagle of liberty to soar"? If Whitman was not serious about *that*, I feel like saying, he wasn't serious about anything. This will sound perverse to the theoretician of speech acts; I am willfully misunderstanding the technical sense of nonseriousness intended by Austin. But *serious* is a word in ordinary language, and it is applied here to ordinary language (Searle: "Austin never denied that plays and novels were written in ordinary language").⁹ I am inclined to use "serious" to describe Whitman's speech act (which we are told is not a "real" speech act), and I want to argue that this inclination follows the vector of ordinary language and Austin's does not.

But why does Austin want to call this language nonserious? Derrida argues that the uses of language defined as parasitic or nonserious by Austin and Searle are all *repetitions* of "serious, literal" language in contexts where we cannot be assured of the full presence of a consciousness as authentic origin of the utterance. An actor on stage, a voice in a poem, an ironic speaker, a deconstructive philosopher citing the formulas of philosophy— all of these would be repeating language, not with the fullness of an originating consciousness which means exactly what it says, so that logos as language would give the true form or essence of logos as psyche, but in a peculiarly "hollow or void" way (*Words*, p. 22), as a mechanical or fictional or irresponsible or unconscious citation or iteration of full speech.¹⁰ Whitman does not really think that there is an eagle of liberty listening to him that can respond to his exhortation; thus he is not serious, not fully present to his utterance in the fullness of ethically committed, knowing consciousness. (Do we not see Austin here returning to the presence of an object as the ultimate index of rationality and seriousness?)

For Derrida, the possibility of full intentional presence to one's meaning is excluded by the essential structure of the sign, its essential repeatability. The sign does not belong to the one who utters it; it is made to be repeated and this repeatability already, at the moment of utterance, makes it structurally incapable of full permeation by the intention of the speaker. If we cut the sign away from the anchor of origin in the authentic and full intention of a present subject, the difference between an actor reciting his lines and someone making a promise *in propria persona* cannot be *essential*, cannot be the difference between "full" and "hollow" or "void" speech.

Wittgenstein is quite in accord with Derrida on this point, denying that there is a "mental act of meaning" that makes the difference between full speech and citation. "If you merely repeat the sentence after someone else," says Wittgenstein's philosophical straight man, "*say in order to mock his way of speaking*, then you say it without this act of meaning" (italics added). He claims that beneath truly meaningful speech he always discovers a "mental undertone." Wittgenstein replies: "And was there no undertone there when you repeated the sentence after someone else? And how is the 'undertone' to be separated from the rest of the experience of speaking?" (*PI* 592). For Wittgenstein, "the rest of the experience of speaking" drowns out the "undertone" that would be the *Geist* of the utterance and distinguish the full from the hollow by its presence (cf. *PI* 331–33).

If there is no essential difference between normal intentional use and parasitic language, then the strategic exclusion of parasitic language for purposes of analysis is called into question. The possibility of theater is not secondary, accidental, not something that befalls the essence of language as an ill from outside. Derrida's conclusion is in a way the most familiar of notions, one which even a speech-act theorist would enjoy while reading Shakespeare, but which sounds shocking in a philosophical essay: the reproduction of "standard" speech acts, their citation or their miming by an actor on stage, is an essential, internal, and permanent part of the "standard" structure of language (*Ltd Inc*, p. 231). "If a form of speech act that was 'serious,' or in general 'nonpretended,' did not, in its initial possibility and its very structure, include the power of giving rise to a 'pretended form,' it would simply not arise itself, it would be impossible" (*Ltd Inc*, p. 234). This is not to subordinate the nonpretended to the pretended, but rather to assert their mutual dependence and mutual derivation from the structure of iterability or repetition-with-a-difference which is essential to language as such. "The possibility of fiction cannot be derived" (*Ltd Inc*, p. 239), writes Derrida; that is, fiction is not an accidental by-product of serious, literal speech, does not have a relation of "logical dependence" to it. Both are structures given within the more general structure of iterability.

IV

Perhaps what we have in this debate is a conflict between modern Anglo-American clean-mindedness or sincerity and a more archaic moral rigor that insists on reminding us of the residue of darkness in man's intention. If there is any skepticism in Derrida, it is a moral, not an epistemological, skepticism—not a doubt about the possibility of morality but about an idealized picture of sincerity that takes insufficient account of the windings and twistings of fear and desire, weakness and lust, sadism and masochism and the will to power, in the mind of even the most sincere man.[11] Now, this idealized picture as presented by Austin is presented not as what we are but as what we can legitimately be expected to live up to, and so far as it goes this demand is just and right. Derrida does not want to lessen this demand; he does not say, "We can never know our intention absolutely; therefore we are not bound by our promises." On the contrary, his argument implies that making promises entangles us in a net of commitments and consequences that go far beyond what Austin is willing to discuss. Austin's account would allow us plausibly to represent ourselves to ourselves as philosophically serious and morally earnest without demanding too much of ourselves; it is by its own definition a *conventional* seriousness and a *conventional* morality. "A man's word is his bond": yes, indeed—but is that all there is to it?

In a way, this is an unfair criticism of Austin, since Austin was not even trying to do anything like what Derrida wants to do. Derrida has more in common with Montaigne and Shakespeare, Nietzsche and Freud, than he does with Austin, the straightforward investigator on the scientific model. On the other hand, in trying to carve out his manageable slice of investigable subject-matter, Austin runs up against other things that he must define out, and in this operation at the boundary of his subject matter, or of what he wants to define as the boundary, he becomes vulnerable to Derrida's criticisms. The operation of excluding poetry and fiction from the fullness of the Logos as field of truth is at least as old as Plato, and philosophers may well feel annoyed at Derrida's insistence on denying that it can be done. But no matter how traditional or well-entrenched the view, it remains that Derrida has worked out a critique and an alternate structure that he claims has a greater range and power, and it is easier to reassert the canonical concepts he criticizes, as Searle has done, in total ignorance of the full range of the conceptual structure Derrida has worked out as its replacement, than it is to master his arguments and his new logic and *then* to show where they fail.

What Derrida calls the insaturability of context could also be called the irony of context. Austin gives us the clear example of Hippolytus' insincerity, but the work of tragedy is typically to show us the limits of conscious intention, the extent to which sincerity and insincerity alike mistake themselves. We need go no farther than *Oedipus Rex* for a demonstration of the impossibility of exhaustively determining the context of a speech act, an impossibility that we could state in archaic, but precise, terms as: the gods know, but men cannot. When Oedipus curses the man who killed Laius and performs the exercitive speech act of forbidding his people to allow him to remain among them, Oedipus commits himself—and later, when he finds out that he himself is the killer, he remains bound by this commitment. Technically speaking, Oedipus' speech act is "happy." He is the proper person correctly executing a properly constituted form of il-locutionary act. The lesson of the play is not that Oedipus is not bound by his commitment (though the *Colonus* complicates this issue) but that men's acts are always essentially shadowed by the illimitable force of a context they cannot see and cannot control and that carries the consequences of acts far away from the will of the doer. To reply, with Searle, that this doesn't *normally* happen, that we are not all Oedipuses, would be to miss what tragedy tells us: that such rupture is part of the *essence* of human life, and that if we do not in fact succumb to it, this is contingent, a lucky acci-dent—perhaps a common accident, but one that bears the inscription of the "necessary possibility" of which we are enjoined to remain always aware.

Consider the terrible monstration of the chorus's final speech: *Leusset', Oidipous hode*, "See, here is Oedipus." If we set the formula *Oidipous hode* next to Aristotle's *tode ti*, we sum up very sharply the difference between deconstruction and philosophy. The *Oedipus Rex* is concerned with the mystery of identity, and when the chorus points to blinded and bleeding Oedipus, it points to something that cannot be subsumed under the philo-sophiс al concept of the thing. First, because he is mortal, and with respect to any mortal we must defer until he ceases to exist the judgment as to the nature of his life, whether it has been happy or unhappy (*mēden' olbizein, prin an terma tou biou perasei*). Again, if Derrida is a skeptic, he is so in the sense that the chorus can be called skeptics when they doubt that we can know the nature of a life before it has ceased to exist. Is tragedy an acci-dent, a deviation from essence? Is not Derrida's formulation absolutely precise: tragedy is a necessary possibility constitutive, as necessary possi-bility, of the essence of human life.

The second reason Oedipus' identity cannot be conceived under the sign of self-identity is that Oedipus confounds the categories, that he is a monstrosity in whom are confused together father and brother, husband and son.[12]

> Ah, the net
> Of incest, mingling fathers, brothers, sons,
> With brides, wives, mothers: the last evil
> That can be known by men: no tongue can say
> How evil![13]

We respond very superficially to tragedy if we suppose that this is merely some weird accident, that there is no essential condition or *law* that it points to.

In "The Law of Genre," an essay that is an extension of the two on speech acts,[14] Derrida discusses "the most general concept of genre" (p. 207) as the concept of a bounded set, thus as the concept of what marks off things having self-identity as things of one kind from things having a different identity as things belonging to a different kind. This most general concept of genre includes both such natural differences of kind as those between male and female ("gender"—in French designated indifferently as *genre*) and "conventional" differences such as those between literary genres. The "law of genre," in whatever sense of *genre*, seems to be that "one must respect a norm, one must not cross a line of demarcation, one must not risk impurity, anomaly, or monstrosity" (pp. 203–4). But, Derrida says, "suppose for a moment that it was impossible not to mix genres. What if there were, lodged within the heart of the law itself, a law of impurity or a principle of contamination?" (p. 204).

These remarks are a prelude to his reading of Blanchot's story "The Madness of the Day," in which Derrida discovers the sort of inquiry into the contamination of categories that we saw in *Oedipus Rex*. In this story there is a confusion or partial indistinction of genders as well as of genres, and the boundaries of beginning and ending of the story are blurred or done away with as well. This is not the place to review the full argument of "The Law of Genre"; I bring it up only to suggest its connection with *Oedipus Rex* and the way that this whole set of problems opens out the more limited issues discussed in the speech-act essays. When Derrida discusses the notion of a literary genre, he does so because "it covers the motif of the law in general, of generation in the natural and symbolic senses, of the generation difference, sexual difference between the feminine and masculine genre-gender, of the hymen between the two, of a relationless relation between the two, of an identity and difference between the feminine and masculine" (p. 221). (As to the question of gender, we should recall the figure of Teiresias in the *Oedipus*.)

It is of the highest significance for the viability of Derrida's project that, although trained as a philosopher and remaining through most of his career primarily a philosopher, he is also one of our most sensitive and sophisticated literary critics. In his exchange with Searle over the nature of fictive discourse, we must keep in mind Derrida's dazzling readings of some of the most difficult modern writers, such as Mallarmé, Valéry, Artaud, and Blanchot. Searle, on the other hand, who assures us that "once one has a general theory of speech acts . . . it is one of the relatively simpler problems to analyze the status of parasitic discourse,"[15] reveals in his own writing on literature a complete innocence of even the orthodox tradition of literary criticism, let alone of the experimental writing of the last hundred years and the theory associated with it. The absurd posturing of Searle's essay "The Logical Structure of Fictional Discourse" is so out of

proportion with what it actually accomplishes that one is moved to wonder, Can Searle (or anybody) really be serious here? Or is this a sly parody
of the critic? I quote from near the end: "Theorists of literature are prone
to make vague remarks about how the author creates a fictional world, a
world of the novel, or some such." (Does Searle refer to Ingarden, Rich-
ards, Bakhtin, Barthes—or even Longinus, Mazzoni, Coleridge—to name
but a very few? Are "vague remarks" really all we have from them and a
multitude of others?) Searle continues:

> *I think we are now in a position to make sense of these remarks.* By *pretend-
> ing to refer* to people and to recount events about them, the author
> creates fictional characters and events. In the case of realistic or natu-
> ralistic fiction, the author will refer to real places and events inter-
> mingling these references with the fictional references, thus making it
> possible to treat the fictional story as an extension of our existing
> knowledge. The author will establish with the reader a set of under-
> standings about *how far the horizontal conventions of fiction break the
> vertical conventions of serious speeches.*[16]

And so on in the same vein. Apart from the platitudes about coherence and
consistency and narrative voice, Searle's contribution to the debate comes
to this: the discovery that fiction is made up, not of real, but of pretended
speech acts, and that this pretense is set in motion by the suspension of the
conventions that relate speech to the real world. I suppose this suspension
could, in Searle's favored formal notation, which marks the fit of words to
the world as ↑ and of the world to words as ↓ , show up as Ⓚ.[17] And for
those who are soothed by such discoveries, and such formalizations, perhaps that would settle the issue.

But for those to whom Searle's analysis appears vacuous, it should be
clear what the provenance is of his claim that the problem of "parasitic discourse" is one of the "relatively simpler problems" once one is equipped
with his theory. It should also begin to seem plausible that Derrida is right
when he suggests that the assumptions behind the strategic exclusion of
nonserious discourse in Austin and Searle are based on an inadequate initial grasp of language's full range of possibility of functioning.

4   Rhetoric, Theater, Death

I

The main theme of our discussion of speech acts has been the question of what Wittgenstein calls "the inner act of meaning" and its relation to the meaning of the words spoken or written. But intertwined with this issue has been the problem of self-identity and of the boundary by which a self is kept identical with itself. In contemporary thought, the boundary of identity is often conceived of as a rule or system of rules. Searle's account of language as a rule-governed activity, for example, gravitates toward Chomsky's picture of grammatical competence.[1] Searle has important disagreements with Chomsky, but for the purposes of the present discussion the differences between Searle and Chomsky are less significant than the differences between both of them on one hand and Wittgenstein on the other. For Wittgenstein, there is no such thing as an implicit rule-entity that can exercise a causal influence over an activity. Implicit-rules theorists want there to be a specifiable *form* to a form of life, a strutwork of invisible rules insuring that the next action of each of the participants, or the next day in the life of the form of life in which they participate, will be identifiable as the same. But for Wittgenstein there is no intelligible soul to be extracted from numerous particulars, or even from *one*, no formula which can speak the unified and unifying act of the knowing mind; boundary operates, but not as what constitutes unity and self-identity out of the many; rather as what restricts consciousness to just this moment in an untotalizable temporal sequence.

We would expect, on the basis of the preceding discussion, that Wittgenstein would call into question the principle of identity, and he does in fact do so. However, he does not criticize it so much as ridicule it; it is a transparent violation of the kind of sensitivity to language that he wants to teach:

> But isn't *the same* at least the same?
> We seem to have an infallible paradigm of identity in the identity of a thing with itself. . . .

Then are two things the same when they are what *one* thing is?
And how am I to apply what the *one* thing shews me to the case of
two things? (*PI* 215)

Wittgenstein here evinces what could be taken as willful obtuseness—
not a constructive attitude at all. These questions can be answered, the sober philosophic mind feels like replying. Indeed, the whole philosophic
tradition is an answer to these questions. Wittgenstein is acting like a refractory pupil, one who refuses to go the way laid out for him, and he sets
himself as a model for other ruffians to follow. He wants to teach us to see
as nonsense, as out of play or useless, a proposition which we have formerly
seen as the foundation of sense—as sense itself. To this end, Wittgenstein
plays the classroom cut-up, citing the austere philosophical principles in
the context of his satirical mimicry of philosophic discourse:

> "A thing is identical with itself." —There is no finer example of a
> useless proposition, which yet is connected with a certain play of the
> imagination. It is as if in imagination we put a thing into its own
> shape and saw that it fitted.
> We might also say: "Every thing fits into itself." Or again: "Every
> thing fits into its own shape." At the same time we look at a thing and
> imagine that there was a blank left for it, and that now it fits into it
> exactly.
> Does this spot ● *'fit'* into its white surrounding? —*But that is just
> how it would look* if there had been a hole in its place and it then fitted
> into the hole. . . .
> "Every coloured patch fits exactly into its surrounding" is a rather
> specialized form of the law of identity. (*PI* 216)

The identity of a thing with itself is its "as-such." To question the formula by which we affirm this as-such is to set the thing adrift. A form of
life, if it is to be a *form*, a bounded structure which would be the context of
repeatable meaning, must not drift away from the boundaries of its own
as-such, its own identity with itself. If it did, no speech-act theorist or
other theorist of implicit rules could recuperate it for the unified formulas
of knowledge. The *form* of a form of life is its thinkable essence, or eidos,
the "outline" into which it must fit. The formulas in which I express this
eidos reassure me that there is indeed a form to a form of life. Conversely,
only because there is a form to the forms of life within which I find myself
can I be sure that there is meaning in the words of the formulas by which I
describe this form. This form is a structure of rules which must be the
same as themselves and the same for everybody who participates in the
form that they define.

The anchor of this whole structure, the most certain of all principles which it seems impossible to escape, is the principle of identity. As Aristotle says, if the boundary which holds the eidos as coincident with itself were to be let down, we could not speak with each other nor, "in truth, even with ourselves" (*Metaphysics* 1006b). It seems as though radical equivocation, an uncontrollable drift of language, would be set in motion if the inviolability of the principle of identity were to be questioned. The "superhardness" of logic is first of all the superhardness of the principle of identity. The equation $2 + 2 = 4$ may be impervious to doubt, but underlying the imperviousness of what it says or shows is the absoluteness of the coincidence of the formula and each of its members with itself. The principle of self/sameness is the strutwork or informing form of all other principles of order: it is the structure of structure, the boundary of boundary, the rule of rule, the hardness of the law.[2] If a rule did not have this ideal structural rigidity, if it were not inhabited by an ideal boundary of identity or determinacy, then the principles of form or order would be essentially different than we had imagined.

> Consider also the following proposition: "The rules of a game may well allow a certain freedom, but all the same they must be quite definite rules." That is as if one were to say: "You may indeed leave a person enclosed by four walls a certain liberty of movement, but the walls must be perfectly rigid"—and that is not true. "Well, the walls may be elastic all right, but in that case they have a perfectly determinate degree of elasticity"—But what does that say? It seems to say that it must be possible to state the elasticity, but that again is not true. "The wall always has *some determinate* degree of elasticity—whether I know it or not": that is really the avowal of adherence to a form of expression. The one that makes use of the *form* of an ideal of accuracy. (*Z* 441)

If we adhere to this "form of expression," Wittgenstein says, it makes an alternative unthinkable (*Z* 442). The notion of determinacy seems unalterably situated within the concept of a boundary or rule—that is, not as what the boundary or rule *determines* but as determination of the boundary itself, as though something must bound boundary in order for boundary to perform its function. The German word for "determinacy" or "definition," *Bestimmung*, suggests by its connection with *Stimme*, "voice," that the notion of determinacy is connected with the ability to state the nature of the determinacy in question, to give its formula. Yet once the form of expression has grasped our minds, we are inclined to retreat from the criterion of determining as knowing and being able to state, and to project "determinacy" as an unknown or even as unknowable. "The wall always has *some determinate* [*bestimmte*] degree of elasticity—whether I know it or not."

According to Wittgenstein a rule, when there is a rule, a boundary, when there is a boundary, determines but need not itself be determinate. We learn to follow it, obey it, or manipulate it, and yet the rule itself is structurally or essentially indeterminate. A rule is best thought of as an object which happens to be used as a standard of comparison within some practice or other. Because any social practice is carried on by different persons who will vary from each other in their sense of how to apply any given rule, any form of life is always transected by diverging lines of possible practice: a form is a transitive essence always in process of essential variation from itself. On this view a form of life has no self-identical and unitary form, nor does a rule, nor do we.

This formulation is not an answer or an explanation or even a theory, but a way of putting a problem. The problem is how to live with other human beings under such circumstances. Wittgenstein says somewhere that an overly simple way of putting a problem is a sure way of involving it in unmanageable complexity later on. As desirable as it might seem to believe in transphenomenal identities which could ground intersubjective agreement, the argument here is that this is an ultimately misleading way of approaching the problem, and that we should at least try to begin from this alternate picture and see where it leads.

II

If language is not to obey truth—if "style," "aesthetic magic" are allowed —is this not a sacrifice of truth to rhetorical effect? In fact, Wittgenstein is quite candid about his rhetorical aim, which follows from his concern not just with ideas but with the person who holds them: "What I'm doing is also persuasion. If someone says: 'There is not a difference,' and I say: 'There is a difference' I am persuading, I am saying 'I don't want you to look at it like that'" (*L&C*, p. 27). He goes on to say that he is "in a sense making propaganda for one style of thinking as opposed to another" that he is "honestly disgusted with" (*L&C*, p. 37). Does he not, then, open the door on an immense arbitrariness by this rhetorical emphasis? Truth forgotten, the question seems to be merely who can win the war of persuasion, who can establish or dispel the "charm" of an idea:

> I would do my utmost to show it is this charm that makes one do it. Being Mathematics or Physics it looks incontrovertible and this gives it a still greater charm. If we explain the surroundings of the expression we see that the thing could have been expressed in an entirely different way. I can put it in a way in which it will lose its charm for a great number of people and certainly will lose its charm for me. (*L&C*, p. 28; cf. *OC* 209, 612)

There are three main dangers that the deconstructive appeal to the arts of language raises for those writers who oppose deconstruction. They are (1) arbitrariness or irrationalism, (2) narcissism or solipsism, and (3) a babble of tongues. These three dangers are interrelated aspects of a single complex phenomenon, the calling into question of "objective norms" which can command isolated individuals to move in concert toward a common goal. "Arbitrariness" and "irrationality" are names for the absence of allegiance to objective norms; narcissism and solipsism are the consequence of such an absence for the mental activity of the individual; and the babble of tongues is the consequence for society of the arbitrariness and narcissism of individuals.

So the crux of the debate is the question of rules or norms—the question of whether it is possible to establish an unmoving standard of measurement which stands outside of the varied and varying perspectives of the individuals involved in the debate. These are, of course, precisely the terms in which Plato decried mimetic representation in that momentous Book X of the *Republic*. The poet, says Plato, "establishes an evil constitution in [a person's] soul; he gratifies the unthinking part of it which does not know the difference between greater and less, but which believes the same things to be now great and now small" (605b–c).[3] The higher part of the soul, on the other hand, "trusts measure and reasoning," which provide a standard against which individual perspectives may be set. But this higher part of the soul is seduced away from objective measure by the charm of language: "The poetic workman dabs on certain colors by using the words and phrases of the various arts . . . so that others, as ignorant as himself, taking their view from words, think he is speaking magnificently. . . . So great is the natural charm in this manner of speaking" (601a). The consequence of this seduction to mere perspectives by the force of cunning language is a divided soul: "In all this, then, is a man of one mind with himself? Or is there rebellion within him, is he at war with himself in his doings—as, where sight was concerned, there was internal strife, and he had contrary opinions within him about the same things at the same time? . . . we have already agreed . . . that our soul is laden with thousands of such contradictions which exist all at once" (603c–d). This anarchic, perspectival, language-susceptible polity of soul is ruled by "pleasure and pain" (607d), and the chief point that Plato wants to make about such a soul is that *it knows no measure in its mourning*, as opposed to the rational man: "'A decent man,' I said, 'whose fortune it is to have lost a son or something he prized very highly, will bear it more easily than any of the others'" (603e).

I have recited Plato's account of this issue because Plato has pursued the question of objective norms into a complex tangle of other issues which are not so obviously our concern, but which we will need to come to terms with if we are to understand the question in its classical context. The concern about standards of measurement, anarchic polities, and childishly self-involved people is, in Plato, involved with questions concerning the charms of language, the division of the self, and the suffering inflicted by the loss of beloved objects.

The problem of the relation between truth and the arts of language is examined in terms very similar to Plato's in the *Confessions* of Saint Augustine. Augustine was trained as a professor of rhetoric, and his conversion to Christianity is perhaps better understood as a conversion from rhetoric than from Manichaeanism. Most of the *Confessions* is structured around the distinction between two sorts of language: language appropriate to human beings and language appropriate to God. Human language, the language which Augustine must learn to leave behind, is most commonly figured as the language of fictions, of poems and the stage; the human world is then understood, analogously, as itself a fiction or stage, and rhetoric as practiced in "real life" as the unreal langauge of fictitious human beings. This equation between the practice of rhetoric and the fictitious language of fictitious characters follows naturally from the practice of training rhetoricians by having them imitate the speeches of characters in fiction:

> The work set was that I should declaim a speech supposed to be made
> by Juno when she was sad and indignant. . . . I had been told that
> Juno in fact had never uttered these words, but we were forced to go
> wandering ourselves in the tracks of these poetic fictions. . . . And the
> declaimer who won most applause was the one who . . . gave in his
> performance the best imitation of the passions of anger and grief and
> found the most appropriate words to express his meaning.[4]

Not only is the human being who allows the itch of emotions which are stimulated by things of this world himself in danger of becoming the actor of a fictitious role, but he finds himself becoming bound in sympathy to the other fictitious characters around him. This begins at the theater: "In those days in the theaters I used to sympathize with the joys of lovers, when they wickedly enjoyed each other, even though this was purely imaginary and just a stage show, and when they were separated from one another, I used to sympathize with their misery" (3.3). And it carries over into "real life," with an increase in suffering. When Augustine's beloved friend dies, Augustine grieves because he has mistakenly loved a mere mutable creature, and he turns for consolation, again mistakenly, to "things which could cause other sorrows": "Now certainly what did me most good and helped most to cure me was the comfort I found in other friends, in whose company I loved all the things which, after this, I did love. And this was one huge fable, one long lie" (4.8). So fictions incite to involvement with the desires of the body, and the desires of the body or desires which are directed at the bodily existence of other human beings are desires for what is also a fiction, a nonbeing. Only the Unchanging truly Is. Fiction is therefore the same as evil, which is defined as nonbeing or distance from God, and to approach God is to escape being nothing or a mere fiction. The rhetorician is an actor, one who addresses untruths to a mutable audience; he exists for the praise and in the eyes of the audience. He is also the audience for them, when it comes their turn to act their parts, and in this reciprocal exchange self and other become one substance, an unreal and mutable substance. "To be sometimes teaching and sometimes learning; to long impatiently for the absent and to welcome them with joy when they returned to us. These and other similar expressions of feeling, which proceed from the hearts of those who love and are loved in return . . . were like a kindling fire to melt our souls together and out of many to make us one" (4.8).

But to love the mutable is to expose oneself to the necessity of being torn: "I was unhappy and so is every soul unhappy which is tied to its love for mortal things; when it loses them, it is torn in pieces. . . . For I felt that my soul and my friend's had been one soul in two bodies, and that was why I had a horror of living, because I did not want to live as a half being" (4.6). So not only does one turn in the direction of nonexistence by existing in the eye of the other and addressing one's discourse to him, but even such substance as one is is torn when the other succumbs to death. Only by existing in the eye of God and addressing one's discourse to him can one escape this nothingness and this torment; and this is what Augustine does in the *Confessions*. The foundation of his conversion to Christianity, the fundamental certainty which marks a limit to his doubt and confusion, is his absolute and unquestionable conviction that "what can be corrupted is inferior to what cannot be corrupted . . . and that what suffers no change is better than what is subject to change" (7.1).

The element which distinguishes divided, suffering, changeable mortality with its language of fictions and lies from the unified, unchanging, immutably blissful Word of Truth is time, to which Augustine devotes so much of his meditation. Human language, "the sounds made by our mouths, where each word has a beginning and an ending" (9.10), becomes for Augustine the paradigm of mutability and mortality—that is, of existence *in time*. This is contrasted with the timeless Word, which has no parts, no tenses, no beginning or ending, and which is the paradigm of God's relation to all of creation. The universe, God's utterance, is extended in time from a human point of view; but to God it is all there at once (11.13). Fictitious or rhetorical language is therefore preeminently language that succumbs to time, to mortality, and which drags the person who uses it or listens to it down to the suffering of mortality in its wake.

Only that which is absolutely unchanging is absolutely real, nonfictitious. As absolutely unchanging, it is absolutely incapable of being moved by the lies of rhetoric (cf. 6.6) and must be addressed with truth, truth even beyond the truth the speaker himself knows.

> Indeed, Lord, to your eyes the very depths of man's conscience are exposed, and there is nothing in me that I could keep secret from you, even if I did not want to confess it. (10.2)

> I will confess what I know of myself, and I will also confess what I do not know of myself; because what I know of myself I know by means of your light shining upon me, and what I do not know remains unknown to me until *my darkness be made as the noonday* in your countenance. (10.5)

On one hand, then, God would be the most critical conceivable audience, the audience that will accept only the language of the greatest probity. He is therefore an audience who sharpens and refines Augustine's language and consciousness, heightening his self-knowledge as no lesser audience possibly could. Augustine's language cannot, in fact, ever quite meet the standards of this audience; hence it must be continually revised, displaced, and deepened. On the other hand, this critic, though he is hypercritical and keeps always in question the unity of Augustine's intention (e.g., "often in our contempt of vainglory we are merely being all the more vainglorious" [10.38]), actually functions as an ultimate and unquestionable guarantee of that unity, because he forgives the shortfall and fills it in. Though the eye of God disquiets the complacency of self, it is the only way to guarantee that this self is my *own*, my true, unified, and integral self, and no mere rhetorical front. At the same time, he guarantees that the self cannot be torn by the pang of separation from what it loves, for, knowing the truth, it can never confuse its selfhood, its substance, with the substance of some other mortal being. It will preserve this selfhood as a unity, which no doubt belongs not to itself but to God, yet which only by belonging to God can remain properly itself, because the Being of God is *its own* Being.

So we find in Augustine, as in Plato, the implication of mimetic fiction with rhetoric, and of both as involved with a deluded attachment to other human beings, who die and are then disproportionately mourned. Maintaining the rectitude of language by the measure of unchanging truth is seen, by Plato and Augustine, as preventing an anarchy of perspectives but also as a rein on grief and a guarantee of the unity and self-identity of the soul. The moveable audience *moves on* clear out of the play, and one who seeks truth and calm and unity must liberate himself both from this language and from this audience—and from time.

III

The question of the speech act has opened out, through Plato and Augustine, onto the question of the audience. The audience must be wary of the character of the speaker and also of the character of his language; conversely, the speaker must be wary of his audience, because if his audience allows itself to be moved by hearing less than truth, it seduces the speaker into speaking less than truth. These problems arise any time we speak or hear, but within the philosophical tradition they arise in particular for fictive speech, which is in its essence a screen or deflection: no amount of sincerity can make it a truthful utterance in the sense of truthfulness demanded.

Thus a peculiar state of affairs develops when literary criticism and literary hermeneutics are conceived (as they have usually been since Aristotle) as truth-preserving enterprises. E. D. Hirsch, the most philosophical and influential exponent of such a conception in contemporary American letters, attempts to recover the presence of the utterance source in fictive discourse, thus in a sense transforming fictive discourse into a full and true speech act. Hirsch's project is classical in all its presuppositions and its stock of concepts: in particular, Aristotle, Augustine, and Husserl provide the form of the argument.

Hirsch's concern in *Validity in Interpretation* is primarily with the ideal of "determinacy" of meaning, which is directly connected with the concept of "communicability" or "sharability" of meaning. Hirsch assumes the standard picture of communication as the transfer from one consciousness to another of a unitary, ideal object as the only possible model of "understanding meaning," and from this picture follows logically (or rather, by definition) the consequence that interpretation must be concerned to identify just such an ideal object.

> Reproducibility is a quality of verbal meaning that makes interpretation possible: if meaning were not reproducible, it could not be actualized by someone else and therefore could not be understood or interpreted. Determinacy, on the other hand, is a quality of meaning required in order that there *be* something to reproduce. Determinacy is a necessary attribute of any sharable meaning, since an indeterminacy cannot be shared: if a meaning were indeterminate, it would have no boundaries, no self-identity, and therefore could have no identity with a meaning entertained by someone else. . . . Determinacy, then, first of all means self-identity.[5]

If the requirement of sharability generates Hirsch's analysis, the concept of self-identity holds it together at every point: meanings must be sharable, but determinacy, which "first of all means self-identity," is a "necessary attribute" of sharability. To "share" a meaning, according to Hirsch, is to have the same meaning that someone else has. Only such a persistence of a unitary and self-identical meaning can fend off a "chaotic democracy of 'readings'" (p. 5) which would not be a communal sharing but an anarchic proliferation of the different.

Both sharability and determinacy, however, depend upon a concept of ownership.

> What had not been noticed in the earliest enthusiasm for going back to "what the text says" was that the text had to represent *somebody's* meaning—if not the author's, then the critic's. (P. 3)

> [A reader] approaches solipsism if he assumes that the text represents a perspicuous meaning simply because it represents an unalterable sequence of words. For if this perspicuous meaning is not verified in some way, it will simply be the *interpreter's own meaning*. (P. 236; italics added)

> I shall be satisfied if this part of my discussion . . . will help revive the half-forgotten truism that interpretation is the construction of *another's* meaning. (P. 244)

This is perhaps an odd sort of "sharing": what I share remains someone else's. He shares it with me, but it is still his. This has its compensations; since what is being established here is rights of ownership, it follows that if I cannot have his meaning for my own, at least I have title to my own meanings: others must respect my property as I respect his. The common thing which language is here finds itself radically restricted, partitioned by laws of private property.

The interesting move in Hirsch's argument (a move which is derived from Husserl) is his definition of the precise nature of this property and this proprietorship. As we saw above, he wants to detach the locus of meaning from the words of the text as words on a page; but he wants also to detach it from the author as psychological subject because the author as mere psychological subject is a casually varying thing, with lapses in attention and memory. The meaning must remain determinate with respect to the variability of any contingent act of consciousness, yet free with respect to the particularity of embodiment in a given physical mark or set of reproductions of such a mark. Here Hirsch invokes the phenomenological distinction between the act of consciousness and the intentional object of consciousness. A building may be viewed from different perspectives and at different times while yet remaining the same building, and "verbal meaning" too may remain stable, as intentional object, across the variety of accidentally varying moments of consciousness in the person who intends it (p. 38).

The theory of verbal meaning leads us straight to the center of the set of conceptual issues which separate traditional epistemology from deconstruction. A verbal meaning is a "type idea," a class concept or essence which is independent of its actual particular embodiments in words. "Since a type is something that can be embodied in more than one instance, it is something whose determining characteristics are common to all instances of the type" (p. 65). This is why verbal meaning is sharable. It is an abstract or ideal object, therefore capable of being repeated as the same in the mind of another (p. 273). Mere words cannot be fixed in self-identity except as objects; with respect to meaning the words themselves are always ambiguous because *there is always a multiplicity of possible contexts surrounding them.* A context is not "simply there" but must be construed by the interpreter, hacked out from the jungle of possibilities which one and the same text will offer. Hence, "determinacy of verbal meaning requires an act of will" (p. 47), both on the part of the author and of the interpreter, because only the willed meaning can fix the actual context for this meaning out of the indefinite range of possible contexts which could be identified in any given case.

So it is by an act of will that my meaning becomes my own. Indeed, strictly speaking, it is only by such an act that there exists any meaning at all. Hirsch suggests that, in its absence, meaning is ambiguous, as attached only to words which can be detached from the unified idea and construed within a proliferation of varying contexts, but elsewhere he implies that meaning which is a function of words alone, detached from an inspiriting intention, is really no meaning at all. "Verbal meaning" is the same as "determinate verbal meaning"; hence it follows that we can have words that look like English, are arranged in English sentences, and seem to make good English sense, yet mean nothing: "Sometimes, of course, it is impossible to detect that the author has bungled, and in that case, even though his text does not represent verbal meaning, we shall go on misconstruing the text as though it did, and no one will be the wiser" (p. 234). Isn't this a startling possibility? It brings to mind the "zombie problem" that crops up now and then in American philosophy, the question of how we can tell zombies from real people when zombies manifest all the outward, behavioral marks of real people. Zombie words—no soul, no life-essence within them, and yet no one will ever be the wiser.

The type idea, then, is inhabited by an essence or soul which is a function of the will of the author. The idea is the goal which guides the author's will, but this will is the "motive force" which "realizes" the idea (p. 101). Once the idea is realized, the will of the author is permanently present within the form of words which he has created. To recreate the type idea which unifies this form of words is also to bring back to life the *will* which is the motive force of the idea. Hirsch is quite explicit on this point: "When we construe another's meaning we are not free agents. So long as the meaning of his utterance is our object, we are *completely subservient to his will*" (p. 142; italics added).

We have seen that Hirsch does not identify the linguistic subject with the psychological subject. By this maneuver he separates out an immortal essence of the subject from the accidents of his variable and contingent personal self. The self is delivered from its fluctuations and contradictions by this objective unity (the type idea), which serves as a guide and focus for a will that can by directing itself to this goal precipitate itself out of its time-bound character and its mortality.

The unity and wholeness of this objective, intentional will depend upon the unity and wholeness of the object or purpose to which it is directed. Verbal meaning is the fulfilled whole, the end, the telos of utterance, and it commands in advance the totality of the temporal sequence of words. "The speaker is able to begin expressing determinate meanings before he finishes his utterance because those meanings (carried by a particular sequence of words) are determined by the kind of meaning he is going to complete in words that have not yet been chosen" (p. 86). This telos, type, or "genre idea," whose motive force is the will of the speaker, is an essence to which all meaning must be referred. If meanings were to be construed apart from this unifying center, they would risk flying off in unpredictable directions. Determinacy is first of all predetermination. Chance and accident must not be allowed to befall the sequence of words as it emerges in time; each word must simply fit into a place that has already been marked out for it in advance. "No one," says Hirsch, "has better described this marvel of consciousness and speech than St. Augustine," and he proceeds to quote a lengthy passage from Augustine's meditation on time in Book IX of the *Confessions*, where Augustine describes how, before he begins, his "expectation alone reaches over the whole" of what he will recite.

Augustine is in fact describing his recitation of a psalm which he already knows, which is in his memory, and Hirsch notes that he does this "to make an analogy with God's foreknowledge." But, Hirsch concludes, "*his observation holds true for all utterances.*" So there is here an implicit analogy between God's foreknowledge and a speaker's, any speaker's, sense of the fulfilled totality of his meaning at the beginning of his speech. And, underlying this leap, there is the comparison of the telos of speech to something that is already there in the memory.

"Determinacy" means predetermination. The "idea" is a totality from which can emerge only those specific characters which are deducible from it as a controlling essence. Hirsch admits the possibility of unconscious meaning, but conceives it as merely that part of the unified essence which is not at this time in the gaze of consciousness.

> Any part of the whole that is not continuous with the mass above the surface cannot be part of the iceberg. *If there is something down below which is separate and discontinuous, then it must either be independent or belong to something else.* . . . The self-identity of a verbal meaning depends on a coherence that is at least partly analogous to physical continuity. If a text has traits that point to subconscious meanings (or even conscious ones), these belong to the verbal meaning of the text only if they are coherent with the consciously willed type which defines the meaning as a whole. (P. 54; italics added)

In the space of the ellipsis above, Hirsch comments: "Physical analogies are dangerous, but in this case the analogy holds." The verbal intention is like a physical object. How? In that the part of it which is not present to the gaze of consciousness is nevertheless already there, out of sight but present and "continuous with," "belonging to," what is visible. The "meaning" belongs to an author because he has willed it; and the "implications" of his act of will belong to its essence by "continuity" or "coherence." There can be no disruption of the unity of this will and this meaning. It is only an accident that we do not see these other "inexplicit" traits, a consequence of the fact that our limited minds cannot see the totality of being, or even of *one* being, spread out before them all at once.

> Our less-than-divine intellect is, as Augustine observed, time-ridden. Some traits of a thing always lie outside our explicit awareness, either because we have not yet experienced those traits or because we are not at the moment attending to them. These unattended or unknown traits constitute a penumbra which may be called a "unifying background" . . . [which] is always present and gives our experience the quality of a type idea. (P. 272)

The type idea has therefore a margin of "vagueness or tolerance" which can fuzz over the differences between particulars and assimilate them to the same class concept.

So from the physical thing we derive the notion of a necessary margin of shadow around the gaze of our mortal consciousness, and of the reassuring, continuous, coherent, already-thereness of what lies in shadow. This makes it possible to conceive by analogy the unity of conscious and unconscious meaning. On the other hand, the unique particularity of the thing must be abstracted from the analogy, for the unique contingent particular is ineffable and unknowable. Those "traits" which lie in shadow, though they are continuous with what is known, nevertheless would confound knowledge if they were all to emerge into the light. The "type experience" includes "inexplicit expectations which, by virtue of their inexplicitness (or vagueness), could be fulfilled by different concrete traits" (p. 272). If this were not so, if the expectation were fully particularized and explicit, only one thing, and not a whole class of things, could fulfill it (p. 270). But this would mean, then, that the mind could not know this thing that is confronted in its full explicitness and particularity, because it could not know what kind of thing it was. The totally explicit thing, the thing in its absolute thingness, would blind consciousness with an excess of light.

Because the human perspective is partial and temporal, it cannot be fully conscious of what it knows, cannot fully know what it knows. But if it *could* fully know what comes before its gaze, *it could not know it at all*. The unity of the essence is like the unity of the object, but its self-identity is repeatable as the same; whereas the self-identity of the object as contingent particular is unrepeatable. The unity of the essence was conceived by analogy with the unity of the object—yet it turns out that the unity of the object must be constituted by the unity of the essence. An individual person, for example, can only be seen as the unified object "person" on the basis of a type idea: "This type idea, which consists of *conditional expectations*, is the ground or background which connects the traits we have observed into the notion of the whole person. It is this unifying ground alone which lends coherence to our scattered explicit observations" (p. 271). The unity of the object, then, is nothing other than the unity of the idea, and to look at the object too closely, to risk seeing it in its complete particularity, its monstrosity, is to risk the disintegration of consciousness. The border of shadow that surrounds the type idea is then the place where a certain inattention, forgetfulness, or unconsciousness transforms the monstrosity of the thing into the typicality of the idea. This is affirmed as necessary to prevent an uncontrolled scattering of the "traits" present to consciousness, a scattering which would result in the fracturing of the unity of the intentional will, which would then be irrecoverable from, incapable of being brought back to life within, the form of words it leaves behind; and, consequently, in the fragmentation of the republic of letters into an anarchy of conflicting readings, a "Babel of interpretations."

Vagueness or unconsciousness attends consciousness as a function of its mortality, yet it makes possible an ideality which ensures the possibility of its transmortal repetition. Furthermore, it makes possible the analogy between human intention and the vision of the divine eye. Human utterance is capable of being present as foreknowledge before speech is actualized because it is a knowledge which is not entirely conscious. If it were entirely present to consciousness, entirely explicit, the object of human consciousness would be utterly mortal, because incapable of being stored in an ideal object which could be brought back as self-identical by another consciousness. But if the implicit were really unknown, and what happens in the next moment of consciousness could not be predetermined by an essence or telos, then the mind would again risk mortality as the fragmentation of its unity across time. What lies in the darkness—"below the surface," as Hirsch describes it in his spatial metaphor for what is really a temporal distinction (that is, the inexplicit is what has not yet emerged or what is not at this moment visible)—could always turn out, if it were not predetermined, to be "independent" from or discontinuous with the consciously willed essence.

Yet the unseen-already-there is not in fact conceived on the model of the spatial, physical thing but on that of the divine panorama, the nontemporal and nonspatial totality which is present to the eye of God; for only this panorama has the ideal wholeness and unity required. The margin of shadow around the thing is a margin which contains not only characters that can be brought into consciousness but also characters which are essentially external to or discontinuous with consciousness, because they would particularize the thing and make it atypical. The object cannot really function as the model of an intentional totalization because to totalize it to the mind would be to make it inaccessible to knowing awareness. The characters which are inexplicit in an ideal object, however, must be essentially internal to consciousness; must be, even if not already within the knowing awareness, essentially capable of being brought before that awareness without disrupting it. The unconscious which Hirsch is willing to allow is unconscious not essentially but perspectivally; it is really the same as consciousness or continuous with the essence of consciousness. "Consciousness" is simply the *now* of this essence; "unconsciousness" the not-now. But at another moment, what was unconscious may emerge into the light and what was conscious recede into the shadow; it is all one. It follows, then, that if we eliminate the now-and-then character of time, what we see is an intentional totalization whose model cannot be the contingent, particular object but must be the intentional totalization, incapable of being fragmented because nothing can possibly be independent of or discontinuous to it, of the divine panorama.

IV

Derrida attacked the "use/mention" and "serious/non-serious" distinctions of speech-act theory by claiming that the structure of language contains, essentially, the possibility of theater. It should now be clear that, far from giving the discussion a quirky or capricious turn, Derrida has brought it back to a classical question. If the possibility of theater seems a side issue for speech-act theory, for Plato and Augustine fiction and theater were the preeminent threat to truth.

Here E. A. Havelock's *Preface to Plato* is an important guide.[6] Havelock argues that Plato's attack on poetry in the *Republic* is no subordinate issue but the fulcrum of the entire effort by philosophy to move Greek culture into a new frame of mind or, as Havelock says, a new "syntax." The description that Havelock gives of the transition from the Homeric to the Platonic syntax could almost be read in reverse as the passage from philosophy to deconstruction. The epic was not a "system" but a "plurality of typical instances" (p. 185), an "associative linkage" of events which were extended in space and time (pp. 180–84); Plato separated out the "I" from the "endless series of moods" into which it had been dispersed (p. 200), creating a tenseless syntax in which the "is" as timeless "being" took precedence; act or event was replaced by "formula" (p. 219). Rules were abstracted from typical instances and "integrated" into essential unities (p. 227).

Austin and Searle's privileging of serious, literal speech is a limited case of the general philosophical mistrust of fiction or *mimesis* which Havelock traces in Plato. Derrida in his reply to Searle raises the question of the unconscious, suggesting that what Searle consciously desires he may unconsciously fear, or vice versa. The speech-act "rule" that we can only "promise" what is desired (not what is feared) is therefore called into question. Derrida thus raises the specter of the self divided against itself that Plato declares is fostered by mimetic representation, and especially by dramatic performance (cf. *Diss.*, pp. 186–87n). Plato characterized the performance of the rhapsode Ion as mechanical or automatic repetition, and Havelock shows how all Greece in its enthrallment by Homer seemed to Plato held in the grip of such an automatism. The fully conscious, rational control of truth-intending utterance is the only safeguard against the fragmentation of the self that goes out into its expressions. Only such a rational volition can insure the unity and self-identity of meaning and thus of the self which expresses itself or finds itself in this meaning. Where, as with Hirsch, fiction as such is not treated as dangerous, this is only because fictive utterance is treated as a form of truth-seeking discourse, subject to the law of identity and capable of maintaining the unity of the self. Plato knew better: he knew that the mimetic impulse leaves behind the transparency of the Logos and loses itself in a swirl of phenomena. The "worse" a speaker is, "the readier he will be to imitate everything; he will think nothing unworthy of himself, so he will try to imitate everything in earnest and before a large audience; even . . . claps of thunder and the sounds of winds and hailstorms . . . and Pan's pipes and all manner of instruments; he will bark like a dog and bleat like a sheep and twitter like a bird" (397a–b).

Mechanical or unknowing repetition is the absence of the subject in his fullness as psyche from the scene of meaning. When I engage in mimesis or in iteration in general, I am not fully present in the fullness of my ethical/rational consciousness, and this means that I may not be preserved in my self-identity—either as a self-contained authentic source of utterance or as a function of some transpersonal system or exhaustively definable context. The self is dispersed across a scene of language which is articulated, broken by intervals of space and time, and which at each juncture of articulation at each level of articulation is capable of being broken into elements that can be carried away into new sequences, new scenes, and new sequences of scenes. *This* scene here means nothing by itself. It is like a picture in a series of pictures which tell a story in a picture language, and the single picture makes whatever sense it makes only in the sequence (*PI*, p. 54n, 536–39; *Z*, 176). There is no transcendental order to this sequence, but an indefinite number of possibilities of such sequences running through them, all at the same time. And when we write or speak, or when we act out scenes, we are essentially exposed to having someone else repeat what we have done or said while "grafting" it into a new context—say, in order to mock us. This essential possibility is the positive condition of being able to say or do anything meaningful, but it ensures that the self that is expressed in the characters of meaning will be illimitably torn and carried away into an illimitable spread of new contexts.

It is not an accident that language is addressed to an audience: the gap in space and time between the sender and receiver of a message constitutes the necessity and the possibility of language. Man alone was given the capacity for speech, says Dante in *De Vulgari Eloquentia*, because he alone needed it.[7] Angels, says Dante, enter immediately into each other's thoughts; animals of the same species are the same as each other and so can know others by themselves—but man is impeded by "the grossness and opacity of his mortal body" and each "takes pleasure in being a species to himself." Human beings are material entities differing from each other and separated by space—a condition which is like that of language and gives rise to language. Derrida traces the intricate relations between proximity and distance in Rousseau's account of the origin of language and comments:

It is remarkable that the original dispersion out of which language began continues to mark its milieu and essence. That language must traverse space, be obliged to be spaced, is not an accidental trait but the mark of its origin. In truth, dispersion will never be a past, a prelinguistic situation in which language would certainly have been born only to break with it. The original dispersion leaves its mark within language . . . . articulation, which seemingly introduces difference as an institution, has for ground and space the dispersion that is natural: space itself. (*Gramma.*, p. 232)

There is difference, disunity, or discontinuity between persons and also between the elements of the medium by which this difference is to be overcome. Further, the medium is also the medium of discourse of the self with itself. If iterability, with all that that implies, structures the discourse of the self with itself, then the self is split from itself even as it is split from others.

The transcendental norm or form as rule, systematic structure, or species idea (*eidos*) would overcome the difference of iteration, unifying the self in its discourse with itself and making possible the unity of different selves with each other in their sharing of a self-identical form.

From the point of view of deconstruction, this unifying movement would be the repression of spacing and differences which are the absence and discontinuity of the self—in a word, death. The spaces in discourse and between subjects are where the self as full conscious presence *is not*, where it ceases to be or is annulled. The possibility of repetition of the selfsame is the possibility that the self as full, conscious presence could leap the gaps of articulation and spacing, preserving itself against the cessation of being that is implied by any discontinuity in self-identity. (In the Lucretian formula, "if ever anything is so transformed as to overstep its own limits, this means the immediate death of what was before.") Hence, the discourse on truth, the demand for an objective form which would stand outside of and command discourse, suppresses otherness and seeks to overcome death. It is governed by the desire to "dispense with passage through the world" (*Gramma.*, p. 153) as that which condemns the self to fragmentation and radical otherness (*Gramma.*, pp. 165–66). It seeks to overcome death, understood as a fragmentation or rending of the self, by the extrication of an ideal self out of the empirical or contingent self through a steady contemplation of the ideal object. This object, essence, or telos overcomes death by negating time and the space of otherness, predetermining as coherence and unity the course of emergence in time and space of the acts or words of the self, a coherence and unity which then may be transferred in their unchanging sameness to other minds. This is the nature of the discourse on truth.

If this self-identity of the ideal object could not be guaranteed, if it were subjected to fragmentation and radical discontinuity by the fissure of iterability, then the staging of the self before an audience of differentiated and mutable beings would be the inscription of the self upon a mutable and fragmentable substance. This would constitute the self as mutable or fictional—that is, as mortal—and as impressed upon the receptive substance of fictional or mortal beings, whose audience we reciprocally become and whose fragmentable substance we share. This is the condition of theater or of the rhetorical use of language. That is, the condition of an animal that possesses language.

5   The Hardness of the Law

The foundational phenomenological principle of primordial presence to intuition of the ideal object, writes Derrida, "signifies the certainty . . . that the universal form of all experience (*Erlebnis*), and therefore of all life, has always been and always will be the *present*" (*S&P*, p. 53). That which is capable of being known must be so under the form of presence, and this presence must be thinkable, repeatable as the same, apart from the existence of any empirical knower. *What is* can only be what is *as such* if it is in principle capable of persisting even though I disappear. This means that in order to imagine the persistence of what is, I must imagine my own absence, and then, Derrida argues, the form of presence which I imagine is shadowed by my death. Thus, the thought of my death is the necessary condition for the thought of presence. The form of presence makes possible the definition of the essence of man as wakeful rationality, because the idealized fullness of living consciousness can be conceived only as the correlate of a presence that transcends the absences to which a merely empirical subject is susceptible (forgetfulness, lapses of attention, sleep, death). But this definition of man as *res cogitans* elides the initiating move by which the possibility of my death had to be imagined in order to constitute the present that persists "before my birth and after my death" (*S&P*, p. 54). Having elided this constitutive thought of death, I can then go on to define nonpresence as an accident that afflicts my essence as living consciousness, as an *I am*. *I am* seems to be original, to have "logical priority." Yet,

> if the possibility of my disappearance in general must somehow be experienced in order for a relationship with presence in general to be instituted, we can no longer say that the experience of the possibility of my absolute disappearance (my death) affects me, occurs to an *I am*, and modifies a subject. The *I am*, being experienced only as

an *I am present*, itself presupposes the relationship with presence in general, with being as presence. The appearing of the *I* to itself in the *I am* is thus originally a relation with its own possible disappearance. Therefore, *I am* originally means *I am mortal*. (*S&P*, p. 54)

From this point of view, all objective forms of presence are covertly imagined as stored-up life or wakeful consciousness, and the condition of their possibility, which they thus also have inscribed within them, is death. The insistence on the pure and enduring self-identity of what is as such, whether as physical object, rule, formula, logical truth, or Living Present, is a repression of this condition that inevitably contaminates presence. This repression makes possible a conception of transphenomenal or superhard identity that is covertly theological. The notion of ideal self-identity, of the super-rigidity of logic, is the modern transformation of something that was once guaranteed by God. Aquinas did not need to be bashful about the super-rigidity of *his* logical forms: they were made of the hardest super-substance of all, the mind of God, which is absolutely wakeful life. To Aquinas it was clear that the form or identity of a this-here was one absolutely determinate *ratio* in the mind of God, and that the order of the totality of particular things was also one *ratio* in that mind. Both Wittgenstein and Derrida have argued that modern philosophy has given up God without giving up any of the benefits for which he formerly stood as surety. Wittgenstein:

We say that people condemn a man to death and then we say the Law condemns him to death. "Although the Jury can pardon [acquit?] him, the Law can't." (This *may* mean the Law can't take bribes, etc.) The idea of something super-strict, something stricter than any Judge can be, super-rigidity. . . .

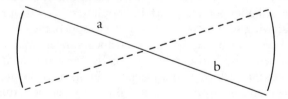

Cf. a lever-fulcrum. The idea of super-hardness. "The geometrical lever is harder than any lever can be. It can't bend." Here you have the case of logical necessity. "Logic is a mechanism made of an infinitely hard material. Logic cannot bend." (Well, no more it can.) This is the way we arrive at a super-something. This is the way certain superlatives come about, how they are used, e.g., the infinite. (*L&C*, pp. 15–16)

It is not the laws of logic that are inexorable, but "*we* that are inexorable in applying the laws" (*RFM* I-118).

Deconstruction is a rethinking of the concepts of law and lawfulness in such a way that law is no longer conceived as a superhardness—but this does not mean that we are now trying just to get away with something, scot-free. The affirmation of the hardness of the law is as much an expression of narcissistic desire as would be the affirmation of infinite freedom. The desire for things to have an ideal unitary self-identity is the desire to be free of the anxiety of what Derrida calls radical otherness. The self-identical thing or logos is precisely what is *always there*, available for us anytime as the opportunity for us as knowers to have full consciousness, full presence, full self-identical wakeful life. On this view, the underlying impulse of the drive for knowledge, objectivity, truth, would be that described by Diotima of Mantineia in the *Symposium*—the desire to have the good thing and to have it always, beyond the boundaries of mortality. To understand the identity of the object or the laws of logic as something *we* have constructed, and to understand this *we* as indefinitely multiple and capable of disagreement, and thus the object and the law as contaminated by our variability, is undoubtedly to picture an anxiety-provoking situation. Anyone who does *not* feel anxious over such a picture has simply not understood or been willing to understand the fearfulness of his plight. Narcissism has almost unlimited resources for denying otherness and can establish itself as well on one side as on the other of deconstruction.

Freud pictures the desire of the narcissistic ego as a desire for an unbroken unity of the self. The ego, he says, is the original "reservoir" of libido, and from this reservoir the soul substance (as we could call libido) is extended out in object cathexes, which Freud compares to the pseudopods of an amoeba.[1] The picture here is formally analogous with that given by Augustine: love, object cathexis, is the extension of one soul into two bodies. The self goes out from itself, but not into otherness: it remains one with itself, having simply "introjected" into its sphere the spatially distinct object. Anxiety, which may be "the fundamental phenomenon and main problem of neurosis,"[2] arises when the self is threatened with the loss of those objects into which it has extended itself, a loss which becomes nothing less than a *sparagmos* of the self. But this separation, this alienation or spacing of parts of the self from itself, is only a derivative of the fundamental "economic" condition *within* the self. The fear of object loss—loss of the mother, of the phallus, or of the goodwill of the superego (with its transformations as social anxiety and the fear of death)—is at bottom fear of "growing tension due to need," against which the organism is originally helpless. "When the infant has found out by experience that an external, perceptible object can put an end to the dangerous situation . . . the content of the danger it fears is displaced from the economic situation . . . onto the condition which determined that situation, viz., the loss of object."[3] But if the ego succeeds in protecting itself against its own instinctual impulses through such processes as projection and repression, what it does is to create a separation between ego and the repressed by the gap of unconsciousness. "The repressed is now, as it were, an outlaw," excluded from the "great organization of the ego."[4]

The pure pleasure ego is present to, conscious of, only that which is homogeneous or continuous with its project of pleasurable unity with itself; the unconscious is the "outside" to which it relegates that within itself which threatens this project. The otherness that separates the pleasure ego from its own instinctual impulses is not, however, created by repression but gives rise to it.[5] Instinctual demand is the demand for satisfaction; without the rising tension of this demand there could be no satisfaction, yet at the same time this rising tension constitutes the threat that has to be avoided.[6] But the unfulfilled demand is already, structurally, an absence even before the psyche is differentiated into conscious and unconscious. It is the not-yet and the not-here, as against the here and now of unity with that which fulfills desire. From the beginning the not-yet and not-here of desire give rise to anxiety, which in turn gives rise to repression. Anxiety is the fear of the otherness within the self, of the space of nonfullness which is marked as such by its relation to a desired object which is not there.[7] And the fear of death is experienced as the fear of the absence or death of the desired *other*. The fear of death is a function of a relation to the self as other and the other as self.

No one can experience his own death: only others can experience one's death. The death we know, the death that is truly *ours*, is the death of the *other*, the one who dies while we live on. Yet this death that is known is one that is somehow outlived. The other death, the one which is not outlived—our "own" death, as it is improperly called—is not known. It can be imagined, perhaps, but the death imagined can only be imagined as nondeath, as though our consciousness had survived the moment of cessation and could now know what this cessation felt like. Thus we imagine ourselves in a casket, lying there with our eyes closed, or buried in a tomb. Or, death can be imagined as though the self were the other: we sit in a funeral house and see ourselves lying dead in the casket. The man who imagines his own death, says Lucretius, does not "oust and pluck himself root and branch out of life, but all unwittingly makes something of himself linger on." Self-pity, pity for one's "own" death, means that he "does not banish himself from the scene nor distinguish sharply enough between himself and that abandoned carcass. He visualizes that object as an on-looker. . . . He does not see that in real death there will be no other self alive to mourn his own decease."[8]

Freud says that what we fear in fearing death is not the nonbeing of the state of being dead, a state which is strictly unimaginable, but a "being overwhelmed and annihilated," a state of complete helplessness in which we feel ourselves abandoned to an overwhelming danger.[9] This annulment of the self is originally the feeling aroused by the disappearance of the mother, and later by other object losses; thus death is experienceable only so far as the self sees itself in the other who goes away or dies. The same effect arises from the other's withdrawal of love. Thus, the anxiety we fig-ure as the fear of death is a constant feature of the relation to any otherness which we cannot enclose in narcissistic unity with ourselves—for example, the audience which we address in speech or in writing, an audience which we know will tear apart the ideal identity we try to project through the meaning which we wish would continue to belong to us.

The narcissistic attempt to develop the unified self-identity of the pure pleasure-ego is the attempt to repress *differance* within the self and so to overcome death as the relation to a mortal other. And it is precisely to the extent that the history of metaphysics is marked by such a project that Der-rida has criticized it. The philosophical project in all its forms insofar as it is determined by the need to posit a structure of "presence"—of an object which in its ideality or concreteness, legality, normality, explicitness, se-riousness, or literality would be simply *there* and available in its persistent self-identity, in fact or in principle, to an empirical or an ideal conscious-ness in its own factual or theoretical self-identity and fullness of presence—this project which presents itself as respect for truth and obedience to the law is to be deconstructed, not in disrespect for truth and disobedience to the law, and certainly not in flight from the demands of a reality which is too stern and fatherly to be faced, but because it is the fantasized fulfill-ment of an infantile wish. Not that there is any purifying ourselves of this wish, but we can see it in its primitive intensity. Derrida's emphasis on the continual movement out of reach of the thing as such must be read in this way, and not as a refusal to face up. For example, he remarks on the "sup-plement" in Rousseau:

> The enjoyment of the *thing itself* is thus undermined, in its act and in its essence, by frustration. One cannot therefore say that it has an es-sence or an act (*eidos, ousia, energeia,* etc.). Something promises itself as it escapes, gives itself as it moves away, and strictly speaking it can-not even be called presence. . . . simple irrationality, the opposite of reason, are less irritating and waylaying for classical logic. The supple-

ment . . . constantly breaches both our pleasure and our virginity. (*Gramma.*, p. 154)

Différance as set forth by Derrida is designed to frustrate the project of repression of frustration and anxiety by describing the relation between self and other—which is not parallel with the relation organism/outer world—as an indissociable synthesis, a structure which is not that of a unity or self-identity but which includes as part of its "identity" its own otherness from itself or inability to fill with its own substance all the space of its "being." This heterogeneous structure contains irreducible tensions between desire and fulfillment, presence and absence, continuity and discontinuity, consciousness and unconsciousness. It does not simply replace or destroy the order and legality of the older organization, but *complicates* them, unsettles the sameness with which we formerly presupposed the structure of our problems and urges us to face up to what has been repressed.

Biological death is only the most striking (and perhaps not the most fearsome) image we have for the anxiety-provoking threat that is an essential aspect of the articulation of all experience. The fear of death is also the fear of theater and rhetoric, of the dispersal of the self across the moveable audience of merely contingent individuals. To attempt to let *différance* be felt is therefore to confront the constitutive contamination of what Heidegger calls the "they" (*das Man*) which makes impossible the authenticity of a pure selfhood, so that otherness and death may exert their necessary force within the self that writes and within the language that is written.

II

Such a deconstructive writing would be related to what Derrida analyzes in Bataille's work as "sovereignty," which is "an absolute risking of death" or the "absolute degree of putting at stake" (*W&D*, p. 256). For Hegel the negative is merely "the reassuring *other* surface of the positive" (*W&D*, p. 259); death or the absolute loss of meaning is never really risked because we always know in advance that through the *Aufhebung* the risk is really an investment that will be recovered in the service of the positive (*W&D*, pp. 255–57).

It does not suffice to risk death if the putting at stake is not permitted to take off, as chance or accident, but is rather invested as the work of the negative. . . .

. . . The poetic or the ecstatic is that *in every discourse* which can open itself up to the absolute loss of its sense, to the (non-) base of

the sacred, of nonmeaning, of un-knowledge or of play, to the swoon
from which it is reawakened by a throw of the dice. (*W&D*, p. 261)

Derrida is here interpreting Bataille's views, and not all the terms used are
terms he himself uses (notably not "the sacred"), but these remarks point
toward the function of language which he has tried to let operate in his
own writing and which is what makes his writing something not quite
philosophy.

I believe it is also the function that operates in Wittgenstein's later work,
and which perhaps he points to when he writes: "Don't *for heaven's sake*, be
afraid [Scheue dich *ja* nicht davor] of talking nonsense! But you must pay
attention to your nonsense" (*Culture*, p. 56). It is true that the second sentence points toward the recuperation of nonsense in the service of sense,
but I have no desire to assimilate Wittgenstein too closely to Bataille; it is
enough to suggest that his willingness to risk nonsense has some kinship
with the "putting at stake" of which Derrida speaks, the allowing of accident or chance to operate in discourse, and that something very different is
operating here from what we normally think of as aiming at truth. Not that
this way of writing is *opposed* to aiming at truth, but that the medium of
language is being worked in a different way. The deconstructive moment
of Wittgenstein's writing is not the whole story, but we have heard too
much about the other, communitarian moment, and not enough about
this one.

Here, the question of skepticism or doubt arises once again. The difficulty is in seeing how deconstructive doubt is not a doubt about things but
about the unrevisability of established linguistic formulas—and not about
just any such formulas, either, but about the ones that are either super-
expressions or that, if we are not careful, tend to lead us toward super-
expressions. Wittgenstein says that if I make an experiment or a calculation
I do not doubt (*OC* 337), and no one is suggesting that we should intro-
duce doubt into, say, the adding up of our bank balance. But if I write
according to the method of deconstruction, then I consider all sorts of
possibilities that I do not consider if I make an experiment or do a calculation. These possibilities are in a sense fictive possibilities, and in a sense
they are not. For I might imagine disappearing chairs, or words that
switch places after I write them, and we could say that these things do not
"really" exist or that I don't "really" believe in them; but they take their
place in this discourse, they have a very real function in the movement of
the investigation, they are part of the deconstructive "calculation." It is at
this point that those who adhere to the "realist" style of metaphysical talk
will say, all right, but that's only language you're talking about, and apart
from that there's the reality which gives us a stable limit, a control over the

multiplication of verbal possibilities. Language may move around as much as you like, but it remains responsible to something that stands still.

The trouble with this way of talking is that the postulated reality is no good whatever unless it can be fixed in a system of concepts, and then we are right back to language again. This does not mean "we can't ever get outside of language"—a remark which I have no idea how to make sense of—but merely that metaphysical propositions are necessarily formulated in language. Hence, in Wittgenstein's way of talking, the interest of remarks like "The chair goes on existing, whether I look at it or not" is conceptual or grammatical; that is, it is primarily an instance of how we talk about what we call "objects":

> But can't it be imagined that there should be no physical objects? I don't know. And yet "There are physical objects" is nonsense. Is it supposed to be an empirical proposition? (*OC* 35)
>
> "A is a physical object" is a piece of instruction which we give only to someone who doesn't yet understand either what "A" means, or what "physical object" means. Thus it is instruction about the use of words, and "physical object" is a logical concept. (Like colour, quantity, . . .) And that is why no such proposition as: "There are physical objects" can be formulated.
>
> Yet we encounter such unsuccessful shots at every turn. (*OC* 36)

This is not in any way to question the accuracy of our ordinary ways of talking about objects—it is, as everyone knows, no part of Wittgenstein's intention to improve or correct our usual ways of talking—but it is a shift of focus that has important consequences. If our interest is in the articulation of concepts like "object" and "reality," we will have no quarrel with the concept or with the uses that follow from that articulation. On the other hand, we will observe that the attempt to limit deconstruction by invocation of "objective reality" is a use whose value or force is not self-evident. What is crucial to be understood is that this invocation is necessarily the bringing into play of a *concept* and not of an unequivocal transcendent something to which the concept refers. The attempt is to draw limits to the play of deconstructive discourse; but no one is questioning whether reality exists, or even whether it draws limits. We are merely asking for the sense of these terms in this context, for the role they play, their articulation and force. The question is whether a discourse that brings into play the concept "objective reality" actually succeeds in enlisting the force of something which cannot be spoken, whether this use is absolutely transparent to its signified, and so quite independent of the rhetorical backgrounds within which it has an unquestioned force, and being thus independent is then capable of exerting a similar force within new contexts; or whether in these contexts its application is none too clear and perhaps quite questionable. Now you might say, "Nevertheless, reality is reality," and perhaps no one will want to quarrel with that—but do we understand what is being said here? Are we being provided with some sort of guide as to the application of this concept in the doubtful spaces of a discourse that seeks to restructure the foundations of our conceptuality? We know that people in love often have illusions about each other, and that eventually they are disillusioned by reality; that a man dying of thirst in the desert may mistake a mirage for reality; that mentally disturbed people must be taught to cope with reality (though this last use begins to create problems). That this word has certain indispensable uses is not in question: what is in question is whether these ordinary uses give the charter to one side of this debate that its proponents rather hastily assume it does (cf. OC 214–15).

Deconstruction probes the boundaries of our concepts, and the sense that these concepts have *within* these boundaries becomes questionable *at* the boundaries. It is as though a concept like "objective reality" provides a clear boundary only when it is looked at from a distance, and then, as we approach closer and closer, the boundary becomes fuzzier and fuzzier and finally disappears altogether. We are then left in a dizzying state of disorientation where our propositions about what is happening look first one way, then another. In *On Certainty* Wittgenstein tries to define the boundary between propositions which are exempt from doubt, as the (perhaps unformulated) framework or unshakeable foundation of all our thinking, and those propositions which lie within the framework and are mutable. Propositions of the former sort are "the earth has existed for a long time," "a table doesn't change or disappear when I am not looking at it," "objects cannot fall upward"; of the second sort, "the earth has existed for X number of years," "it is not possible to fly to the moon," and so on (cf. OC 96–97).

But "there is no sharp division" between the unmoving framework and the moveable contents. This lack of a sharp boundary always, in Wittgenstein, opens up the possibility of radical questioning, since it is impossible to tell in advance where this questioning should stop. Hence the double movement of *On Certainty*, towards the affirmation of base propositions which it would be madness to doubt and towards the calling into question of these very propositions.

The firm framework of beliefs which Wittgenstein ponders in *On Certainty* is clearly closely related to his concept of "ordinary language": it is the assemblage of judgments common to a culture, or to humanity, which is implied by our ordinary uses of language and ways of acting. But this emphasis on "agreement in judgments" which gives us an indubitable framework that we hold in common is complicated by repeated questions of this form: "Might it not be possible for something to happen that threw me entirely off the rails?" (*OC* 517). In fact, Wittgenstein claims what is perhaps not so easy for everyone else as it is for him, that "it is easy to imagine and work out in full detail events which, if they actually came about, would throw us out in all our judgments" (*Z* 393). He is certain, for instance, that he is now in England—to doubt it would be madness—and yet,

> would it not be possible that people came into my room and all declared the opposite? . . . so that I suddenly stood there like a madman? [etc.] (*OC* 420)

> Might I not be shaken if things such as I don't dream of at present were to happen? (*OC* 421)

For Wittgenstein, the "important thing" about such a situation is that "there isn't any sharp line between such a condition and the normal one" (*Z* 393). "If I were sometime to see quite new surroundings from my window instead of the long familiar ones, if things, humans and animals were to behave as they never did before, then I should say something like 'I have gone mad'; *but that would merely be an expression of giving up the attempt to know my way about* [*das wäre nur ein Ausdruck dafür, dass ich es aufgebe, mich auszukennen*]" (*Z* 393; italics added).

There is proof, confirmation, evidence—and then there is what grounds proof, and is in itself incapable of being proved. "Giving grounds . . . comes to an end," and the ground which cannot itself be grounded "is not a kind of *seeing* on our part, it is our *acting*" (*OC* 204). We may, if we like, take a certain perhaps anti-intellectual comfort in the notion that *action* is the ground of our language games. Wittgenstein himself is not entirely free of such an inclination. But if acting is the ground of our language game—if "unshakeable conviction" is "anchored in all my *questions and answers*," that is, already presupposed and implied by not only my answers but my questions, "so anchored that I cannot touch it" (*OC* 103)—then our language games would be beyond the reach of philosophical investigation, and we would be unable to form new concepts which could escape the ossified form of the substratum. Yet that is precisely what "imagining certain very general facts of nature to be different from what we are used to" is designed to do. Looked at one way, the normal way, the foundations are unshakeable; but it is possible to devise other ways of seeing.

> I am not saying: if such-and-such facts of nature were different people would have different concepts (in the sense of a hypothesis). But: if anyone believes that certain concepts are absolutely the correct ones,

and that having different ones would mean not realizing something that we realize—then let him imagine certain very general facts of nature to be different from what we are used to, and the formation of concepts different from the usual ones will become intelligible to him. (*PI*, p. 230)

For deconstruction, the entity is monstrous. The scene and every element of the scene before us swarm with accidental characters that threaten to squirm away in every direction—a Medusa's head alive with snakes that could get away. But are snakes really so horrifying? And suppose they did get away; suppose the scene before me, always threatening to get out of control now that the hardness of the law has been questioned, exploded into its characters and left me completely disoriented before apparent chaos and anarchy? "Then I should say something like 'I have gone mad'; *but that would merely be an expression of giving up the attempt to know my way about.*"

Notes

Preface

1. See my review of two of these books, *Deconstruction: Theory and Practice*, by Christopher Norris (London and New York: Methuen, 1982) and *On Deconstruction: Theory and Criticism after Structuralism*, by Jonathan Culler (Ithaca: Cornell University Press, 1982), in *Modern Language Notes* 100, no. 4 (May 1985).

2. Thus my project here is to some degree parallel with that of Richard Rorty in his *Philosophy and the Mirror of Nature* (Princeton: Princeton University Press, 1979). However, my reading of Wittgenstein differs fundamentally from Rorty's. Rorty, a true philosopher, pays no attention to the problem of the materiality of the signifier; indeed, he thinks no such problem exists.

3. For the interpretation of Wittgenstein as therapist, see John Wisdom, *Philosophy and Psycho-Analysis* (Berkeley and Los Angeles: University of California Press, 1969), especially the essays "Philosophy, Anxiety, and Novelty" (pp. 112–19), "Philosophy and Psycho-Analysis" (pp. 169–81), and the remarkable "Philosophy, Metaphysics, and Psycho-Analysis" (pp. 248–82); O. K. Bouwsma, "The Blue Book," in Bouwsma, *Philosophical Essays* (Lincoln: University of Nebraska Press, 1965), pp. 175–201; and Bouwsma, "A Difference between Ryle and Wittgenstein," in *Towards a New Sensibility*, ed. J. L. Craft and Ronald E. Hustwit (Lincoln: University of Nebraska Press, 1983), pp. 17–32.

4. An interesting attempt at using ordinary language to tease more meaning out of obscure metaphysical texts (in this case, Heidegger's) is Stephen Erickson, *Language and Being: An Analytic Phenomenology* (New Haven: Yale University Press, 1970).

5. J. N. Findlay, "My Encounters with Wittgenstein," *Philosophical Forum* 4 (1973): 167–85.

6. For discussion and bibliography on this point, see Nicholas Gier, *Wittgenstein and Phenomenology* (Dordrecht, Holland: D. Reidel, 1979). Gier does not mention an interesting article on the subject that brings Derrida in as well: Wataru Kuroda, "Phenomenology and Grammar: A Consideration of the Relation between Husserl's *Logical Investigations* and Wittgenstein's Later Philosophy," *Analecta Husserliana* 7 (1978): 90–108.

161

Introduction

1. David Pole, who missed the mark in most of his criticisms of Wittgenstein, asked exactly the right question when he remarked that "it is hard not to ask oneself what sort of linguistic activity Wittgenstein himself is engaged in, what game is this, and where are we to look for its rules?" (David Pole, *The Later Philosophy of Wittgenstein* [London: Athlone Press, 1958], p. 97). See the devastating critique of Pole's book by Stanley Cavell in his well-known essay, "The Availability of Wittgenstein's Later Philosophy," in *Must We Mean What We Say?* (New York: Charles Scribner's Sons, 1969), pp. 44–72.

2. See E. K. Specht, *The Foundations of Wittgenstein's Late Philosophy* (New York: Barnes and Noble, 1969), pp. 29–37. Specht comments that "the problems arising from Aristotle's approach to the philosophy of language have remained amazingly unchanged to the present day" (p. 35n).

3. See David Pears, "The Relation between Wittgenstein's Picture Theory of Propositions and Russell's Theories of Judgment," in *Wittgenstein: Sources and Perspectives*, ed. C. G. Luckhardt (Ithaca: Cornell University Press, 1979), pp. 190–212. Pears concludes that the "metaphysics" of the *Tractatus*, "unlike Russell's, is 'Aristotelian'" (p. 211).

4. Anthony Kenny, *Wittgenstein* (London: Allen Lane, Penguin Press, 1973), p. 59.

5. My account of Aristotle mainly follows Joseph Owens, *The Doctrine of Being in the Aristotelian Metaphysics* (1951), 3d ed., rev. (Toronto: Pontifical Institute of Medieval Studies, 1978). Hereafter cited in the text.

   In an article, "Aristotle on Categories," Owens explains that "in Aristotelian logic the concrete individual is indeed the primary substance. It is the basic subject of all predication. From the logician's viewpoint, accordingly, it is the primary being (*ousia*). But that does not at all mean that the concrete individual is primary being or primary substance in the real order. In the *Metaphysics*, Aristotle's doctrine to the contrary is explicit. Form is the primary substance" (*Aristotle: The Collected Papers of Joseph Owens*, ed. John R. Catan [Albany: State University of New York Press, 1981], p. 19). "The Stagirite's explanation is given wholly in terms of actuality and potentiality within a formal (as contrasted with existential) order—the one Aristotelian term *eidos* serves for the object of both the potential knowledge given by the 'species' and the actual knowledge by way of 'form.' Of itself the Aristotelian form is actual. It is multiplied by matter and thereby assumes singularity; it is able to give universal knowledge of the other singulars in which it may be found, and so is potentially universal" (pp. 184–185n). See also Owens, *The Doctrine of Being*, p. 393n.

6. The question of precisely how we get from the intuition of essence in direct perception of an object to the discursive formula of essence is difficult and appears not to be resolved by Aristotle. See J. M. LeBlond, "Aristotle on Definition," in *Articles on Aristotle*, vol. 3, *Metaphysics*, ed. Jonathan Barnes, Malcolm Schofield, and Richard Sorabji (London: Gerald Duckworth and Co., 1979), pp. 63–79. LeBlond concludes that Aristotle, "given his conception of knowl-

edge," remains "oblivious" of the "chasm between being and knowing" (p. 76).

7. This is roughly the notion of "presence" criticized by Heidegger, the "enduring" in "outward appearance" of individual *beings* which had obscured the more primal sense of *Being* (Heidegger, *The End of Philosophy* [New York: Harper & Row, 1973], pp. 5–10). Heidegger says that the *energeia* of the individual *this* is "incomprehensible in its beingness" when thought in terms of the eidos (p. 9).

8. Werner Jaeger, *Aristotle: Fundamentals of the History of His Development* (1934), 2d ed., trans. Richard Robinson (Oxford: Clarendon Press, 1948), p. 382.

9. Curt Arpe, *Das Ti En Einai Bei Aristoteles*, rpt. ed. (New York: Arno Press, 1976), p. 8n.

10. Cf. Werner Marx, *Heidegger and the Tradition*, trans. Theodore Kisiel and Murray Greene (Evanston: Northwestern University Press, 1971), chap. 1, "The Form and Meaning of the Aristotelian Ousia." Marx writes that "for Aristotle, the Being and essence of the particular being was in principle unconditionally and unobstructedly intelligible. This intelligibility resulted for Aristotle from the supposition of an unconditional sovereignty of the principle of complete transparence. The early Greeks had already termed this principle the *nous* [mind]. . . . only because *ousia* is thinkable, because it is ready for thinking, man, through the intuitive beholding *noesis*, is able to think it" (p. 38).

11. Derrida sounds very Heideggerian in passages like this one. It is beyond the range of the present study to investigate the enormously complex question of Derrida's relation to Heidegger. Here let us simply note that Derrida believes Heidegger in some profound way remains within that "thought of presence" whose critique Heidegger himself has elaborated (*Pos.*, p. 55). Derrida argues that "if Heidegger has radically deconstructed the domination of metaphysics by the *present*, he has done so in order to lead us to think the presence of the present" (*Margins*, p. 131).

12. See the extensive discussion of this point in Karl Bärthlein's *Die Transzendentalienlehre der alten Ontologie* (Berlin and New York: de Gruyter, 1972), pp. 210–71. Bärthlein concludes that through all the obscurities of Aristotle's presentation, the principle he is defending has to be the principle of identity, which can be stated in either a positive form (A is A) or a negative one (A is not not-A); the negative form is often called the principle of contradiction.

13. Cf. "White Mythology," *Margins*, pp. 247–48.

14. J. F. Mora, "On the Early History of Ontology," *Philosophy and Phenomenological Research* 24, no. 1 (September 1963): 36–47.

15. Paul Natorp in 1888 remarked the kinship between Aristotle's being qua being and Kant's "object-in-general." Aristotle says that the science he is seeking is that of the "first causes and principles" which are themselves knowable in the highest degree and the cause of the knowability of things. Natorp comments: "The word 'first' (*protos*) of course has here the established technical Aristotelian sense of the conceptually fundamental . . . ; it is therefore a question of what is most universal, most abstract, with respect to that which can in general be the object of a scientific investigation. This highest, because most universal and abstract, object, is, however, . . . the fundamental concept of an 'object-

in-general,' as we might almost render in the Kantian expression the Aristotelian being qua being." Then Natorp adds, in a footnote, that there remains an "essential difference": Aristotle does not realize that an investigation of the object-in-general has meaning only as an investigation into the conditions and laws of the objectivity of the understanding (Natorp, "Thema und Disposition der aristotelischen Metaphysik," *Philosophische Monatshefte* 24 [1888]: 39).

Bärthlein has recently worked out in great detail the historical and conceptual connections of the Aristotelian "transcendental doctrine" with that of Kant. In addition to the *Transzendentalienlehre*, cited above (n. 12), see his "Von der 'Transzendentalphilosophie der Alten' zu der Kants," *Archiv für Geschichte der Philosophie* 57 (1976): 353–93. Bärthlein argues that the kind of knowledge sought by Aristotle in his search for a science of being qua being must be knowledge of the universal conditions that must be valid for any existent thing in general. Such knowledge cannot be abstracted from concrete particulars, but must be implicit in our knowing as its condition of possibility; thus Aristotle's inquiry is implicitly transcendental (*Transzendentalienlehre*, pp. 155–56).

Heidegger argues the continuity between classical ontology and Kant's transcendental inquiry in *Kant and the Problem of Metaphysics*, trans. James S. Churchill (Bloomington: Indiana University Press, 1962), esp. pp. 9–22. According to Heidegger, what we know when we know the *a priori* principles of knowledge is the "constitution of the being of the Essent," with Essent understood as an object in general, prior to the knowledge of any determinate object; thus Kant's *a priori* knowledge is really ontological. Heidegger's argument is the converse of Bärthlein's.

16. See Ronald P. Morrison, "Kant, Husserl, and Heidegger on Time and the Unity of 'Consciousness,'" *Philosophy and Phenomenological Research* 39, no. 2 (December 1978): 182–98.

17. Immanuel Kant, *Critique of Pure Reason*, trans. Norman Kemp Smith (1929; New York: Humanities Press, 1950).

18. Cf. Morrison, "Kant, Husserl, and Heidegger on Time."

19. Bärthlein, "Transzendentalphilosophie," p. 374. In this article Bärthlein concludes that the persistence of the transcendental validity of the principle of contradiction forms the connecting link between Kant and his predecessors (p. 374). Like Natorp, however, Bärthlein holds that Kant's predecessors failed to realize clearly that the study of the highest principles of the possibility of objects necessarily refers us back to the understanding as synthesizing and unifying faculty (p. 383; cf. *Transzendentalienlehre*, pp. 155–56).

20. There are two major forms of idealization from which I want to distinguish Wittgenstein's view. (1) The notion that the order of an activity is determined by our intending a rule, with the rule conceived as intrinsically linked, by virtue of its identity as just that rule, to the steps of the activity it governs. This picture can be criticized either by focusing on the mode of being of the rule itself, as Gordon Baker does ("Following Wittgenstein," in *Wittgenstein: To Follow a Rule*, ed. Steven H. Holtzman and Christopher M. Leich [London: Routledge & Kegan Paul, 1981], pp. 31–71), or by focusing on the psycho-

logical side, the realization of the rule in the mental or brain-state of the person who follows it, as Saul Kripke does (*Wittgenstein: On Rules and Private Language* [Cambridge: Harvard University Press, 1982]). These two critiques seem to me valid, faithful to Wittgenstein, and for the most part compatible with each other; both are ultimately "communitarian" interpretations of Wittgenstein that take as given and fundamental the contingent fact of community agreement and deny the causality of the rule or rule-intention. However, Baker's emphasis is closer to the deconstructive emphasis proposed in the present study (see the next note). (2) The notion that the order of an activity is determined by a rule which exists, not in our minds, but in some sense in the activity itself, as a sociological rather than psychological reality. This is Peter Winch's adaptation of Wittgenstein's critique of (1) above (*The Idea of a Social Science and Its Relation to Philosophy*, ed. R. E. Holland [New York: Humanities Press, 1965]). Though Winch denies that human activities can be "summed up in a set of explicit precepts" (p. 55), he nevertheless holds that "human actions exemplify rules" and can be grasped only as an "embodiment of principles" (pp. 58–63). For a Wittgenstein critique of Winch's form of "Wittgensteinian" account, see Hannah Pitkin, *Wittgenstein and Justice* (Berkeley and Los Angeles: University of California Press, 1972), pp. 254–63.

21. This point is laid out in detail in Chapter 2 below. See also Baker, "Following Wittgenstein." Baker argues that Wittgenstein's goal in the *Investigations* is "to render transparently ridiculous the idea of a hidden or unconscious *following* of a *rule*" (pp. 42–43). In his middle period, Baker says, Wittgenstein did move from his *Tractatus* mythology of objects to a mythology of rules, according to which the meaning of a word was the "totality of rules for its use" (p. 45). But in the later work Wittgenstein moved away from the rules mythology and showed that "the idea of a rule functioning as a transcendent standard of correctness is incoherent" (p. 54). Rules are not "abstract entities" (p. 59). Christopher Peacocke thinks Baker's interpretation misses Wittgenstein's main point, which is that we cannot follow a rule privately ("Reply: Rule Following: The Nature of Wittgenstein's Arguments," in Holtzman and Leich, *Wittgenstein*, pp. 72–95), but Baker's argument cuts deeper than Peacocke sees. The "communitarian" interpretation of Peacocke and Kripke is accurate so far as it goes (though Baker rejects it), but requires supplementing and filling out in the fashion Baker pursues. Baker is concerned not just with what "following a rule" is, but with what *rules* are, or rather, with what, if we don't subject the concept to critical examination, we are likely to imagine that rules are. Baker correctly emphasizes what Henry LeRoy Finch has called Wittgenstein's "phenomenalism" (*Wittgenstein: The Later Philosophy* [Atlantic Highlands, N.J.: Humanities Press, 1977], pp. 169–91). Rules are best conceived as objects used in a particular way, without any intrinsic properties that make them rules (Baker, pp. 58–64). This view breaks down the sense of a rule as having a "*form*" that makes it identical with itself (p. 60), and thus brings out the radical way in which Wittgenstein rejects the classical metaphysics of entity. All of this is ignored when we focus merely on the agreement of the community as the determinant of correct rule-following. Baker's interpretation is therapy against

views that are widely but inexplicitly held, and is the necessary prelude to an investigation into how agreement is underlain by the possibility of multiplicity (cf. Chapter 4, below); whereas the communitarian view by itself tends to imply that Wittgenstein is committed to the status quo and has nothing to say about the emergence of new practices.

22. All of this has an obviously Hegelian sound to it. The difference between deconstruction and Hegelian dialectic is fundamental, however, and can be summed up by saying that in deconstruction there is no *Aufhebung*.

23. Cf. *Margins*, p. 318: "This structural possibility of being severed from its referent or signified . . . seems to me to make of every mark, even if oral, a grapheme in general, that is, . . . the nonpresent *remaining* of a differential mark cut off from its alleged 'production' or origin. And I will extend the law even to all experience in general, if it is granted that there is no experience of *pure* presence, but only chains of differential marks."

24. In "Ousia and Grammē," one of his most important essays, Derrida characterizes the "vulgar concept of time" exposed by Heidegger in *Being and Time* as follows:

> Time is defined according to its relation to an elementary part, the now, which itself is affected—as if it were not already temporal—by a time which negates it in determining it as a past now or a future now. The *nun* [now], the element of time, in this sense is not in itself temporal. It is temporal only in becoming temporal, that is, in ceasing to be, in passing over to nothingness in the form of being-past or being-future. Even if it is envisaged as (past or future) nonbeing, the now is determined as the intemporal kernel of time, the nonmodifiable nucleus of temporal modification, the inalterable form of temporalization. (*Margins*, p. 40)

> The current now is not time, because it is present; time is not (a being) to the extent that it is not (present). This means that it appears one already has determined the origin and essence of no-thing as time, as nonpresent under the heading of the 'not yet' or 'already no longer.' (P. 50)

> Thus, because time, in its Being, is thought on the basis of the present, it is also strangely thought as nonbeing (or as an impure, composite being). (P. 52).

> In repeating the question of being in the transcendental horizon of time, *Being and Time* thus brings to light the omission which permitted metaphysics to believe that it could think time on the basis of a being already silently predetermined in its relation to time. If all of metaphysics is engaged by this gesture, *Being and Time*, in this regard at least, constitutes a decisive step beyond or within metaphysics. The question was evaded [by metaphysics] because it was put in terms of belonging to being or to nonbeing, being already determined as being-present. It is what the question evades that Heidegger puts back into play from the first part of *Being and Time* on: time, then, will be that on the basis of which the Being of beings is indicated, and not that whose possibility will be derived on the basis of a

being already constituted (and in secret temporally predetermined), as a present being . . . , that is, as substance or object. (P. 47)

However, Derrida argues against Heidegger that the texts of Aristotle and Hegel yield up not only the "vulgar concept of time" that Heidegger in *Being and Time* finds there, but also the resources that Heidegger uses in order to construct the other concept of time that he opposes to the "vulgar concept" (*Margins*, pp. 62–63).

25. Husserl's version of retention of a past Now, however, abides by "a linear, objective, and mundane model" according to which Now B retains an *immediately preceding* Now A and no possibility exists for a Now X to take the place of Now A. Husserl's model "would prohibit that, by a delay that is inadmissible to consciousness, an experience be determined, in its very present, by a present which would not have preceded it immediately but would be considerably 'anterior' to it. It is the problem of the deferred effect (*Nachträglichkeit*) of which Freud speaks" (*Gramma.*, p. 67). Furthermore, Derrida wants to speak of this Now X as *never* having been present, as retrospectively constituted. See "Freud and the Scene of Writing," in *W&D*, pp. 202–3.

26. Roman Ingarden, *The Literary Work of Art*, trans. George G. Grabowicz (Evanston: Northwestern University Press, 1973), p. 38.

27. Ibid.

28. Don Ihde, "Wittgenstein's 'Phenomenological Reduction,'" in Ihde, *Sense and Significance* (Pittsburgh: Duquesne University Press, 1973), p. 156.

29. See the discussion of "transitive essences" in Chapter 3.

30. See Joseph Owens, "The Grounds of Universality in Aristotle," in *Aristotle*, pp. 48–58. "Where being is explained ultimately by form, as in Aristotle, the difficulty that each act of being means existential distinction is not felt. Within its own metaphysical framework, therefore, his notion of sameness in form does not seem to run into self-contradiction. But it can hardly hope to prove complete or satisfactory when questions in terms of existence are encountered" (p. 55).

31. Derrida remarks on Aristotle's assigning metaphor a status inferior to truth in "White Mythology," *Margins*, pp. 230–50.

32. Philosophy's concern with beings leads to the fixing of the essence of words as their capacity to name or refer; thus, for Aristotle only those words are fully meaningful "which have meaning in themselves," which "have an immediate relation to an object or rather to a unity of meaning"—the noun and verb. Other words belong to the semantic order so far as they are nominalizable, that is, so far as they can claim "complete and independent signification . . . outside any syntactic relation" (*Margins*, p. 233). Derrida urges the semantic fertility of syntax and syncategoremes in "The Double Session," *Diss.*, pp. 172–285. There Derrida speaks of the "irreducible excess of the syntactic over the semantic" in the text of Mallarmé.

33. James Bogen, arguing against the notion that Wittgenstein provides a "language-game theory of meaning," points out that in the later work Wittgenstein has given up the idea of a "rule-calculus" as characteristic of meaningful language-use, and can no longer use it to distinguish meaning and under-

standing from stimulus response. "A language-game theory of meaning would somehow have to distinguish linguistic use of signs from stimulus-response mechanisms by appeal to the kinds of practice which constitute them. This in turn presupposes a distinction between linguistic and non-linguistic practices, and the later works do not tell us how to draw this distinction. They do not tell us the difference between a language and a nonlanguage game" (*Wittgenstein's Philosophy of Language: Some Aspects of Its Development* [New York: Humanities Press, 1972], p. 201).

Chapter 1

1. This situation shows signs of changing. With the increased availability of Husserl's work in English, especially the *Logical Investigations* (Findlay's translation appeared in 1970), Husserl is beginning to attract the attention he deserves from analytic philosophers.
2. Husserl's vision of the chain of philosophical projects, forming an unfolding unity despite their opposition to one another (*Crisis*, pp. 70–73), would seem to have influenced Derrida's own view of the unity of the great philosophical text.
3. For a discussion of the problem with Hume's account of perception and Husserl's solution to the problem, see Aron Gurwitsch, "On the Intentionality of Consciousness," in *Philosophical Essays in Memory of Edmund Husserl*, ed. Marvin Faber (New York: Greenwood Press, 1968), pp. 65–83.
4. Husserl's use of the expression "content [*Inhalt*] of consciousness" here is a bit puzzling, since one is not *conscious* of this content. The sensational content is "had" or "experienced," but one is conscious, not of it, but of the object which is its source. The explanation of Husserl's usage comes in his peculiar definition of "content": "Whatever can be regarded as part of a whole, and as truly constituting it in real (*reell*) fashion, belongs to the content of the whole" (*LI*, p. 540). Thus, sense data are part of the real, psychological constitution of consciousness, and in this sense "content" of consciousness, though not conscious.
5. Husserl later revised his conception of the meaning-bestowing activity of consciousness, rejecting the notion of raw sense-data in favor of a more radical view, according to which consciousness "constitutes" the being of the object at a preverbal level. Conceptual grasping of an object thus operates not upon raw material but upon material that has already been given implicit conceptual form. See Robert Sokolowski, *The Formation of Husserl's Concept of Constitution* (The Hague: Martinus Nijhoff, 1970), for a lucid account of this development in Husserl's thought. Sokolowski concludes that even in the later doctrine, there remains a "facticity" which consciousness encounters and does not create. The advantage of the doctrine of constitution is that it overcomes the "abruptness" of the sense-data schema, making possible a more finely differentiated account of experience (Sokolowski, pp. 195–214). He thus sees the process of constitution as a sort of gestation culminating in the conceptually formed object. For another view, see the first two essays in Ludwig Land-

grebe, *The Phenomenology of Edmund Husserl*, ed. Donn Welton (Ithaca: Cornell University Press, 1981). Landgrebe argues that "the hyle . . . belongs to the immanence of transcendental becoming itself" (p. 63). See also the eloquent concluding pages of Welton's essay "Intentionality and Language in Husserl's Phenomenology," *Review of Metaphysics* 27 (December 1973): 260–97. Welton emphasizes the productive role of language in a dialectical encounter with objects.

6. J. N. Findlay, Translator's Introduction to *LI*, p. 10.

7. Gurwitsch, "Intentionality," p. 77.

8. See Dallas Willard, "The Paradox of Logical Psychologism: Husserl's Way Out," in *Husserl: Expositions and Appraisals*, ed. Frederick Elliston and Peter McCormick (Notre Dame: University of Notre Dame Press, 1977), pp. 11–17. Willard identifies nine features of the "standard, anti-Psychologistic view of propositions" found in a variety of modern works.

9. That is, intentional objects are not a "real part or moment of consciousness" or a "psychic Datum"; nevertheless, their transcendence is constituted "in the immanent sphere," in mental acts, but as an "ideality" or "irreality" (*Logic*, pp. 165–66).

10. See the concise survey of interpretations of Husserl's idealism by Joseph J. Kockelmans, "Husserl's Transcendental Idealism," in *Phenomenology*, ed. Kockelmans (Garden City, N.Y.: Anchor Books, 1967), pp. 183–93.

11. Iso Kern, "The Three Ways to the Transcendental Phenomenological Reduction," in Elliston and McCormick, *Husserl*, p. 144.

12. Dagfinn Føllesdal, "Husserl's Notion of Noema," *Journal of Philosophy* 66, no. 20 (October, 1969): 681.

13. The possibility of this formalism depends upon the distinction between what Frege called "sense" (*Sinn*) and "reference" (*Bedeutung*). Though Husserl never used the terms as Frege did (in *LI*, *Sinn* and *Bedeutung* are synonyms, and "reference" is *Gegenstand*), the distinction is fundamental to the *Logical Investigations*. It has been thought that Husserl learned it from Frege, but J. N. Mohanty has recently argued that Husserl may have arrived at it independently. See "Husserl and Frege: A New Look at Their Relationship," in *Readings on Husserl's Logical Investigations*, ed. Mohanty (The Hague: Martinus Nijhoff, 1977), pp. 22–32.

14. Roman Ingarden (*The Literary Work of Art*, trans. George G. Grabowicz [Evanston: Northwestern University Press, 1973], p. 191) points out that it is always possible to "thematize" in its own right that which performs the representing function; yet this thematization would occur, for phenomenology, as a possibility whose intrinsic sense would be determined by its place within the larger framework in which the representer is predestined to pass over into the represented.

15. Ernst Tugendhat, "Phenomenology and Linguistic Analysis," in Elliston and McCormick, *Husserl*, pp. 325–37.

16. Ibid., p. 336. Suzanne Cunningham similarly argues that language is essential to the consciousness that performs the eidetic reduction, and that language necessarily brings intersubjectivity into the phenomenological consciousness,

precluding the complete bracketing of the world (*Language and the Phenomenological Reductions of Edmund Husserl* [The Hague: Martinus Nijhoff, 1976]).

17. Tugendhat, "Phenomenology and Linguistic Analysis," p. 326.

18. The conflict between Tugendhat's philosophically orthodox view of linguistic analysis and a more radical Wittgensteinian approach is brought out very sharply in the papers by Tugendhat and Anthony Manser in *Linguistic Analysis and Phenomenology*, ed. Wolfe Mays and S. C. Brown (Lewisburg, Pa.: Bucknell University Press, 1972), pp. 256–66 and 273–80. Manser's view of Wittgenstein is in fundamental ways close to deconstruction.

19. Welton, "Intentionality and Language," p. 278.

20. Ibid., pp. 289, 293.

21. J. N. Mohanty, *Edmund Husserl's Theory of Meaning* (The Hague: Martinus Nijhoff, 1976), p. xix n. Mohanty seems to me correct in this assessment of Husserl's theory of meaning. If so, Suzanne Cunningham would have missed the mark in trying to convict Husserl of having overlooked the essential role of intersubjectivity. (For a reply to Cunningham, see Peter Hutcheson, "Husserl and Private Languages," *Philosophy and Phenomenological Research* 57, no. 1 [September 1981]: 111–19.)

Mohanty rejects Husserl's use of interior monologue to reveal the essence of meaning as "ruinous" in its potential "psychologism," which undermines Husserl's own belief in the "objectivity of meaning": "The true nature of thought . . . manifests itself in reflection upon its communicative function; for here in communicative speech, subjectivity is overcome and thought exhibits itself as an objective, over-individual process" (Mohanty, p. 15). Derrida's point is completely different. He is not concerned with privacy versus intersubjectivity but with the question of whether meaning can be immediately present to thought, a question which opens a revision of the concepts of both privacy and intersubjectivity.

22. From Derrida's perspective, there is no essential difference between "fulfillment" as a real possibility and as an unachievable telos. Even as telos, fulfillment dominates philosophical discourse, lining up its terms like iron filings in obedience to a magnet. Welton's interpretation of perception as a dialectic of presence and absence is still oriented toward this telos: "The in-itself drawing perception is the presence of the object as future" (Welton, "Structure and Genesis in Husserl's Phenomenology," in Elliston and McCormick, *Husserl*, p. 66). Cf. Derrida:

> Horizon is the always-already-there of a future which keeps the indetermination of its infinite openness intact (even though this future was *announced* to consciousness). As the structured determination of every material indeterminacy, a horizon is always virtually present in every experience; for it is at once the unity and the incompletion of that experience—the anticipated unity in every incompletion. The notion of horizon converts critical philosophy's state of abstract possibility into the concrete infinite potentiality secretly presupposed therein. The notion of horizon thus makes the *a priori* and the teleological coincide. (*Intro.*, p. 117)

The last sentence seems to me to contain one of Derrida's most important insights.

23. See the Introduction.

24. "The accomplishment of the turning-toward is what we call *the being-awake of the ego*. More precisely, it is necessary to distinguish being-awake as (the factual accomplishment of an act from being-awake as) potentiality. . . . To be awake is to direct one's regard to something" (*EJ*, p. 79). Cf. Aristotle, *De Anima*, 412b–413a: "As, then, the cutting of the axe or the seeing of the eye is full actuality [*entelecheia*], so, too, is the waking state; while the soul is actuality in the same sense as eyesight and the capacity [*dynamis*] of the instrument" (trans. R. D. Hicks [Cambridge: Cambridge University Press, 1907]).

25. Ferdinand Saussure, *Course in General Linguistics* (New York: McGraw-Hill, 1959), pp. 113, 118. It is not clear what Saussure means when he says we are "conscious" of the *a/b* difference. To say that this difference constitutes the meaning of the term does not imply that we therefore are "conscious" of it. Difference is just the sort of thing that evades the perceptual mode of consciousness—and what other model is Saussure relying on?

26. We could compare Derrida's position with respect to phenomenology, when he asserts the essential character of "constitutive spacing," to that of Leucippus when he asserted the *diastema* against the plenum of the Eleatics.

27. See Chapter 3.

28. I must emphasize once again that from the deconstructive standpoint most of what is called "linguistic analysis" is open to the charge of having an uncritical attitude toward the role of language.

29. The problematic or self-deconstructing character of his usage of the "as such" must be in the foreground of any reading of Derrida. In a recent, important essay, Rodolphe Gasché ("Deconstruction as Criticism," *Glyph* 6 [1979]: 177–215) correctly emphasizes the importance of a knowledge of phenomenology to the understanding of deconstruction, but pushes so hard in the direction of philosophy that he assimilates deconstruction too closely to it. In repeatedly asserting that the arche-trace manifests itself *as such*, Gasché seems to me to stop short of the radical questioning of the concept of as-suchness which would keep the arche-trace from becoming another metaphysical principle. Thus Gasché is able to say that Derrida has identified a "primordial structure" which "functions indeed like a sort of *deep structure*" underlying the conceptual systems of philosophy (p. 193). It is true that Derrida does often work with the kind of conceptual move Gasché describes, of formulating a generative principle which encompasses the "conceptual dyads" of philosophy while baffling definition in their terms. But this move is, as Richard Rorty has seen ("Philosophy as a Kind of Writing: An Essay on Derrida," *New Literary History* 10 [1978–79]: 141–60), just that moment in Derrida's discourse that is most in danger of being reabsorbed into the tradition against which he is working: "That tradition is kept going by the following dialectical movement: first one notices that something all-encompassing and unconditioned is being treated as if it were just one more limited and conditioned thing. Then one explains that this thing is so distinctive that it requires an entirely different

vocabulary. . . . Finally, one's disciples become so bemused by one's new vocabulary that they think one has invented a new field of inquiry, and the whole sequence starts up again" (p. 151). "One can comment cynically on this passage that, if you want to know what notion takes the place of God for a writer in the onto-theological tradition, always look for the one which he says does not exist" (p. 153).

30. See Gerald Else, "The Terminology of the Ideas," *Harvard Studies in Classical Philology* 47 (1936): 17–55, esp. sec. IV, pp. 38–42.

Chapter 2

1. See Rush Rhees, *Without Answers* (New York: Schocken Books, 1969), pp. 169 ff., on Wittgenstein's repeated admonitions to him to "Go the bloody *hard* way" in philosophy.

2. Wittgenstein, "Remarks on Frazer's *Golden Bough*," in *Wittgenstein: Sources and Perspectives*, ed. C. G. Luckhardt (Ithaca: Cornell University Press, 1979).

3. A. M. Quinton, "Excerpt from 'Contemporary British Philosophy,'" in *Wittgenstein: The "Philosophical Investigations*," ed. George Pitcher (Garden City, N.Y.: Anchor Books, 1966), pp. 9–10. Quinton goes on to say that "the two generations of British philosophers who have come under [Wittgenstein's] influence have in effect simply ignored" the "self-denying ordinances" by which Wittgenstein tried to dissociate what he was doing from the usual theorizing activity of philosophers.

4. On the "graft" see Chapter 3.

5. On the tortuous process of composition of the *Investigations*, see the detailed account by G. H. von Wright, "The Origin and Composition of Wittgenstein's *Investigations*," in Luckhardt, *Wittgenstein*, pp. 138–60. Because he wrote in "remarks," Wittgenstein was able to detach them from numerous manuscripts and arrange them into various combinations, one of which eventually became the published version of the *Investigations*. With the increasing availability of the mass of Wittgenstein's unpublished material, there is a danger that the integrity of this carefully honed text will be entirely lost in the detail of responsible historical and textual scholarship. More attention needs to be paid to why Wittgenstein chose just *these* remarks in just *this* sequence, and did not publish the rest. On this topic see Gordon Baker, "Following Wittgenstein," in *Wittgenstein: To Follow a Rule*, ed. Steven H. Holtzman and Christopher M. Leich (London: Routledge & Kegan Paul, 1981), pp. 33–36. One very important suggestion made by von Wright is that Wittgenstein may have been planning to use the volume now published as *Zettel* as the middle part of a trilogy of which the present Part One of the *Investigations* would have been the first part and the present Part Two the third.

6. See O. K. Bouwsma, "A Difference between Ryle and Wittgenstein," *Rice University Studies* 58, no. 3 (Summer 1972): 77–87.

7. Kripke is undoubtedly right, however, in his argument that the private language problem discussed later in the *Investigations* has already been resolved by 242. See Saul Kripke, *Wittgenstein: On Rules and Private Language* (Cambridge, Mass.: Harvard University Press, 1982).

8. Cf. *Culture*, p. 17: "What has to be overcome is a difficulty having to do with the will, rather than with the intellect."

9. See Robert L. Arrington, "*Mechanism* and *Calculus*: Wittgenstein on Augustein's Theory of Ostension," in Luckhardt, *Wittgenstein*, pp. 303–38. Arrington shows how for Wittgenstein "even in an ostensive definition the meaning equation is purely linguistic" (p. 338).

10. The notion of "absorption" is taken from David Pears, "The Relation between Wittgenstein's Picture Theory of Propositions and Russell's Theories of Judgment," in Luckhardt, *Wittgenstein*, pp. 190–212. Another lucid discussion of the "picture theory," and of its background, is chapters 2–4 of Anthony Kenny, *Wittgenstein* (London: Allen Lane, Penguin Press, 1973). See also Peter Barker, "Hertz and Wittgenstein," *Studies in the History and Philosophy of Science* 2, no. 3 (1980): 243–56.

11. Wittgenstein, *Tractatus Logico-philosophicus*, trans. D. F. Pears and B. F. McGuinness (New York: Humanities Press, 1961).

12. Let us keep in mind, however, that Wittgenstein is not in process of reducing everything to language, because he will make no distinction between word language—the Logos—and other sorts of objects, any of which can function as signifiers. The argument here is that Wittgenstein's overall strategy is best understood in terms of Derrida's argument that all experience is structured like a sign sequence.

13. Wittgenstein's argument does not, of course, apply to Husserl, who anticipated him in criticizing and discarding the notion of the mental picture. J. N. Mohanty compares Husserl's view with what he takes to be Wittgenstein's in *Edmund Husserl's Theory of Meaning* (The Hague: Martinus Nijhoff, 1976), pp. 38–43, but is mistaken about Wittgenstein on several crucial points. For example, he thinks Wittgenstein is concerned with "the nature of understanding," rather than with the grammar of the concept "understanding," and thus mistakenly assumes that Wittgenstein denies that the "experience" of understanding consists of anything more than an "operation undertaken." Wittgenstein's point is, rather, that though there are many experiences *characteristic of* situations in which we understand something, these experiences are not the *essence* of understanding (understanding has no essence) and do not determine whether we will correctly be said to "understand" in those situations. This conclusion does not keep Wittgenstein from taking the liveliest interest in experiences of various kinds. Nevertheless, Mohanty is right in concluding that Wittgenstein's account "does not decide any of the philosophical issues" with which he is concerned (p. 42). Mohanty is looking for an account of understanding *as such*, and Wittgenstein makes only "grammatical remarks." Noam Chomsky too has remarked on several occasions about the inadequacy of Wittgenstein's view—but Wittgenstein is simply not interested in what Mohanty or Chomsky is interested in, and he does not offer a competing view of the same thing. He is talking in an entirely different way and about something else.

14. J. N. Findlay, "My Encounters with Wittgenstein," *Philosophical Forum* 4 (1973): 177–78.

15. Charles Altieri, "Wittgenstein on Consciousness and Language: A Challenge to Derridean Literary Theory," *Modern Language Notes* 91, no. 6 (Decem-

ber 1976): 1409. Altieri has marshalled the "normalizing" view of Wittgenstein against Derrida in a way that, as the converse of the view presented here, makes it an illuminating comparison-piece. Altieri repeats a view that is traditional, both among Wittgenstein's supporters and his critics. See E. K. Specht, *The Foundations of Wittgenstein's Late Philosophy* (New York: Barnes and Noble, 1969), p. 49, and the critical view (cited by Specht) of H. R. Smart, "Language-Games," *Philosophical Quarterly* 7 (1957): 232. Altieri's view is basically the "communitarian" interpretation of Wittgenstein, and Kripke's influential reading of Wittgenstein on rules (*Wittgenstein: On Rules*, pp. 96–97) falls generally into the same camp. Kripke does not take the plunge that Altieri does and call "forms of life" an "ontological base," but whatever sort of ultimate they might be taken as, there appears, on the communitarian reading, no way of getting beyond them.

16. The notion of "Übersichtlichkeit" is crucial to understanding Wittgenstein's thought and its connection with and difference from classical philosophical views of understanding, which have been concerned with *in*-sight, with vision of the essence. See the discussion by G. P. Baker and P.M.S. Hacker in *Wittgenstein: Understanding and Meaning* (Chicago: University of Chicago Press, 1980), pp. 531–45. See also Frank Cioffi, "Wittgenstein and the Fire-Festivals," in *Perspectives on Wittgenstein's Philosophy*, ed. Irving Block (Cambridge, Mass.: MIT Press, 1981), pp. 212–37. Cioffi's discussion of Wittgenstein's "Remarks on Frazer" is the most illuminating I have seen on Wittgenstein's way of resolving puzzlement by "surveyable" (*übersichtlich*) rearrangement. A related essay by Cioffi is "Wittgenstein's Freud," in *Studies in the Philosophy of Wittgenstein*, ed. Peter Winch (New York: Humanities Press, 1969).

17. For this way of approaching Descartes' sentence, see O. K. Bouwsma, *Philosophical Essays* (Lincoln: University of Nebraska Press, 1965), pp. 149–73.

18. Ferdinand Saussure, *Course in General Linguistics* (New York: McGraw-Hill, 1959), p. 110.

19. Stanley Cavell makes this point very forcefully in "The Availability of Wittgenstein's Later Philosophy," in *Must We Mean What We Say?* (New York: Charles Scribner's Sons, 1969), pp. 105–7.

20. Thus Specht misleads when he speaks of Wittgenstein's "grammatical propositions" as "necessarily true" and a priori, and says that they "refer to reality without being dependent on this reality in their truth value" (*Foundations*, p. 153). Nothing could be more contrary to Wittgenstein's conception of grammatical propositions than to suppose, as Specht does, that the statement "every rod has length" makes an "assertion" about "particular objects" (p. 149), or even about a class of objects. Specht correctly observes that language games are "neither true nor false," but slides from this to the notions that they are "prior" to truth and falsity and from there to the notions of necessity and apriority (p. 171). But for Wittgenstein, the priority of grammar to truth and falsity is not priority of the sort that bestows transcendental dignity: it is the priority of not having gotten anywhere yet.

21. Cf. Kent Linville, "Wittgenstein on 'Moore's Paradox,'" in Luckhardt, *Wittgenstein*, pp. 286–302.

22. The aesthetic bent of Wittgenstein's sensibility is evident from the beginning. The concept of the "picture" as developed in the *Tractatus* already contains a strong aesthetic element. A recent essay that has discussed the implications of the picture theory for aesthetics is James D. Carney, "Wittgenstein's Theory of Picture Representation," *Journal of Aesthetics* 60, no. 2 (Winter 1981): 179–85.

23. Again, it should be kept in mind that this is not a "theory of language acquisition," as Chomsky takes it to be, but a descriptive account of what it looks like to an eye that does not penetrate to what is hidden.

24. Cf. Cioffi, "Fire-Festivals."

25. Cf. Northrop Frye's remarks on "doodle" and "babble" in *Anatomy of Criticism* (New York: Atheneum, 1967), pp. 275 ff.

26. Derrida discusses this aspect of Rousseau in the *Grammatology*, esp. pp. 195–203.

27. Bouwsma's "Expression Theory of Art" (*Philosophical Essays*, pp. 21–50) is a development of this aspect of the *Investigations*.

28. Cf. *Culture*, p. 44: "If Freud's theory of the interpretation of dreams has anything in it, it shows how *complicated* is the way the human mind represents the facts in pictures." We may contrast this complexity with the limpid directness of the picturing relation which Wittgenstein had sought in the *Tractatus*.

29. "Ordinary language" is thus to Wittgenstein something like what Derrida in "Plato's Pharmacy" (*Diss.*, pp. 61–171) calls the *pharmakon*. The word *Mittel* does not, like *pharmakon*, have contradictory meanings; the opposite senses we can read for it in Wittgenstein's sentence are a function of syntax, of placement, rather than of the word's intrinsic semantic content.

30. Wittgenstein, "Remarks," in Luckhardt, *Wittgenstein*, p. 69. On this subject see Cioffi, "Fire-Festivals," pp. 219–20.

31. Derrida points out that Aristotle in the *Rhetoric* assigns metaphor to the poet and homonymy to the sophist. Commenting on *Rhetoric* 1404b37–1405a1, Derrida writes: "While the philosopher is interested only in the truth of meaning, beyond even signs and names; and the sophist manipulates empty signs and draws his effects from the contingency of signifiers (whence his taste for equivocality, and primarily for homonymy, the deceptive identity of signifiers), the poet plays on the multiplicity of signifieds, but in order to return to the identity of meaning" (*Margins*, p. 248n). Derrida reads this as Aristotle's attempt to yoke poetry to the labor of truth as against "dissemination." In his study of Mallarmé, Derrida speaks of rhyme as "the general law of textual effects"—it is the "folding-together of an identity and a difference," and the "raw material" for its operation need not be sound. "All 'substances' (phonic and graphic) and all 'forms' can be linked together at any distance and under any rule in order to produce new versions of 'that which in discourse does not speak'" (*Diss.*, p. 277).

32. Cf. Stephen Erickson, *Language and Being* (New Haven: Yale University Press, 1970).

33. Cavell, "The Availability of Wittgenstein's Later Philosophy," p. 71.

34. Barry Stroud, "Wittgenstein and Logical Necessity," in Pitcher, *Wittgenstein*,

pp. 477–96. Cf. Kripke, *Wittgenstein*, p. 98, and James Bogen, *Wittgenstein's Philosophy of Language* (New York: Humanities Press, 1972), pp. 196–98.

35. This is, in fact, one of Wittgenstein's most celebrated arguments; it is basically the notion of "being held captive by a picture." Now the communitarian interpreters want us to believe that Wittgenstein thought captivity to the pictures embedded in our communal practices was natural, inevitable, and inescapable.

36. Cf. Cavell, "Must We Mean What We Say?," in the volume of the same name, pp. 28–29: "Rules tell you what to do when you do the thing at all; principles tell you how to do the thing well, with skill or understanding. In competitive games, acting well amounts to doing the sort of thing that will win, so the principles of games recommend strategy." A difference between Cavell and Wittgenstein may be illustrated by Cavell's remark that "the Britannica 'rules' tell us what we *must* do in *playing* chess, not what we ought to do *if* we play" (p. 30). While Cavell is right on the difference in usage between "ought" and "must," my sense of the matter is that Cavell's "must" is functionless. The rules tell us what we do in playing chess—or, as most of us would say, how chess is played. Cavell's "must" seems to me to come from his lingering preoccupation with "necessity" as it functions in traditional philosophical discourse, though for him moral rather than logical compulsion is usually the real issue (not, of course, in the case of chess). In this, Cavell seems to be more influenced by Austin than by Wittgenstein.

37. Rodolphe Gasché, "Deconstruction as Criticism," *Glyph* 6 (1979): 192.

38. Richard Rorty, "Philosophy as a Kind of Writing," *New Literary History* 10 (1978–79): 158.

Chapter 3

1. This does not mean consensus is impossible, only that the possibility of consensus cannot be purified of the possibility of misunderstanding, not even by a strategic idealization.

2. This is not so because my thoughts as I speak are different from your thoughts as you speak, but because we are differently situated and our words thus have a different context, different surroundings, a different before and after. Obviously words *can* still be said to mean identically the same in different contexts, if we define their identity in such a way that it is not essentially affected by context. But it would be merely dogmatic to claim that such a definition is compulsory or given in the "facts." Meaning is not an observable, and as soon as we try to formalize its sense we enter the realm of theory.

3. J. L. Austin, *How to Do Things with Words*, ed. J. O. Urmson and Marina Sbisa, 2d ed. (Cambridge, Mass.: Harvard University Press, 1975), pp. 134–35. Hereafter cited in the text as *Words*.

4. John Searle has pointed out that Austin's analysis here suffers from his failure to distinguish clearly between kinds of illocutionary verbs and kinds of illocutionary acts. See "A Taxonomy of Illocutionary Acts," in Searle, *Expression and Meaning* (Cambridge: Cambridge University Press, 1979), pp. 9–10. This

valuable essay makes the analysis of illocutionary acts more accurate and nuanced and at the same time begins to lose the synoptic clarity of Austin's approach, moving away from ordinary language toward a formal notation that can hold on to the complex of new distinctions. The stylistic difference between Austin and Searle is of considerable interest from a deconstructive as well as a psychoanalytic point of view. Some philosophers love standardized jargon and formal notation; others, like the later Wittgenstein, consider it largely a way of avoiding thought.

5. We have the pure generality "successful performative." Then we have particular events, which can be ranged in a spectrum from the most problematic to the clearest. In between, we have generalizations which attempt to specify the content of the pure generality. On this intermediate level, contamination is inevitable. No flawless formula can be given. But we can effect a marriage between the pure generality and particular successful speech-events in which the telos seems to be actualized. The whole set of illocutionary acts escapes exhaustive specification in formulas, but a subset of "successful" speech acts norms the set. The criteria that Austin searches for are those by which particular speech-events can be identified *as* something. On one hand, Austin finds that the criteria always fail to keep out complicating possibilities that render the identification problematic. On the other hand, it is always sure *as what* the identification is supposed to, or fails to, identify the cases.

6. John R. Searle, "Reiterating the Differences: A Reply to Derrida," *Glyph* 1 (1977): 202.

7. Searle explicitly acknowledges the function of idealization in his own work. Derrida cites Searle to this effect and criticizes the way the idealization is set up in *Ltd Inc*, pp. 207 ff.

8. Searle, "Reply," p. 205.

9. Ibid., p. 206.

10. Searle objects to Derrida's generalization of the term "citation" to include poems and theatrical performance. Derrida's own more precise term is "iteration"; however, he also uses "citation" in this new sense, undoubtedly not the standard sense, but one he defines clearly. See *Ltd Inc*, pp. 241–43.

11. Thus Derrida seems to be impertinent in the extreme when he suggests that Searle's unconscious may desire what Searle's consciousness rejects (*Ltd Inc*, p. 215), or that there are Oedipal motives in Searle's relation to Austin (*Ltd Inc*, p. 177).

12. And yet Aristotle, whose ideal model of tragedy is the *Oedipus*, tells us that tragedy is an imitation, and that imitation pleases people "because in their viewing they find they are learning, inferring what class each object belongs to: for example that 'this individual is a so-and-so (*houtos ekeinos*)'" (*Poetics*, 48b16–18, trans. Gerald Else in his *Aristotle's Poetics: The Argument* [Cambridge, Mass.: Harvard University Press, 1963], p. 125). This passage is often mistranslated, as Else points out: "What Aristotle means by 'learning' and 'inferring' is not the recognition that 'this person is that person,' but that he is 'that *kind* of creature,' or as Rhys Roberts puts it in the Oxford translation of the *Rhetoric*, 'That is a so-and-so.' . . . In Aristotle's terms, if you have merely rec-

ognized the semblance of one individual (the portrayed one: *houtos*) to another individual (the original: *ekeinos*) you have not learned anything. Learning and knowledge are of universals; the individual *per se* is unknowable" (p. 132). Butcher's widely used translation is one of those that misleads on this point.

13. Sophocles, *Oedipus Rex*, trans. D. Fitts and R. Fitzgerald (New York: Harcourt, Brace, 1949), p. 103.

14. Derrida, "The Law of Genre," *Glyph* 7 (1980): 176–229. Hereafter cited in the text.

15. Searle, "Reply," p. 205.

16. John R. Searle, "The Logical Structure of Fictional Discourse," in *Expression and Meaning*, p. 73. Italics added.

17. Searle proposes the arrow symbols in "A Taxonomy of Illocutionary Acts."

Chapter 4

1. See John R. Searle, *Speech Acts* (London: Cambridge University Press, 1969), pp. 12–15, 41–42. Compare Searle's account of speech acts with Austin's: Austin, in classical philosophical form, speaks of the "necessary conditions" for the execution of speech acts; Searle, utilizing the modern picture of which Chomsky is the leading exponent, speaks of the "underlying rules" that "govern" the performance of speech acts. Searle believes that there exist rules that we follow though we are unaware of their existence or their form, and he characterizes their effect on our behavior as "causal" (John R. Searle, "Rules and Causation," a commentary on Noam Chomsky's "Rules and Representations," both in *Behavioral and Brain Sciences* 3 [1980]: 1–61). I believe Chomsky's version of implicit rules is plausibly tied to a "scientific" research project, and that it is not vulnerable to refutation by a purely philosophical critique, as is Searle's project, or Jonathan Culler's in *Structuralist Poetics* (Ithaca: Cornell University Press, 1975). Chomsky's project is not privileged merely through his claim to be scientific, but because his text has been minutely and rigorously tied to the text of scientific investigation (see the many criticisms and replies in the *Behavioral and Brain Sciences* forum cited above).

2. It may be that, as J. Lucasiewicz argues, modern logic shows the law of contradiction to be untenable, but even this author concludes that we must in practice hold on to it because it remains "our only weapon against error and falsehood" ("Aristotle on the Law of Contradiction," in *Articles on Aristotle*, vol. 3, *Metaphysics*, ed. Jonathan Barnes, Malcolm Schofield, and Richard Sorabji [London: Gerald Duckworth and Co., 1979], p. 62).

3. *Great Dialogues of Plato*, trans. W.H.D. Rouse (New York: New American Library, 1956).

4. Augustine, *Confessions*, trans. Rex Warner (New York: New American Library, 1963), book 1, chap. 17. Hereafter cited in the text.

5. E. D. Hirsch, *Validity in Interpretation* (New Haven: Yale University Press, 1967), pp. 44–45. Hereafter cited in the text.

6. E. A. Havelock, *Preface to Plato*, Universal Library Edition (New York: Grosset and Dunlap, 1967). Hereafter cited in the text.

7. *Literary Criticism of Dante Alighieri*, trans. and ed. Robert S. Haller (Lincoln: University of Nebraska, 1973).

Chapter 5

1. Freud, "On Narcissism: An Introduction," in *Complete Psychological Works*, ed. and trans. James Strachey (New York: W. W. Norton, 1957), 14: 75.
2. Freud, "Inhibitions, Symptoms, and Anxiety," *Works*, 20: 144.
3. Ibid., p. 138.
4. Ibid., p. 153.
5. "It was anxiety which produced repression and not, as I formerly believed, repression which produced anxiety" (Freud, "Inhibitions," pp. 180–9).
6. Cf. Derrida, "Speculations: On Freud," *Oxford Literary Review* 3, no. 2 (1978): 93–94.
7. "Anxiety is a reaction to a situation of danger" (Freud, "Inhibitions," p. 128). "Since the danger is so often one of castration, it appears to us as a reaction to a loss, a separation" (ibid., p. 130). "All [anxiety-provoking danger situations] retain a common quality in so far as they signify in a certain sense a separation from the mother" (ibid., p. 151). It should be noted that all these remarks are speculative, and Freud confesses that he does not know how far they take him toward a solution of the problem of anxiety (ibid., pp. 152–53).
8. Lucretius, *On the Nature of the Universe*, trans. R. E. Latham (Baltimore: Penguin Books, 1971), pp. 122–23.
9. Freud, "The Ego and the Id," *Works*, 19: 57–58.

Index

181